5-10-83

REAGANOMICS
IN THE
STAGFLATION
ECONOMY

POST KEYNESIAN ECONOMICS

A series edited by
Sidney Weintraub

REAGANOMICS
IN THE
STAGFLATION
ECONOMY

Edited by

Sidney Weintraub

and

Marvin Goodstein

University of Pennsylvania Press
Philadelphia
1983

Library of Congress Cataloging in Publication Data

Main entry under title:

Reaganomics in the stagflation economy.

(Post Keynesian economics)
Mostly papers presented during the Third Annual
Sewanee Economics Symposium, Oct. 1–3, 1981; sponsored
by the Economics Dept. of the University of the South
at Sewanee in cooperation with Sidney Weintraub, visiting
appointee to the Kennedy Distinguished Professorship in
Economics.
1. United States—Economic policy—1981– —
congresses. 2. Unemployment—United States—Effect of
inflation on— Congresses. I. Weintraub, Sidney,
1914–   . II. Goodstein, Marvin E.   III. Sewanee
Economics Symposium (3rd : 1981 : University of the
South)   IV. University of the South. Economic Dept.
V. Series.
HC106.8.R423 1982   338.973   82–60305
ISBN 0–8122–7858–5
ISBN 0–8122–1133–2 (pbk.)

Printed in the United States of America

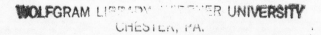

CONTENTS

PREFACE

Most of the essays in this volume were papers presented at the Third Annual Sewanee Economics Symposium on October 1–3, 1981. These symposiums are organized by the Economics Department of the University of the South at Sewanee in cooperation with the person holding a visiting appointment to the Kennedy Distinguished Professorship in Economics. In the fall semester of 1981 the holder of the chair was Dr. Sidney Weintraub of the University of Pennsylvania. The objective of the symposiums is to provide a forum for outstanding people in economics and related fields to present their views on issues of importance to the South and to the nation. Publication is designed to help fulfill that objective.[1]

Probably the only topics that have been discussed more than stagflation are Shakespeare, the American Civil War, and the New York Yankees, so why yet another discussion? As long as stagflation is with us, like the weather we will always talk about it. Indeed, this is healthy; continuing appraisal of economic policy is always necessary and useful. And it is a fact that, at least in principle, more can be done about stagflation than the weather, even though we are not always sure what that "more" is. In the presidential election of 1980 many people voted for Ronald Reagan simply in the belief that we needed to "try something new," despite some vagueness on what that should be. Whether the blame for this feeling of futility lies with economists or politicians can be left to the reader's own contemplation. But because we are at a point where there has been a dramatic change in the rhetoric and policy concerning stagflation, this is an opportune time to examine the topic once again.

The symposium was organized to encompass varied perspectives on stagflation. While the potential subject matter can never be considered exhaustively in the various groups of essays, several questions might be kept in mind as they are read.

The two aspects of the economy receiving the widest current attention probably are productivity and the federal budget. Sluggish productivity has been blamed for both inflation and relative stagnation in production and employment. Obviously there are important questions to be asked about productivity. What, in fact, has happened to it, and in which sectors of the economy? What are the specific factors affecting productivity, and what is the relative significance of each? What are the precise relationships between the inflation and stagnation that have been occurring and changes in productivity?

The federal budget has been at the center of debate about stagflation under President Ronald Reagan's exercise in fiscal fitness. The budgetary deficit, government spending versus taxes, particular spending and tax items, and federal versus state and local budgets are all matters of controversy, both in terms of what is efficient and in terms of what is equitable.

No discussion of stagflation would be complete without a monetary perspective. To illustrate our conflicting ideas about money, we stress that it does not grow on trees yet claim that it is the root of all evil. Aside from contention over what direction and force monetary policy should take, there is debate over its effectiveness and fairness compared to other methods of dealing with stagflation.

In recent years the monetary debate has been full of sound and fury. But even though the noise may signify something, it does not signify everything. There are other ways of dealing with sluggish production, high levels of unemployment, and rising prices—such as through energy policy, price and wage controls, and a tax-based incomes policy.

Another direction in which our perspectives could profitably expand is geographically. Too often we are either ignorant of events in other countries or use their experience selectively to reinforce our own biases. It is therefore appropriate to consider other economies and the mutual impacts.

While the topic of the symposium is stagflation, some of the essays are directed more to the stabilization of prices than to the expansion of production and employment, that is, more concerned with the "flation" rather than the "stag." This does not imply that the former should necessarily take precedence, or even that full employment and reasonably stable prices are to be viewed as incompatible objectives. It is simply a matter of individual emphasis and judgment.

Mention was made of the widespread frustration that seems to exist about fighting stagflation. Perhaps the large number of difficult questions that have been raised here will serve only to strengthen that feeling. Yet instead of being discouraged by the complexities, we can be encouraged by the fruitful thought reflected in the essays.

The successful organization of the symposium and the preparation of the essays for publication are due in no small part to the efforts of

Professor Sidney Weintraub and the invaluable participation at Sewanee of Vice-Chancellor Robert Ayres, Provost Arthur Schaefer, Dean Brown Patterson, departmental colleagues Robert Degen, Werner Hochwald, Jerry Ingles, and Yasmeen Mohiuddin, and Mary Howard Smith and Eileen Degen. I must also thank colleague and wife Anita for her exercise of a meliorating invisible hand during the days of planning and execution.

Sewanee, 1982   MARVIN GOODSTEIN

NOTE

1. The papers of the First Annual Sewanee Economics Symposium, *Business in the New South: A Historical Perspective,* edited by Fred Bateman, were published in 1981 by the University Press at Sewanee. The second set, *Continuity Versus Change in Southern Economic Development: A Multidisciplinary Perspective,* edited by Marvin Goodstein and Werner Hochwald, is currently being prepared for publication.

PART ONE

THE
STAGFLATION
SETTING

1

America's Inflation

FRANCIS M. BATOR

Just over four years ago in Plains, Georgia, the late Arthur Okun told the president-elect that if the new administration did not institute some form of direct wage restraint, by 1980 the underlying rate of inflation would have risen from 6.5 percent to around 10 percent and the Carter presidency would be judged a failure. Someone in Ronald Reagan's government should tell that story to the new president. There is nothing in the Reagan program to prevent *either* a deep recession followed by stagnation *or* a repetition of the Carter result.

There are, broadly speaking, only three choices available to meet inflation.

• We can curb it by traditional means, a relentless monetary and fiscal squeeze on demand that works by creating a reserve army of unemployed and a lot of idle capacity. As Prime Minister Thatcher is discovering, that is an agonizingly slow and expensive cure. Supply-side measures can make it only marginally less painful, even if they achieve a spectacular success in accelerating productivity growth.

• If that kind of economic trench warfare is unacceptable, we can instead try to live with inflation at double-digit rates, limiting the damage by widespread indexing. The pace of inflation would, however, keep ratcheting up everytime there is a serious harvest failure or a large price increase from the Organization of Petroleum Exporting Countries (OPEC).

• We can try to reinforce a policy of moderate monetary and fiscal restraint, and a variety of steps to reduce costs and boost productivity, with some inevitably meddlesome scheme of price oversight and direct, mandatory wage restraint.

Reprinted with some minor alterations with permission from *The Economist*, March 21, 1981. Copyright © 1981 *The Economist*, Newspaper Ltd., London. Professor Bator's address to the Sewanee conference was drawn from this essay.

There is no other, happier, choice. People who say otherwise are in my opinion fooling themselves.

The rate of inflation at any particular time—the rate of change of the price level—is likely to reflect a variety of short-lived events such as a temporary spurt in the price of fuel or a harvest-related movement in farm prices. But the current inflation rate will also reflect the rate of inflation experienced during the recent past. In the last fifteen years inflation in the United States has exhibited a growing inertia, a tendency, once it has been speeded up by some transient event, to persist at the faster rate long after the cause of the acceleration has run its course.

The explanation for the inertia of the inflation rate has to do with wages. Since the mid-1960s, wage increases have become increasingly sensitive to the speed of inflation that employers and employees have recently experienced. As a result, the economy behaves as though it were indexed: wage rates chase prices and thereby push up labor costs; labor costs push up prices; prices pull wages after them again. It is like a dog that keeps chasing its own tail, at whatever speed it got used to yesterday.

To make the underlying inflation slow down, one must slow down the rise in labor costs. To do that, one must somehow shrink the gap between the rate of increase in wages and the rate of increase in productivity. Counting fringe benefits, wage rates have been rising at about 10 percent per year; labor productivity is thought to be rising at a rate of about 1 percent. As a result, standard unit labor costs (wages per hour divided by output per hour) is rising at 10 percent − 1 percent = 9 percent. As long as that continues, prices will keep rising at 9 percent—if real oil and food prices do not change. Labor costs absorb about 84 percent of corporate revenues net of depreciation and of sales and excise taxes. Pre-tax profits take only 12 percent; interest accounts for the rest. There is no room for businesses to absorb cumulative annual increments in standard labor costs of 9 percent; they mark up prices instead.

One way to slow down the rise in labor costs would be to speed up productivity growth by stimulating investment, regulatory reform, and a variety of other, mainly microeconomic, supply-side steps. Unfortunately that is uncertain business and a matter of years, not months. Besides, even a dramatic result, say a doubling of productivity growth from an annual 1 percent to 2 percent—though it would double the rate at which the standard of living improves—would initially diminish the rise in labor costs, and therefore in prices, only by a point, from 9 percent to 8 percent. Such a deceleration in prices would tend in time to slow wages down, and that would slow prices down some more. But the process of winding down would be gradual and would be aborted by any large increase in the price of oil or food or foreign exchange. We would be lucky indeed if "merely" by improving productivity growth we managed to reduce the core inflation rate from 9 percent to 6 or 7 percent by 1984.

To slow down inflation more reliably and quickly than that, one must find a more direct method for curbing wage rates. Labor is right that wages have not been even the proximate cause of the acceleration of inflation, at least not since the mid-1960s, and also that real wage rates are barely higher than they were in 1970. Both points are right but immaterial. If in response to a prior spurt in prices—thanks to an increase in the price of oil or food—wage rates accelerate, that is, if the initial increase in the price level triggers a (futile) catch-up response in pay, then wage costs will perpetuate the faster inflation by continuing to push up prices even after the initiating rise in real oil or food prices has come to a stop. Once such a wage-price spiral gets under way, what started it is irrelevant (except to all of us whose real incomes have fallen behind, in favor of OPEC or farmers).

How to slow down wages? Anyone claiming a cure for the underlying inflation must confront that question. In particular, all the talk about money supply and deficits is largely beside the point—if inflation is the point—except as it bears on the rate of increase in wages.

WHAT CAN FISCAL AND MONETARY POLICY DO?

Tightening money, reducing government spending, and increasing tax rates will reduce aggregate spending for goods and services—the quantities of goods and services demanded multiplied by their current prices. How the decrease in spending will be split between lower prices (which we want) and lower physical output (which we do not want) depends on how producers respond to the decline in orders and sales and the resulting pileup of unwanted stocks. Typically, they will respond by reducing output, cutting back overtime, and, if the slump in sales persists, laying off workers. As long as wage rates and therefore labor costs keep rising, they will not mark down prices or even stop raising them, at least not for long. In time, however, the extra unemployment will cause wage rates to slow down. The crucial question is: How much unemployment, maintained for how long, would it take to reduce the average yearly increase in wage rates from 10 percent to 6 percent, or 4 percent, or—for zero inflation, if there is no improvement in productivity growth—to 1 percent?

The postwar evidence is disheartening. If past regularities remain firm and OPEC price shocks and bad harvests do not intervene, it would take about 9 percent unemployment maintained for two years to compress core inflation by three points, say from 10 percent to 7 percent. The cumulative two-year cost of operating the economy with that much slack, with unemployment at 9 percent rather than 6 percent, would run to about $400 billion of unproduced output and real income ($6,000 per family). And that does not take into account the continuing loss in productivity that would follow the recession-caused reduction in capital formation. It seems a poor bargain.

Some economists believe that monetary stringency will curb wages much faster than it has during the past thirty-five years, if the government is visibly determined to keep restraining demand until inflation subsides. The causal chain is alleged to run from the government's fiscal and monetary determination to employers' and employees' expectations about inflation, and then to wages and prices. On this optimistic view the momentum of wage inflation is due to allegedly numerical "inflationary expectations." Change those expectations by credibly determined fiscal-monetary stringency, and wage inflation will quickly abate.

In the optimists' view, in its most plausible form, wage inflation has persisted in the recent past despite high and rising unemployment and idle capacity because both employers and employees have expected that the government would respond by stimulating demand—by speeding up money growth, taxing less, and spending more. Given that expectation, neither employers nor employees have had much incentive to scale down wage settlements.

The remedy? The government must behave in such a way as to change expectations "directly." Were Paul Volcker to set his money-printing machine to produce annual increments in the monetary base of, say, 5 percent, and to attach to the controls a tamper-proof lock— and especially if the administration and Congress adopted a similarly stringent fiscal rule—even the most skeptical might be convinced that spending for goods and services could grow no faster than an annual 5 to 6 percent. If so, the optimists believe, wages and prices would quickly decelerate to produce an inflation rate of 2.5 to 3.5 percent, and real growth would proceed at the 2.5 percent rate warranted by growth in the labor force and productivity.

The prescription raises two questions. Can a democratic government credibly commit itself to adhere to a policy no matter what its consequences—to guarantee that the monetary base will not be allowed to grow faster than x percent, even if the optimists should turn out to be wrong and the policy leads to massive unemployment and idle capacity quickly, and slows down inflation only very gradually? Catch-22: Maybe the theory is right, but the only way to test it is to convince people that the government would persist even if it is wrong.

The second question goes to the hypothesis itself.[1] Even if the government makes the threat of unemployment credible by convincing everyone that it will not allow aggregate spending to increase by more than 5 percent each year, how fast will the rate of wage increase diminish? If markets were perfectly competitive, a wage-price spiral could not persist in the face of involuntary unemployment and idle capacity. Reductions in nominal demand, brought about by monetary and/or fiscal policy, would immediately make prices and then wage rates decelerate and then fall. But the economy is a good deal less than perfectly competitive: Many producers can pass on costs, and labor markets are characterized by industry-wide bargaining, staggered multiyear contracts, employer reluctance to risk prolonged strikes, a relatively protected status for senior employees, much public employment, wage patterns that reflect strongly held notions of equity, pervasive career relationships between employers and employees, and extensive income support for the unemployed. As Keynes pointed out, in modern industrial economies wages are "sticky" downward. So recently has been their rate of change, much stickier in the United States than in, for instance, Britain, West Germany, or Japan.

The experiment has not been tried; the belief that it would work relatively painlessly rests on faith. During the past thirty years, retarding inflation has required much actual unemployment and idle capacity. To be sure, the evidence is tainted; it is drawn from a policy environment in which both employers and employees expected that the government would not persist. But that brings one back to Catch-22 and whether it is reasonable to believe that the threat of persistent unemployment would work any better than has the fact of unemployment, for instance, during 1974–76. (Measured inflation between 1974 and 1976 decelerated mainly because mortgage rates and food and oil prices stopped rising. The core rate of wage-price inflation was around 4.2 percent in 1973 and close to 6.5 percent in 1976. The first OPEC price shock way overmatched, in its effect on labor costs, the effect of the increase in unemployment from 4.9 percent in 1973 to 8.5 percent in 1975 and 7.7 percent in 1976.)

THE REAGAN PLAN

The Reagan administration plainly believes that both double-digit inflation and any form of wage-price controls are intolerable. That leaves only one option: a monetary-fiscal policy tight enough to threaten massive unemployment and idle capacity and, if necessary (in my opinion it would be necessary), to make good on that threat. Unemployment and idle capacity, or at least the credible threat thereof, is how a tight fiscal and monetary policy works to slow wage and price rises; there is no other, nonmagical connection. Yet Mr. Reagan is on record as being against unemployment and idle capacity. More to the point—one should not expect a serious politician seeking office explicitly to advocate either—it is not clear that the Reagan program entails a tight demand policy, or at least a tight fiscal policy.

If Reagan-Kemp-Roth tax reductions exceed reductions in federal spending by an appreciable margin, the result will be to increase aggregate demand. At least that will be the result unless the Federal Reserve, by tightening money, causes real interest rates to rise enough to offset the fiscal effect on demand by compressing its credit-sensitive components: residential construction and, notably, business investment—the process is called "crowding out." The looser is fiscal policy, the tighter money has to become and the higher real interest rates, to bring about the restraint on the total spending that would be necessary to create the unemployment needed to slow down inflation.

Is the Reagan administration counting on the Federal Reserve to make money so tight as to override a relatively loose fiscal policy? Or will it throw demand restraint to the wind, relying on alleged supply effects somehow to do the job? The universe is inconveniently designed; most policies affect both demand and supply. To judge which way a policy will cut, one must estimate the relative size of the effect on each, and the quarter-by-quarter timing as well. A reduction in personal income-tax rates, not offset by expenditure cuts, will slow down wages only if it causes the supply of labor to increase by more than the demand for labor. Research suggests that it will do the opposite:

• The supply of labor may not increase at all. Faced by higher after-tax wage rates, some workers will work more, others less—work becomes more lucrative, but one needs to work less to achieve any particular after-tax income goal. Many workers, institutionally locked into a pattern of fixed hours, will not respond at all. The evidence suggests that overall there will be at best only a small positive effect.

• In contrast, the evidence is clear that the tax-cut induced increase in spending would cause the demand for labor to increase by a multiple of any conceivable increase in its supply. Labor markets would become tighter and wage inflation would get worse.

• Since there seems to be strong supply-side support for betting on miracles, it is worth pointing out that even if, contrary to experience, the supply-enlarging effect of a personal tax cut were to dominate its effect on demand—and, I repeat, that is an absurdly poor bet—the size of any impact on inflation would depend on the sensitivity of wage rates to the resulting increase in unemployment. We know that in a range of 6.0 to 8.5 percent unemployment the wage response is small and gradual. (Whether it takes an increase or a decrease in income tax to give rise to an excess of aggregate supply over demand, it is that excess supply—unemployment and idle capacity—that produces the antiinflationary effect on wages and prices.)

Supply-side advocates of cutting taxes usually have in mind not labor supply but saving and investment. Here again one must be careful. Unmatched reductions in personal taxes (i.e., increases in public dis-saving) will give rise to a lot of consumption and little extra private saving, crowd out some investment, and aggravate inflation. Even the right kind of tax combination, one that brings forth extra investment and neutralizes its inflationary effect on demand by eliciting a matching upward shift in private or public saving, will retard inflation only gradually. The supply effect of investment works on inflation by raising labor productivity and thereby reducing labor costs. In relation to an inflation at 9 to 10 percent, the initial effect can only be small.

It does not follow that to encourage investment is a mistake. More capital formation, of the right sort, will speed up the rate at which real living standards improve. It will make a gradual contribution to getting inflation under better control. But a cure for inflation it is not.

In discussing the effect of a Kemp-Roth tax cut, I have assumed that the Federal Reserve does not respond to fiscal acceleration by stepping hard on the monetary brakes. If it does, it can override an expansionary fiscal policy, cause spending to go down and unemployment and idle capacity to rise, and depending on the magnitudes, make inflation gradually decelerate. But that is just old-fashioned, neo-Keynesian demand-and-supply economics. In its tight-money-loose-fiscal-policy version, it will compress especially the investment spending we need for supply-side productivity growth.

It should be said, parenthetically, that a large tax cut not neutralized either by spending cuts or by tightening money may be just the medicine we shall need to counter a nasty second dose of recession, if it comes. The consensus forecast for 1981–82 promises a flat economy and then gradual real growth. But a second decline cannot be ruled out. The object of a tax cut, in that event, would be to increase demand to counter the increase in unemployment and idle capacity that would otherwise occur. It would not make inflation better; indeed, it would make it a little worse than if, instead, we allowed the unemployment rate to rise to 8.5 percent or 9 percent and kept it there. (A sophisticated, supply-and-demand-oriented fiscal policy would entail cutting excise, sales, and employer payroll taxes. While stimulating demand, it would also reduce "costs" and thus mitigate the inflationary effect.)

That is the dilemma. Curbing inflation, without direct control over wages, requires a draconian fiscal and/or monetary policy: severe demand compression and high unemployment and idle capacity. There is no supply-side free lunch. It is not without irony that counsel to the contrary should have become the stock-in-trade of supposedly conservative Republicans.

Margaret Thatcher is closer to the truth, if beating inflation at any cost, without wage controls, is the right truth. Most of the people who say she is failing because she has not made fiscal and monetary policy tight enough only half know what it is they are saying. (Professor Hayek is an exception.) If she had, aggregate spending and output would be lower still, and unemployment and idle capacity worse, with even more disastrous consequences for investment and future productivity growth, not to speak of social and political comity. But to give the policy its due, inflation would probably be slowing down faster. The strategy has an old name; it works by creating a "reserve army of unemployed."

ANOTHER WAY OUT?

Free-lunch conservatives have their liberal counterparts, people who believe that wage and price controls provide a cheerful way out. They are fooling themselves too. Even a well-designed incomes policy would be inefficient and inequitable. In order to work, it would have to be combined with fiscal-monetary demand restraint that would keep the economy uncomfortably slack for quite a while, with unemployment at around 7 percent and the use of capacity at only 75 to 80 percent. It would have to be combined also with serious supply-side measures, not Laffer-style snake oil, and encouragement for business investment, not easy in an environment of slack. None of it would be enjoyable, at least not soon; it comes down to a question of "compared with what?" In comparison with demand compression without direct wage restraint, even an experimental and messy mixed strategy commends itself.

To cure inflation, we have to do something about wage—and salary—setting. There lies the key to the one-way inertia of the inflation rate that has made coping with external supply-price shocks so difficult. The need is for procedures that will allow flexibility of movement in relative wages, and especially in relative prices, yet will limit the average rate of nominal wage and salary increase to what productivity warrants and thus prevent the dog-and-tail phenomenon.

Though prices and profit margins also need to be watched, wages are the key. If labor costs behave, the price level will too, as long as the economy is not too tightly stretched by demand. Increases in the price of fuel, and fluctuation in the prices of other imports and of domestic commodities, will of course be reflected in the price level. For instance, a 50 percent increase in the price of oil would raise the price indexes by about 3 percent, causing "inflation" to speed up for a year by three points. But those effects should not be suppressed by a scheme of controls. They serve to signal changing scarcities, and, in the case of OPEC oil, the transfer of real income from us to them.

Still, even if *price* controls are not needed, why not adopt a fully parallel scheme that protects the appearance as well as the reality of equity? The danger is that controls on prices that really bind would freeze *relative* prices. That would soon create an unholy mess. There would be excess demands and supplies all over the place, with informal rationing, queues, and endless complaints. The chances are that the controls would break down long before the underlying inflation had cooled down. (There is a danger of that even with wage controls. But changes in relative wages, though for equity they matter a great deal, play a much smaller role than price movements in mediating changes in supply and demand.)

One reasonable compromise would be to control increases in dividends. In any case, it is essential to keep in mind the distinction between things nominal and real. The purpose of a scheme of wage restraint is not to reduce the share of wages in real income. It is, rather, to stop and then avoid pointless increases in nominal wages that bear no real fruit, and serve only to push up the price level. Indeed, the predictable consequence of nominal wage increases that, on average, ex-

ceed average productivity growth, is to *reduce* real wage *incomes*. The
natural reaction of governments to increases in the price level is to
tighten money and fiscal policy, compress demand, and drive a lot of
people out of work. Even if the real wage rate doesn't go down, the real
wage bill—the average wage rate times the number of hours worked—
certainly will.

Is a flexible scheme of wage and dividend controls feasible, or is the
choice between no wage restraint and some monstrosity? This is not
the place to explore that very large subject. My guess would be that
a "tax-based incomes policy" (TIP) of some sort offers considerable
promise. There are many variants. One version would entail imposing
a surtax on the profits of any employer who gives raises that, on average, exceed a specified national norm.[2] After a period of transition, the
norm would be set to equal the national growth rate of average productivity. The effect would be to discourage, but not forbid, wage increases
that put upward pressure on labor costs. Administration would be a
headache, but so it is with the ordinary income tax or, for that matter,
with the enforcement of contracts and the national defense.

Even with a proper wages policy, we will have to keep restraining
demand. And we shall have to decide whether to continue trying to
slow inflation only gradually or attempt a rapid cure. It is my belief
that a gradual, five-year program to wind down inflation cannot work
in a world of asymmetrically one-sided commodity shocks. Progress on
prices, if any, would be too slow. People would feel cheated; support
for the wage standard would inevitably erode. The alternative would
be a severe wage norm, with a stiff surtax to back it up, that would drive
down the rate of increase in labor costs quickly to an annual 2 to 3 percent.

Many of my wisest colleagues think that impossible because it
would create too great a sense of retroactive inequity. I am inclined
to disagree. If there is prompt progress on prices—and, with some luck
on oil and food, prices in a slack economy would decelerate in step with
labor costs—I would suppose that most people would welcome the result. But that is a guess. And obviously the proviso about oil and food
is important and would entail both skill and luck.

There is a third choice, which avoids both Thatcherite trench warfare and wage controls. We could instead decide to live with a baseline
inflation of 9 to 10 percent, recognizing that periodically it would be
ratcheted up by supply-price shocks. In light of the alternatives, that
is not an unthinkable choice, especially if we make inflation less damaging by indexing.

A balanced, anticipated inflation has only negligible real economic effects. Granted, a lot of people would not see it that way; when the price of what I buy goes up, it's inflation; when the price of what I sell goes up, that's justice. In any event, they would not distinguish between the "pure" inflation part of what is happening and the relative price changes that reflect real or, in some cases (e.g., OPEC oil), monopoly-contrived scarcities. But to many economists it seems a shame to impose on ourselves massive real economic costs in order to stop what is mainly a monetary disease. Indeed, it can be argued that the worst consequence of an inherited inflation consists in what we do to ourselves to slow it down.

I think the live-with-it school, or its gradualist near-equivalent, is profoundly wrong. That is not a professional judgment; it is a guess about the likely temper of our politics if inflation continues at double-digit rates, is periodically speeded up by supply shocks, and, in any event, remains uneven in its incidence because technical and political constraints limit the scope of indexing. I do not believe that it is possible, by whatever clever devices, sufficiently to alleviate the insecurity that most people would feel if the price level were to keep doubling every six or seven years. People would feel insecure even though it is likely that, over time, most would keep level at least with respect to income. The result is likely to be an ungenerous, conflicted politics, the opposite of benign.

There is another point too. Inflation of 10 percent need not deteriorate into hyperinflation; certainly, high single-digit inflation has been made a way of life by countries whose real economic performance has not been bad. But with supply-price shocks mostly positive and sometimes large, a true live-with-it strategy is likely to result in an inflation that keeps speeding up; 10 percent would be only the starting rate. Moreover, we are talking here about the United States; size and power dictate that we try to be different. For safety, and relative decency, we must play a leading and constructive international role. If we are seen, at home and abroad, as incompetent in managing our domestic affairs, we will not play that role very effectively.

So for that reason too, vanquishing inflation has to remain a primary goal. It is not a goal we can achieve merely by compressing demand and trying to boost productivity. However distasteful to business and labor (and to most economists), we must supplement fiscal, monetary, and supply-side policies with a flexible but mandatory incomes policy. There is no tolerable alternative.

Harvard University

NOTES

1. See F. M. Bator, "Fiscal and Monetary Policy: In Search of a Doctrine," in *Economic Choices: Studies in Tax-Fiscal Policy* (Washington, D.C.: Center for National Policy, 1982), pp. 25–42.
2. This is the essence of the original Wallich-Weintraub TIP. See *Journal of Economic Issues* 5 (June 1971): 1–19.

PART TWO

SUPPLY-SIDERS, MINORITIES, AND PRODUCTIVITY

INTRODUCTION

MARSHALL E. MCMAHON

Stephen Rousseas has reviewed the history of the U.S. economy since World War II and concluded that significant gains in stability and equality have resulted from the postwar decision that government should be held responsible for the overall performance of the economy. In terms of two specific goals—the avoidance of another Great Depression and the amelioration of poverty—the postwar experience involving a growth in government transfer payments has been a success.

However, one of the consequences has been the building of an inflationary bias into the economy. The supply-side shocks of the 1970s interacted with this bias to produce several years of double-digit inflation and levels of chronic unemployment that are high by the standards of the 1960s. At the end of the 1970s, the time was ripe for a simple-minded counterrevolution in economic theory. And it came on the supply side.

Rousseas sees supply-side theory, grounded in the Laffer curve and the empirical claim that a large reduction in marginal personal income-tax rates would generate an increase in government tax revenues, as wanting. Most of his remarks concerned the inconsistency between supply-side theory and supply-side praxis.

According to supply-side theory, reducing marginal tax rates on the most productive social class, the wealthy, would unleash a reservoir of talent that would accelerate growth and development and therefore carry *all* the members of society to higher levels of well-being. However, if tax cuts based upon supply-side theory are combined with a determination of other economic conservatives to move the budget toward a balance in the short run, then expenditures must be cut. And if defense expenditures are to rise, nondefense expenditures must fall drastically. This means that the transfer programs that contributed to increased stability and the amelioration of poverty in the postwar era are destined to be undone.

17

Rousseas believes that the consequence of this supply-side praxis will undo the stability of the postwar era. Capitalism's flexibility is being discarded in a return to an earlier unfettered capitalism. Rousseas' conclusion is that "the Reagan administration's program . . . is a raid on the public treasury. It is a massive redistribution gambit with a reverse twist, not a growth scenario based on supply-side theory, no matter how addle-brained." It is, further, a "return of the economic royalists" and a "legitimation crisis in the making."

Eileen Collins has examined one part of the Reagan program: the tax incentive for research and development (R & D) in the Economic Recovery Tax Act of 1981. Collins readily admits that we do not understand all the factors that influence R & D expenditures. Her analysis leads her to conclude that a tax incentive, at the margin, might indeed affect R & D expenditures positively, although the magnitude of the effect cannot be reliably estimated. And the effects are not likely to be large in "old-line manufacturing firms in the industrial Northeast and Midwest and new innovative ventures which are not yet profitable." Hence the tax incentives are not likely to help those industries or those regions of the country that need the most help, nor are they likely to help the new firms that are the vehicles of the supply-side mechanism described by George Gilder in particular.[1]

Collins' conclusion is that, while the effects of the tax-incentive component are quite uncertain, there are plenty of reasons to doubt that this component will induce much additional R & D under present conditions. There may well be other incentives that would be more effective, and they might be targeted in ways to improve their impact on specific sectors and regions.

Two essays deal with the outlook for specific segments of the population—women and blacks.

Eileen Appelbaum has raised doubts about the traditional explanation of postwar changes in women's work patterns and expresses concerns about the economic position of women in the 1980s.

The growth of the economy from 1948 through most of the 1960s (the period during which expansion was most influenced by postwar government economic intervention) provided employment opportunities previously not available for women, as the supply of male workers failed to keep pace with the demand for labor, especially in the types of jobs that expanded most rapidly—clerical, sales, services—which were considered "appropriate" for women.

Nevertheless, the work patterns of females showed that women moved in and out of the work force as their family situations changed.

With the advent of stagflation in the late 1960s, women's work patterns changed once again. By 1981, not only were married women working, but married women with young children were working, as female labor force participation rates continued to rise and the differences between male and female lifetime work patterns further diminished.

The 1980s may well produce a slowdown in the growth of "female jobs," even an absolute decline in the number of these jobs, if office automation reduces the amount of "female labor" required. If stagflation persists, this could mean that the American family will experience more and more difficulty trying to maintain its standard of living, while women are unlikely to make much progress in penetrating "male jobs" without economic growth sufficient to produce tight labor markets. While Appelbaum does not mention the administration's stance on equal employment opportunity and affirmative action, it seems likely that backing off from this commitment to opening "male positions" to women can only exacerbate the problem. Although Gilder might welcome the forced return of women to their domestic chores as a positive step,[2] many women will not find this prospect so alluring.

William Darity cast doubts upon the positive effects of the liberal agenda. He questions whether the programs of the past two decades have really benefited the majority of blacks; they have suited the black elite, but not the black masses.

In Darity's model, society is divided into three classes: workers, capitalists, and "social managers." The price of saving capitalism in the postwar era was the development of the managerial class to use government to promote the social welfare, as defined by the social managers. Darity sees the Reagan phenomenon as a counterrevolution in which the capitalist class is trying to wrest control from the social managers. Since government in general, and transfer programs in particular, are the social manager's source of power, this capitalist counterrevolution must reduce the power of government and cut back transfer programs in order to regain control over the economy, and particularly over labor markets and wages.

While Darity is not enthusiastic about the liberal program, he is troubled over how blacks can survive the Reagan administration. This will depend upon the ability of the black masses to develop their own ideology which, Darity thinks, must come from below, not from above, and which must be inclusive rather than exclusive. Darity fears that otherwise some rebellion will come closer to being a reality.

Whether they are in agreement or not, all of the essays in this part deal with major issues and important economic, political, and social blocs in our economy. Individually and collectively they can enlighten the public debate on matters that cloud our future.

Southwestern at Memphis

NOTES

1. See George Gilder, *Wealth and Poverty* (New York: Basic Books, 1981).
2. Ibid., pp. 9–20.

The Ideology of Supply-Side Economics

STEPHEN ROUSSEAS

Our revenue laws have operated in many ways to the unfair advantage of the few, and they have done little to prevent an unjust concentration of wealth and power.

—FRANKLIN D. ROOSEVELT

The taxing power of the government must not be used to regulate the economy or bring about social change.

—RONALD REAGAN

The Great Depression, half a century ago, was by far the greatest challenge American capitalism had to face since the Civil War. The stock market crash wiped out the paper wealth of the newly rich, and massive bank failures cleaned out the life savings of many of the not-so-rich. Real output fell by one-third, and unemployment soared to 25 percent. According to the conventional economic theory of the time, it could not happen.

True, panics and cycles were a part of our past, but cycles were seen as an unavoidable part of "creative" capitalism to be borne in stoic silence. There could thus be no moral public responsibility for the short-run suffering of the mass of people, for American capitalism in the 1920s was seen by the economics profession as marching forward resolutely on a plateau of infinite albeit occasionally interrupted prosperity.

Then came the collapse. One of the great axioms of our existence is *What is, is possible.* The Great Depression was there in all its black majesty, and it was not just another rainy day but a storm that threatened the very survival of the market system. And there was no new theory to provide a quick fix; John Maynard Keynes' *General Theory* came later. The political response in the United States was purely pragmatic, a groping for solutions that led to that amalgam of policies called the New Deal. Its public works projects, its relief for the poor, its civilian conservation program for unemployed youth, the National Recovery Act (NRA), and the establishment of a social security system—all these gave some measure of hope to a dispirited nation. Yet in retrospect the New Deal did too little rather than too much. After a slow recovery, the U.S. economy dropped sharply once again in 1937. Full recovery came only with the 1939 onset of World War II in Europe and our direct involvement in 1941.

After World War II victory was assured, the old fears resurfaced. As a warning to its corporate subscribers, Leo Cherne's Research Institute of America predicted (on expensive linen paper) 11 million people unemployed in the immediate postwar period. The Pabst Blue Ribbon Beer Company announced a competition, with a $25,000 first prize, for the best two-thousand-word essay on how to avoid the mass unemployment of the prewar period. The National Planning Association was established in Washington, and it quickly recruited a staff of professional economists to work on a national plan for the postwar reconversion of the economy. The British White Paper of 1945 for the first time in modern history officially proclaimed the government's *responsibility* to provide for *full* employment; in the United States, the Employment Act of 1946 committed the federal government to the maintenance of *maximum* employment (full employment being too controversial for the U.S. Congress). And in the late 1940s the United Nations convened a Committee of Experts (Nicholas Kaldor, Arthur Smithies, John Maurice Clark, Pierre Uri, and E. Ronald Walker) to propose *National and International Measures for Full Employment.*

Governments (particularly the United States) were to be clearly responsible for adopting appropriately stabilizing fiscal measures. It was on this basis that we entered the postwar era, with some trepidation but, now that Keynes had conveyed his message, armed with a new theory for managing aggregate demand. Government was to "compensate" for the occasional job failings of the capitalist system.

On the occasion of its sixtieth anniversary in 1980, the National Bureau of Economic Research (NBER) held a conference on "The American Economy in Transition."[1] Its participants were asked to review the overall postwar performance of the American economy. The year 1980 was not a good one. The economy was once again in serious trouble.

Martin Feldstein, host of the conference as director of the NBER, attributed the poor performance of the American economy to government interference. The worm had turned. "There can be no doubt," he wrote, "that government policies . . . deserve substantial blame for [our] adverse experience."[2] Government regulations, income transfer and social insurance programs, and the inhibiting tax effects on capital accumulation had sapped the vitality of capitalism. Feldstein's views, however, were hardly reflected in the papers of his main participants. Instead of a return to "the years of chaos and depression," the postwar economy, according to Benjamin Friedman, "entered an era of stability and prosperity" with not only a higher average growth rate in the postwar years "but also a smaller variability of that growth."[3] The "categorical imperative" of postwar policymakers, in the opinion of the late Arthur Okun, was the avoidance of the Great Depression, and in that, he argued, they largely succeeded. The business cycle had been tamed, or at least brought within politically tolerable limits. "The standard deviation of real GNP [Gross National Product] around its growth trend," wrote Okun, "was about one-fourth as large as it had been in 1900–45, and only half as large as in the 'golden age' of 1900–16, 1920–29."[4]

Where expansions averaged 26 months and contractions 21 months, from 1854 to 1937, the postwar expansions had an average duration of 48 months with contractions compressed to an average of 11 months. "This quantum jump in stability," said Okun, "must . . . be credited to public policy. *It was made in Washington,*" and it was "the compositional shift" to a larger public sector GNP share that constituted "the largest single stabilizing element." In this context the growth of government transfer payments was another contributing factor to the marked reduction in cyclical instability. To Okun, the signal success of postwar economic policy was to be measured *"not in dollars of real GNP, but in the survival of United States Capitalism."*[5]

Okun's assessment is amply reinforced in Alan S. Blinder's analysis of the postwar distribution of income.[6] From 1947 to 1977, "real consumption per capita increased by more than 80 percent." At the same time, "the basic necessities of life—food, clothing, and shelter— commanded ever decreasing shares of the consumer budget." The net result was a drastic improvement in the "average level of economic well-being" as well as in its content.[7] Nonetheless, the distribution of income remained virtually unchanged, with a Gini ratio (the area of a Lorenz curve under the line of perfect equality as a proportion of the total area) ranging from a low of 0.40 to a high of 0.42 with the mean smack in the middle at 0.41. Still, it was "noticeably more equal than the distribution of 1929."[8] It remains, however, that the United States continues to have a higher inequality of income distribution than many other industrialized countries, with the dubious distinction of competing with France for the worst record among Organization for Economic Cooperation and Development (OECD) nations. In 1977, according to Blinder, "the richest fifth of American families received eight times as much income as the poorest fifth."[9]

The constancy of the postwar income distribution is in large part due to government transfer payments which rose, as a proportion of GNP, from 0.7 percent in the 1920s to more than 10 percent for 1973–79. To Robert Gordon, "the growth in the size of government after 1947 was mainly reflected in transfer payments rather than in goods and services."[10] The combined spending on goods and services by federal, state, and local governments as a precentage of GNP "exhibited no increase at all between the 1957–67 decade and the most recent 1973–79 subperiod." Since "the lower income strata receive a disproportionately large share of transfers," according to Blinder, "it is clear that cash transfers pushed the distribution of income in the direction of greater equality during the postwar period."[11]

As Blinder points out, "to decide who is poor, we must place a 'poverty line' somewhere in the income distribution . . . and count how many families (or people) fall below it."[12] He finds that *when transfers are deducted from income,* poverty goes up from 11.8 to 21.0 percent on an absolute consumption standard, and from 15.4 to 24.1 percent on a relative poverty standard with incomes 44.0 percent below the median income. Government transfer payments must therefore also be seen as a critical factor in the amelioration of poverty.

There was a marked decline in officially defined poverty during the 1960s largely because of the War on Poverty programs of the Lyndon Johnson administration. Blinder found that between 1965 and 1976 "the poverty rate for all persons declined by 24.4 percent," but on an *"income minus (cash) transfers"* basis, there was "almost no trend in the poverty rate."[13] In summary, transfer payments are clearly responsible, in great part, for the improvement of the postwar distribution of income over its *prewar* distribution, for its constancy over the past thirty-five years, and for the amelioration of poverty. In conjunction with macroeconomic policies, they also contributed to the greater stability of the postwar economy.

Economists stress that income is a *flow,* while wealth is a *stock.* What of the distribution of wealth in the United States? The distribution of wealth is far worse. Blinder cites one study, based on the same 1966 population, which found a Gini ratio of 0.76 for wealth compared to 0.43 for income distribution.[14] The available evidence also seems to indicate that wealth inequality is relatively stable with no ameliorating trend discernible. It should be obvious that an increase in the inequality of wealth would have a marked impact on the distribution of income, particularly if government tax policies were drastically changed to favor the accumulation of wealth, and the welfare aspects of government transfer payment were subject to substantial cuts. There is more to social welfare programs, as Wilber J. Cohen has emphasized, than Gini ratios and Lorenz-curve shifts,[15] for a "larger context" of hopes and aspirations, and the very *legitimation* of capitalism, is at stake.

Capitalism has survived as long as it has because of one unique aspect of its historical development: its flexibility in responding to changed circumstances. Unlike the Bourbons and the Romanovs, capitalism has been able to defuse potentially threatening situations and to adapt along lines that assure its continuation. It has been this enormous elasticity of capitalism, within a relatively democratic context, that has confounded Marxian analyses of its "internal contradictions," which according to a mechanical dialectic assured its demise in a bloody collapse. It has been capitalism's ability to place "an iron bit in nature's mouth" that has enabled it to co-opt its opponents through growing levels of real income. Growth has served, up to now, to defuse the distribution of income and wealth as politically destabilizing factors, for the system is seen as just. Only when growth becomes the "problematic" is distribution repoliticized.

This happened in the 1930s when the economic crisis was transformed into a social and political crisis with class antagonisms—as Britain is now experiencing in the wake of Margaret Thatcher's policies.

During the late 1950s up to the U.S. involvement in the Vietnam War, the postwar performance of the economy was, as we have seen, largely successful—compared to the trauma of the 1930s. The business cycle was still with us, but brief recessions were now followed by larger expansions. Liberal ideologues were quite satisfied with themselves. Political sociologists, such as Seymour Martin Lipset and Daniel Bell, seconded by John Fitzgerald Kennedy in his famous Yale speech, loudly proclaimed *the end of ideology*. Historians such as Arthur Schlesinger, Jr., were writing articles asking, "Where does the liberal go here?"[16]

Schlesinger described the two sources of liberalism as "the vindication of the individual against economic privation and despair [and] the vindication of the individual against moral and spiritual frustration." He then went on to state that the vindication of the individual against privation and despair had been largely achieved in the postwar period by "the most brilliant explosion of creative social thought this country has ever seen." He was convinced that modern mixed capitalism had solved its major economic problems. "Few liberals," he argued, "would seriously wish today to alter the mix in our present economy." Hence, what we now needed was a "new" liberalism which would "recover [its] deeper roots in the American cultural tradition by shifting [its] focus from economics and politics to the general style and quality of our civilization." Creative spontaneity could now be let loose in an economically secure world for the problem was no longer economic unemployment but that no less terrible, though more intangible, problem of "spiritual unemployment." What the new liberalism must do is "to help prime the pump, not economically, but ethically." As one defeated Democrat in the elections of 1952 was heard to lament, "The trouble is, we ran out of poor people."

To a large extent, this celebration of the status quo is reflected in the sixtieth anniversary celebration of the NBER, except for one troubling development: the 1970s. The consensus politics of the 1950s and early 1960s began unraveling with the guns *and* butter policies of the Johnson administration, which generated the inflationary impact of the Vietnam War. And it was during this traumatic time that monetarism challenged the conventional wisdom of Keynesian economics with its famous restatement of the quantity theory of money. Then came a series of supply shocks that made a shambles of the Phillips curve and the fine-tuning nostrums of orthodox, neoclassical Keynesians as well as the steady-as-you-go monetary growth rule of the monetarists. Inflation was now linked with a chronic level of unemployment that made "stagflation" the faddish neologism of our time. The supply shocks started with the worldwide crop failures of 1972, quickly followed by the devastating 1973 crisis brought on by the Organization of Petroleum Exporting Countries (OPEC) which led to a rapid acceleration of the inflation rate. Recession was now associated with jumping price levels. "When an economy is made depression proof," wrote Okun, "private expectations and conventions become asymmetrical, introducing an inflationary bias into the system."[17] The underlying inflation rate of about 5 percent in the 1960s was, in retrospect, politically tolerable. Now double-digit inflation occurred at the same time that employment and economic growth were seriously constrained.

Invariably, during periods of great crisis when conventional theoretical explanations no longer serve, the ground is laid for the rise of crackpots and assorted runaway ideologues with simple explanations for complex problems designed for popular appeal. This is the stuff of manipulated mass movements, where generally a single cause is attributed to all society's ills. And for single causes there are singular panaceas for piping us into the good society. The 1970s gave birth to the ideology of supply-side economics.

The two major popularizers of the supply-side theory are Jude Wanniski[18] and George Gilder.[19] The foremost practitioner is Ronald Reagan. Mainly, supply-side theory idealizes a past that never was and forces past history into its ideological mold.

Supply-side economics abhors the welfare state and all its redistributive programs. Indeed, it attributes all current ills to a misguided compassionate state, in nostalgia for the *prewar* period of unencumbered capitalism. Its program is to repeal the last half-century.

Essentially, supply-side economics is a theory of growth, taxation, and fiscal policy—all wedded to a largely discredited theory of human motivation and behavior which would render moot the divisive problem of redistribution. Its intellectual anchor is the Laffer curve, a distended belly framed by tax rates on the vertical axis and total tax revenues on the other, where in its upper, negatively sloped reaches the tax elasticity of revenue exceeds 1. On the lower, positively sloped portion, elasticity is less than 1—it is 1 at the point of maximum revenue. Consequently two rates of taxation produce the *same* revenue. Supply-siders are convinced, on the basis of contrived "historical" evidence, that the American economy is already on the upper portion of the Laffer curve, so that a reduction in the tax rate will *enhance* government tax revenue. That is what the curve says, but it is the explanation of this putative phenomenon that reveals the heart of supply-side theory. Part of the explanation of this inverse relationship between tax rates and tax revenues lies in the effect of high marginal tax rates in encouraging an "underground" economy. Lower the tax rate, therefore, and the process reverses itself, so that with more and more people reentering the visible tax-paying economy, tax revenues will rise.

But apart from this underground economy effect, lower tax rates (over the elastic portion of the Laffer curve) increase output and hence revenues by an *incentive effect*. And it is here that a convenient theory of human behavior comes into full view.

Human beings, we are told, are hypersensitive to tax rates, especially at the margin—so much so that their behavior is obsessively dominated by taxes. And since economic growth is the result of human behavior, it is *uniquely* dependent on the level of the marginal tax rate. A neoclassical labor market humming along is assumed, with after-tax income substituted for the real wage rate. *All* unemployment is *voluntary,* and involuntary unemployment is dismissed. The government with its taxing power inserts a "wedge" between what a worker gets and what he is paid. The greater the wedge, the less the individual after-tax income and the less he is willing to work. It follows, therefore, that by reducing the government wedge the incentive to work will soar, leading to such a disproportionate increase in output that tax revenues will actually be magnified despite the tax cut. A remarkably powerful relationship is discovered between work effort and taxes—and a highly doubtful one at that.

But there is more to this parable of human motivation than first appears. The higher one's income, the greater one's tax sensitivity. And in supply-side theory, those who earn more are more productive; actually they are the cutting edge of capitalism. It is the rich, as owners and creators of the physical means of production, who take the risks in an uncertain world. It is they, on the supply-side telling, who save, invest, and make capitalist growth possible, thereby providing for the poor through growth. Sap the energies of the rich, and the system founders in an orgy of welfare programs—and, supply-side theory claims, it is the poor who suffer most; nothing demoralizes the rich more than high marginal tax rates whose proceeds are used to finance the welfare state in grandiose redistribution schemes. To make matters worse, economic egalitarianism only serves to make the great unwashed more greedy. The supply-side axiom is that the nonrich are not creative, only the rich are. And it is "the experimental competition of elites" that generates the dynamism of capitalism that causes the rising tide of growth to raise *all* ships to a higher level—to use Jack Kemp's favorite John Kennedy metaphor. Capitalism is seen as a boiling cauldron of great convection currents where the *natural* elite rise from the bottom and the tired, worn-out elite, having done their thing, are cast down from whence they came. Social Darwinism at its boiling

... words, is "ineluctably elitist" and

... moving again requires only a tax cut
... powerful. And the poor would be the
... nly be helped by lifting the rate of in-
... ke place only if a greater inequality of
... wealth is fostered. It is *regressive* taxes,
... s, which help the poor most! On supply-

side logic, the only way out of our current malaise is to dismantle the welfare state.

High marginal tax rates, especially on the rich, are denominated as the primary cause of low growth rates, the decline in labor productivity, high unemployment, inflation, and everything else that is wrong with the economy. Manifestly, the simpler the cause, the simpler the solution! Herbert Stein, a conservative former chairman of the Nixon Council of Economic Advisors, has accurately characterized supply-side economics: "Businessmen have a strong propensity to argue for supply-side solutions to demand-side problems because they like to argue that if you will cut taxes on us we will produce more and that will cure both unemployment and inflation. The supply-side argument is a way of arguing that what is good for us is good for you."[20]

Supply-side theory suffers from an acute case of tax fetishism, with tax cuts an object of irrational reverence. Taxes are the cause of all our problems, and tax cuts will solve them—especially if they favor the rich. Supply-side economics is the *reductio ad absurdum* of capitalism. It is vulgar capitalism trying hard to vindicate vulgar Marxism. And in the hands of Ronald Reagan and his administration, it is a counterrevolution of the first order.

The Reagan administration's *Program for Economic Recovery*[21] is basically a supply-side document. Its goal is to "rekindle . . . entrepreneurial instincts and creativity" by cutting taxes drastically. Government regulation is to be undone. Nondefense expenditures are to be slashed, particularly the transfer payments which improved (slightly) the distribution of income in the postwar period. Cuts in nondefense spending will certainly do wonders for the work incentives of the poor, according to the canons of supply-side theory. There will be cuts in Medicaid, child nutrition programs, social security benefits, food stamps, unemployment benefits, youth training and employment programs, public service employment, income-assistance payments (Aid to Families with Dependent Children), and so on down the welfare handout line. On the other hand, defense expenditures will increase *in real terms* between 1980 and 1984 by an annual average of 7 percent, compared to a nondefense spending rate of growth of 1 percent *in nominal terms*. Real nondefense spending will be 15 percent lower in 1984 than in 1980, according to the Congressional Budget Office.

Clearly the cuts in nondefense expenditures will finance the planned increases in defense expenditures, and the main features of the Kemp-Roth tax cut will serve as an *offset* to the inflation-induced income tax increase (bracket creep) and the scheduled rise in social security taxes. In effect, there will be a substantial redistribution of the social product to the rich.

On the key issues of unemployment, inflation, stagflation, and money, supply-side economics is mostly confused. Unemployment is caused by the tax wedge effect of high taxes on the rich, provoking the incentive effect. But since high taxes also *cause* inflation, supply-side theory has a convenient theory of stagflation as well. Cut taxes on the rich, output will rise dramatically, unemployment will dwindle, and prices will fall. At one fell swoop we have the solution to unemployment, inflation, and stagflation!

That is the simplistic side of supply-side economics. The confusion comes in through the money window. What about money in inflation? Some supply-siders disdain Milton Friedman's monetarism.[22] Prices are a function of taxes, and not the money supply—or deficits. Monetarists are classed as closet Keynesians, working the demand side of the street. Monetary restraint serves only to inhibit private-sector growth and adds to inflationary pressures. Tight money's effect is sited on output and employment, not on prices, and as along Post Keynesian lines, in a curious juxtaposition, the money supply is *passive*.

Wanniski explains the *initial* inflationary price increases by relating them directly to money supply increase in excess of the real rate of growth, with the Laffer wedge inducing secondary price increases by way of progressive *ad valorem* taxes.[23] Tax cuts *plus* tight money are therefore seen as *the* solution to stagflation. Congressman Kemp, whose football career has made him an instant economic prophet, proposes the adoption of a strict gold standard as the only way of stopping inflation dead in its tracks—even if it destroys the economy as in a Great Depression!

The Reagan administration favors "a predictable steady growth in the money supply" while attributing inflation to government spending and the crowding out of the private sector in loan markets. Deficit spending is the *primary* cause of inflation, with easy money compounding the problem with *secondary* effects on the price level. This was the early confident assertion before the mounting Reagan deficits led to a comfortable rationalization that deficits scarcely mattered for inflation. The deep-think theory is subject to instant revision to fit its 1981 and 1982 deficit failures.

In the early Reagan scenario, inflation was programmed to fall from 9.9 percent in 1981 to 4.9 percent in 1986. As a result, interest rates are supposed to fall dramatically, as the fall in the expected rate of inflation (interest rates being simply a markup over the rate of price level change)—from 11.1 percent for 91-day Treasury bills in 1981 to 5.6 percent in 1986. So far, in mid-1982, financial markets continue to express skepticism, especially in the face of colossal deficits. But the money slowdown and the continued high growth projections imply a strong increase in the velocity of money. The administration is caught in a bind: How can an excess demand for money lead to a *fall* in its interest rate price?

The revolution in economic policy now under way transcends theoretical niceties. It is prepared to bend "reality" to the needs of its beliefs, no matter how incoherent it makes its supporting theory. The role of established social theory is to rationalize whatever is, after the fact. It serves those who hold power. Revolutionary theories are future-oriented and entail a vision of the good society. In those few instances when revolutionary theories succeed in gaining power, they are invariably corrupted by the need to consolidate that power. Praxis and theory are torn apart in the ensuing struggle, as purists demand that the revolution be realized immediately in its full dimension. Pragmatists advise caution and the tempering of theory.

The struggle currently going on in supply-side economics is between its theorists and its pragmatists. According to supply-side "theory," a cut in taxes is all that is needed. The rich will be stimulated to work harder (the incentive effect), real output will increase relative to demand, and prices will be stabilized or even fall. There is no danger that a tax cut will generate a counterproductive, inflationary deficit, for government revenues will increase because of the Laffer-curve effect. In short, deficits are irrelevant.

It is on the issue of deficits that supply-side economics has met its first defeat. More traditionally conservative economists, such as Arthur F. Burns, Alan Greenspan, and George P. Schultz, have not been sold on the wonders of the Laffer curve and, backed by doubts on the part of powerful members of the Senate and the House, they have pressured the Reagan administration with incomplete success into linking cuts in government expenditures to cuts in taxes. Deficits are to be avoided and the budget balanced by 1984—*at all costs.*

At all costs, of course, means massive cuts in nondefense expenditures. Defense expenditures, given the Reagan administration's foreign policy, have become sacrosanct.

Supply-side economics, in mid-1982, is in a state of shambles, with recession growing and deficits ballooning. Moreover, the administration's projection of a balanced budget by 1984 has already been withdrawn as beyond realization. Under continued high interest rates, the housing and the automobile and steel industries have all but collapsed. Supply-side theory has collided head-on with supply-side praxis. David Stockman has publicly confessed its failures in its early overoptimism. Doubts in the competence of Reaganomics are widespread. The Federal Reserve System is under administration criticism, and a second round of slashes in nondefense expenditures is in the making.

With the unemployment rate of black youth over 50 percent and with further cuts in welfare transfer payments, the American economy is headed for the polarization of classes. The fears of the Kerner Commission loom larger than ever. Should the economy falter, competition for scarce jobs among whites, blacks, and the disenfranchised will become more strident, and the gains of the last twenty years will go by the board, followed by a search for scapegoats and an even more violent political lurch, with American capitalism losing its facility to adapt to changing circumstances. Progress made in the postwar period is being undone with the maldistribution of income and wealth being deliberately skewed on the pretext of making everyone better off.

Supply-side praxis has by now left supply-side theory at the altar. What we are faced with is a rampant ideology of economic royalists engaged in their own Vendée—ideologists cynically using simple-minded theories as their prop because of their easy appeal to the uninformed. The Reagan administration's program, to put it baldly, is a calculated raid on the public treasury. It is a massive redistribution gambit with a reverse twist, not a growth scenario based on supply-side theory, no matter how addle-brained.

It is in the nature of ideological visionaries to sacrifice the present and the past in the name of a utopian future, even if it means an increase in human suffering and the sacrifice of the powerless and the disenfranchised on the way to that good society. Chiliasts are not famous for their tolerance or for their sensitivity to human suffering. Robespierre, Stalin, and the Ayatollah Khomeini, to take a few extreme examples, come immediately to mind. They are not idols that a democratic society will easily emulate. On this reading, supply-side economics will have a rocky future that can still be detoured. But it will require a more decent vision of humanity and its desires for a fair shake.

Vassar College

NOTES

1. See Martin Feldstein, ed., *The American Economy in Transition* (Chicago: University of Chicago Press, 1980).
2. Ibid. p. 3.
3. Benjamin Friedman, "Postwar Changes in the American Financial Markets," in Feldstein, *American Economy in Transition*, pp. 9–78.
4. Arthur Okun, "Postwar Economic Performance," in Feldstein, *American Economy in Transition*, pp. 162–69.
5. Ibid., pp. 162–63, 168. Italics added.
6. Alan S. Blinder, "The Level and Distribution of Well-Being," in Feldstein, *American Economy in Transition*, pp. 415–79.
7. Ibid., p. 433.
8. Ibid., p. 435.
9. Ibid., p. 436.
10. Robert J. Gordon, "Postwar Macroeconomics: The Evolution of Events and Ideas," in Feldstein, *American Economy in Transition*, pp. 101–62.
11. Blinder, "Level and Distribution of Well-Being," p. 446.
12. Ibid., p. 454.
13. Ibid., p. 459.
14. Ibid., p. 466.
15. Wilber J. Cohen, "Economic Well-Being and Income Distribution," in Feldstein, *American Economy in Transition*, pp. 486–93.
16. Arthur M. Schlesinger, Jr., "Where Do the Liberals Go from Here?" *New York Times Sunday Magazine*, August 4, 1957.
17. Okun, "Postwar Economic Performance," p. 169.
18. Jude Wanniski, *The Way the World Works* (New York: Simon & Schuster, 1979).
19. I have treated the Wanniski-Gilder supply-side theory more fully in a review article, "The Poverty of Wealth," for the *Journal of Post-Keynesian Economics* 4 (Winter 1981–82): 192–213.
20. Herbert Stein, "Changes in Macroeconomic Conditions," in Feldstein, *American Economy in Transition*, pp. 170–77.
21. *America's New Beginning: A Program for Economic Recovery*, The White House, February 1981.
22. George Gilder, *Wealth and Poverty* (New York: Basic Books, 1981).
23. Wanniski, *The Way the World Works*, pp. 113–15.

3

Women in the Stagflation Economy

EILEEN APPELBAUM

Although the emergence of the stagflation economy in 1969 had important implications for the economic position of women, its role in the subtle revolution[1] in women's relationship to work, marriage, and family has rarely been noted. This is true despite recognition by economists that women's participation in production and the nature of the work they perform have been shaped in significant ways by the economic opportunities confronting them. The role of stagflation has gone largely unnoticed, however, because of the narrow terms in which economists have conceptualized the chain of incentives. "Opportunities" are identified in standard economic theory with women's wages,[2] and the conclusion is reached that women's real wages will increase when job prospects are abundant. Rising real wages for women, in turn, induce a "substitution effect," causing women to substitute paid employment for housework or for leisure-time activities, thus increasing their participation in the labor force. Standard theory identifies "incentives" with family income net of the woman's own earnings. The theory then argues that a rise in family income as husbands' real wages increase induces an "income effect," reducing work incentives for married women and leading them out of the labor force. The impact of more than a decade of high levels of inflation and unemployment on the changing economic role of women has hardly been investigated.

This standard economic approach, largely devoid of reference to historically specific phenomena, has obscured some major changes in women's employment patterns since World War II. Thus, observing the steady increase in husbands' real wages during the 1950s and early 1960s,[3] economists consistently underestimated the labor force participation rate for married women. Undaunted by their poor prediction

34

record, economists simply concluded *ex post* that the substitution effect had outweighed the income effect in shaping women's decisions. Not only were men's real wages increasing, but women's real wages were also going up. This, economists concluded, was why women were working outside the home in ever-increasing numbers. With the fall in real wages between 1965 and 1969, and the sharp decline that began in 1972, the logic of the economists' argument suggested a slowdown in female labor force participation after 1965 as married women substituted home production for paid employment. Yet the influx of wives into the labor force continued through the 1970s.[4] In particular, economists did not foresee the large increase after 1965 in the proportion of married women with young children who sought paid employment. Despite declining real wages, the labor force participation rate for wives with children under the age of six increased from 23.3 percent in 1965 to 43.2 percent in 1979.[5]

The argument that will be developed in this essay is that both women's participation in economic activity and the kinds of jobs they hold are conditioned by the nature of the production process and by the pattern of economic growth. For married women, the question of whether husbands' earnings in combination with wives' home production activities are adequate to meet family needs must also be considered.

Changes in the work and family roles of women began during the first half of the 1940s with the wartime need for women workers and developed in earnest after 1950. Our analysis must therefore begin at that point. Changes in production processes imply that simple extrapolation from the previous work experience of women will not be an adequate guide to the future.

The traditional view of the division of labor between the sexes, in which men work in the marketplace while women perform unpaid housework and child care within the family, rested on two premises. The first was that labor requirements could largely be met out of the available pool of male workers. The second was that men could command a market wage sufficient to meet the market purchase needs of their families. Each of these assumptions has been challenged during the last three decades.

Paid employment of women obviously did occur during the longer past—18.9 percent of women in 1890 and 25.8 percent in 1940 were in the labor force.[6] It was, however, mainly single women who were employed, for after marriage women were expected to assume lifelong responsibilities for home and family. The low labor force participation rate for married women—still only 13.8 percent in 1940—confirms that most did.

Two factors in particular led women to leave paid employment upon marriage. Women's wages were viewed as supplementing the family's income. They were low both in comparison with men's wages and with the cost of the woman's own subsistence, encouraging productive activity in the household in the service of husbands who could command a higher market wage. At the same time, employers preferred to hire young single girls, many of whom migrated to the cities from rural areas in response to the availability of jobs. Clerical and sales positions were often restricted to single women, domestic servants were often required to live in, and nurses and teachers were discouraged from marrying. Thus marriage closed off employment opportunities.

For women, then, there was no real choice. Paid employment was simply the stage in the life cycle between leaving school and marriage. The differential between the wages of men and women, and the lack of jobs for married women, reinforced a sexual division of labor in which women were destined to perform unpaid labor in the home and, after marriage, were economically dependent on their husbands. Young single women were hired for jobs that were viewed as consistent with their primary role in society. Thus jobs in domestic service, making apparel, canning fruits, nursing, and teaching young children were labeled "women's work." Occupational segregation buttressed traditional sex roles and reinforced the existing division of labor within the home.

The "baby-bust" of the Depression decade meant that by 1940 families had relatively fewer young children to care for. The absolute number of children under the age of ten was about the same in 1941 as in 1917, but the proportion per 1,000 women age fourteen and older had fallen from 642 in 1917 to 425 in 1941. The percentage of married women between the ages of eighteen and forty-four who lived with their husbands and had no children under ten years of age rose from 37.5 percent in 1930 to 45.5 percent in 1940. Yet the labor force participation rate of women never increased as much as the drop in the number of children cared for by the average woman would allow. A wartime estimate of the potential reserve of female labor by Clarence D. Long suggested that the reduction in child-care responsibilities would have "allowed" a female labor force participation rate of 35.5 percent.[7] Census data, however, indicate a labor force participation rate of women in 1940 of 25.8 percent, up only slightly from 23.7 percent in 1920.[8] The traditional view that women belonged in the home continued to prevail.

The large wartime draft of men from the civilian labor force during 1942, followed by a smaller but still substantial draft during 1943, created both pressure and opportunity for women to seek jobs, even forcing a temporary relaxation of social pressures against hiring married women. The civilian male labor force declined from 40.3 million in December 1941 to 37.8 million a year later; this was just about offset by the 2.3 million increase in the civilian female labor force which rose from 14.6 to 16.9 million. Of the 5.0 million women that Long estimated as potential job recruits, at least 2.5 million entered the labor force within two years of Pearl Harbor.[9] The labor force participation rate of wives, which was only 13.8 percent in 1940, increased by 1944 to 22.0 percent.[10]

The end of the war, amid gloomy predictions of renewed recession, brought numerous calls for women to return to their traditional roles in order to facilitate the demobilization of veterans. The participation rate for wives declined between 1944 and 1947, though it remained well above its 1940 level.

It was the unprecedented expansion of the economy and the resulting postwar labor shortage that provided both job opportunities and a sympathetic environment for some shift in ideology that enabled married women to enter the labor force in large numbers.[11]

The supply of male workers grew slowly between 1945 and 1965 as a result of the low Depression birthrate, the increased proportion of men in school, and the inevitable war casualties. Growth in the pool of male workers just kept pace with the growth of traditionally male jobs. Lower birthrates and increased school enrollment affected the supply of young single women as well. In addition, age at first marriage declined and birthrates jumped. Employment of single women declined from 6.7 million in 1940 to 5.1 million in 1955, and went up to only 5.9 million in 1965.

Rapid growth in clerical, sales, and service employment resulted as government sectors expanded together with an enlarged distribution network necessitated by expanded output of durables and food products. Available jobs occurred just as the pool of single women, ordinarily preferred for these jobs, was declining. Employers closed the labor deficit by hiring married women for jobs ordinarily labeled "female." Labor force participation for married women increased from 22 percent in 1948 to 35 percent in 1965 and 41 percent in 1970.[12] By 1970 a married woman with children could expect to spend twenty-five years in the labor force.[13]

A complicated dynamic was set in motion during these two decades by the tension between the high demand for female labor generated by a rapidly expanding economy and the expectation that married women would continue to fulfill their traditional role as housewives. The dominant view that emerged, held not only by husbands but also by employers and often by the women themselves, was that female employment was acceptable, subordinated, however, to the claims of domesticity in their primary roles as wives and mothers. As a result, married women tended to work intermittently, moving into and out of the labor force in response to changes in their situation at home. Whatever their personal aspirations, many of them found it difficult to exhibit a commitment to a career, job seniority, or long-term promotion. Essentially, it was employment outside the home by childless married women or those with children in school that came to be viewed as consistent with the more compelling obligations of marriage.

The structure of jobs and the economic position of women within the labor market were both affected by the fact that married women were the main pool of available labor from 1948 to 1965. Prevailing sex-role attitudes provided a rationale for denying women promotion to supervisory responsibilities. As the employment of married women increased, employers embraced the incentive to structure new jobs to be performed by a low-paid, intermittent work force through fragmentation and "de-skilling" of tasks, denoting them as female. Women were seldom hired directly for jobs previously identified as "male." Women were integrated into the work force by way of enlarging the number of low-paying, dead-end jobs; labor market segmentation increased.

Despite the increase in paid employment of married women, their second-class status within the labor market remained largely unchanged. Nonetheless, there were significant changes in the social fabric wrought by the increased number of working wives. While a wife's earnings were usually below even her own subsistence level, they were nevertheless high enough to affect the family's standard of living. The advent of the multiple-earner family has had a major impact in augmenting family income and consumption expenditures. The average upper-middle-income household with a working wife would have dropped to middle-income status without the wife's paycheck, while the average middle-income family with a working wife would have fallen to lower-middle-income status if the wife stopped working.[14] The importance of this development did not become fully apparent until inflation, recession, and slow productivity growth threatened the living scales of American families in the 1970s.

Female labor force developments have had numerous ramifications—some obvious, like the change in employers' willingness to hire married women; others subtle, like the changes in abortion laws as women assumed greater responsibility for the timing of their children. Economists attempted to capture these phenomena through the real wage variable, focusing on the rise in women's real wages as the primary determinant of the postwar increase in the labor force participation rate of married women. This explanation seemed sufficient so long as women's real wages increased in tandem with the growth in jobs sex-stereotyped as "female." Inflation in the mid-1960s, however, caused real wages to decline between 1965 and 1970, with a more precipitous drop in real wages since 1972. Yet despite three recessions since 1969 and productivity stagnation since 1973, employment in clerical work, food service, health service, and retail sales continued to increase and even accelerated in the 1970s.[15] Perversely, jobs labeled "female" continued to grow even as real wages fell. The growth in the labor force participation of women has likewise continued, confounding economists by the "perverse" supply behavior.

As stated earlier, one of the basic assumptions underlying the traditional conceptualization of the division of labor between the sexes was the supposition that men were able to command a market wage sufficient, in conjunction with the unpaid labor by wives within the home, to meet the needs of their families. In the 1970s, economic events conspired to violate that assumption. Unlike the Depression era, however, there was no scarcity of jobs for women this time.

Though the economy continued to expand through the 1960s, buoyed up by the Vietnam War, inflation began to erode real income. Spendable average weekly earnings of a worker with three dependents peaked in 1965 at $91.67 in real terms (1967 dollars), declining slowly but steadily to $90.20 in 1970. They rose to $97.11 in 1972 before dropping to $90.35 in 1975. The price increases over the last six years have obliterated twenty years of money wage gains, depressing real wages in the first half of 1981 to about their 1960 level, leaving real wages of a worker with three dependents in April 1981 at $81.39.[16] Thus the ability of a male wage earner to command an income sufficient to support himself and his family was seriously impaired by inflation during the last decade.

Nonetheless, continued growth in the feminized sectors of the economy provided women with job opportunities, despite the deep recession of 1973–75 and the general economic malaise that characterized the decade. About 12.7 million new jobs were created between 1972 and

1978, and 7.8 million were filled by women. Some 4.1 million were hired for clerical or service jobs, and another 1 million in sales or as registered nurses or health technicians.[17] Women increased their participation in the labor force by more than 1 million workers each year between 1971 and 1979.[18]

For many families, economic survival in the 1970s depended on having two incomes. As recently as 1960 the husband was the only wage earner in most husband-wife families. By 1967, however, half of all such families were two-earner families, with wives contributing the second income in nearly 40 percent of the families and other family members working in another 11 percent. In 1976, for the first time, half of all wives in families in which the husband worked also worked. By 1979 only 36 percent of families were supported solely by the husband's earnings; in 55.5 percent of the families both adult members worked.[19]

Augmenting the number of wage earners per family succeeded in offsetting the decline in real wages between 1965 and 1969. Median family income increased steadily, by 35.4 percent in real terms between 1960 and 1969. In 1970 and 1971, however, median family income fell despite the growth in the number of families with more than one wage earner; median family income increased less than 7 percent between 1970 and 1979.[20] This leveling off of real income occurred despite the increase in the number of families in which other members in addition to the husband worked, from 53 percent of families in 1970 to 64 percent in 1979. Thus, after 1970 the extra family wage earner barely kept real family income from declining.

Empirical support for the argument that employment opportunities and inflation exert an influence on female labor force participation can be found in recent econometric studies by Beth Niemi and Cynthia Lloyd.[21] They found that inflation, measured by the consumer price index, had a positive and significant effect on the labor supply of young and prime-age women and a significant negative effect on women over the age of fifty-five. This finding is consistent with other evidence that the pattern of women's labor force participation has undergone a revision in the last fifteen years.[22] Prior to 1965, most female labor force growth occurred in the over-thirty-five age-group, among women who had completed childbearing. Notable increases in the labor force participation of women under age thirty-five first occurred in the 1965–69 period, coinciding with the onset of inflation and the decline in husbands' real wages. Since 1970, women between the ages of twenty-five and thirty-four have become the major source of increases in the women's labor force pool. Their participation rate rose from 38.6 percent in 1965 to 63.9 percent in 1979.[23] In 1975, for the first time, the dip in labor participation rates among women twenty-five to twenty-nine years of age was no longer observable. For women between twenty and twenty-four years of age in 1970, it was 57.8 percent; in 1975, when these women were twenty-five to twenty-nine years of age, the labor force participation rate for that age category was 57.0 percent.[24] Some women in this age category had postponed marriage and childbearing, but to a large extent the change reflected the fact that the proportion of young married women who had preschool age children and continued to work increased. The number of married women who had children under the age of six and worked outside the home had climbed steadily during the 1950s but had reached only 18.6 percent of such mothers by 1960. By 1970 the proportion stood at 30.3 percent, and by 1979 it had reached 43.2 percent.[25] The work-life expectancy of women registered a substantial increase. By 1977 the average woman could look forward to spending 27.6 years in paid employment (the comparable figure for men is 38.3 years).[26]

An argument developed by Richard Easterlin and extended by Michael Wachter[27] attributes these changes to a desire by young people to achieve a targeted standard of living during their prime working years that equals or exceeds what their parents accomplished. In light of the 1970s stagflation, the only way to achieve such affluence was through a shift to two-earner families, involving more continuous work patterns for young married women.

Young families are no longer able to sacrifice the wife's earnings. In families in which the wife was employed, her earnings accounted for 26 percent of family income in 1970, 1975, and 1977 (38 percent in 1977 if she worked full-time).[28] Moreover, median family income of married-couple families in which the wife had a job substantially exceeded that in families in which she was a full-time homemaker, with the ratio being 1.35 in 1977.[29] The contribution of wives to family income has become indispensable.

Families headed by women increased dramatically during the 1970s. Women headed 9.4 percent of all families in 1950, 10.0 percent in 1960, 10.9 percent in 1970, and 14.4 percent in 1978.[30] Such families have been at a double disadvantage in coping with rising prices and declining real wages, and their incomes have lagged because of the substantial wage differentials, with median usual weekly earnings in May 1978 at $166 for women and $272 for men. Hence households that lack an adult male wage earner are more likely to be poor.

In 1977, median family income for families headed by women was about $7,700, or 44 percent of the $17,720 total for husband-wife families. While 45 percent of such families had incomes under $7,000, and only 19 percent had incomes of $15,000 or more, for married-couple families the situation was quite different: Only 11.5 percent had incomes under $7,000, while 60.5 percent had incomes of $15,000 or more. Lacking either a male wage earner or multiple wage earners, nearly one-third of families headed by women had incomes below the poverty line. The comparable figure for families headed by men is one-ninth, and for husband-wife families, one-nineteenth. After declining steadily through the 1960s, the number of poor families increased during the stagflation decade of the 1970s; all the increase in the number living in poverty during this decade has been among families headed by women.

As with other groups of women, labor force participation for those who head families rose during the last decade. Here again, most of the increase came from those under the age of thirty-five. The largest group of female household heads who work consists of divorced women, whose occupational distribution and unemployment experience is similar to that of women living with their husbands. White collar occupations sex-stereotyped as "female" also opened up job opportunities for black women. Black female family heads employed in white collar jobs (secretaries, stenographers, typists, and teachers, etc.) rose from 24 percent in 1970 to 41 percent in 1978. Service workers (especially domestic service) decreased from 51 to 37 percent.

The increase in the incidence of poverty among households headed by women cannot be attributed either to a reduced commitment to paid employment or to differences in occupational distribution as compared with other women. Stagflation, compounded by the clustering of women in traditionally lower-paying female jobs, bears the onus.

The slowdown in labor productivity growth has contributed both to inflation and to the erosion of real income growth. Vagueness over the causes for the slowdown remains. We consider here the contention that effective labor services have declined relative to measured labor hours because of the increased employment of women and young people (including, of course, young women).

This contention rests not on the premise that women (or young people) are intrinsically less productive than prime-age males, but on the premise that women (and young people) are less productive than men because they have less experience. It is also argued that women (and young people) are consigned to low productivity jobs in the secondary labor market and that women are denied access to more productive jobs through the sex-labeling of occupations.

Martin Baily examines this hypothesis using a demographically adjusted measure of labor input for the nonfarm business sector (carrying the strong assumption that lower wages for women are an accurate reflection of their lower productivities). His conclusion is that demographic changes make only a small difference in the growth of labor productivity, and cannot explain the productivity slowdown between the 1968–73 and 1973–79 periods.

As for young workers today being somehow less productive than young people a generation ago, Baily estimates that for this explanation to hold would require workers born in 1963 to be intrinsically less than *half* as productive as those born in 1943. As this seems patently implausible, Baily concludes that a decline in cohort quality "can at most explain a small fraction of the slowdown."[31]

Thus the trend toward a younger and increasingly female labor force is not likely to "explain" the slowdown in labor productivity growth, especially since 1973.

Clerical work has been the fastest-growing job sector. By 1985, one-fifth of our work force will consist of clerical workers, compared with one-seventh in 1960. Nearly 8 million women found clerical work between 1960 and 1979 in the explosive growth in a demand for bank tellers, bookkeepers, cashiers, secretaries, and typists. This expansion of clerical jobs enabled many families to protect themselves against the worst ravages of inflation during the 1970s despite steep declines in real wages. But what of the future? Women's employment prospects are closely tied to developments in the clerical sector, where one-third of women workers are employed. Compression in clerical jobs could obviously have serious ramifications.

Computers are already widely used in large enterprises for such clerical functions as the creation, filing, retrieval, copying, moving, and transforming of information. Some enterprises are even moving in the direction of keeping and transmitting information electronically, making the futuristic "paperless office" a present reality. Automation promises to revolutionize the traditional clerical function.

While it is unlikely that office microelectronics will cause the bottom to fall out of the clerical labor market, J. Rada gives three persuasive reasons to anticipate rapid office automation in the developed countries:[32] (1) The sector is badly undercapitalized in comparison with manufacturing or agriculture. (2) The sector has shown low productivity increases in the past; for some firms, office automation can yield stronger overall productivity gains than equivalent investment in manufacturing operations. (3) Office labor costs are high and rising, and unionization is increasing. Moreover, much repetitive office work has already been computerized, and word processors are commonplace.

Studies of technological displacement conducted in Western Europe suggest that 40 percent of the work done in offices is suitable for automation. The Siemens Report (West Germany) estimates a reduction in labor requirements of 25 to 30 percent if such automation is implemented; the French Nora Report reaches similar conclusions about the French banking industry; and the International Federation of Commercial, Clerical, and Technical Employees estimates that European office employment could fall 20 to 25 percent over a ten-year period. Informed observers, such as Bell Laboratories executive Victor Vyssotsky, expect a U.S. reduction of the total clerical effort of about 20 to 30 percent in large firms.[33]

It must be borne in mind that office automation does not necessarily mean a reduction in staff. Additional clerical services may be provided; office automation, to date, has been accompanied by increases in the hiring of clerical workers. Nevertheless, automation has already changed the relationship of employment growth to increased volume in such growth industries as insurance and banking. Thus while bank transactions increased 8.3 percent annually between 1960 and 1973, employment grew by just 4.5 percent per year. Between 1973 and 1976, with transactions up by 7.2 percent annually, jobs grew by 3.2 percent. By 1990, employment in finance, insurance, and real estate is expected to climb at an annual rate of only 1.8 percent.[34]

The ultimate impact of automation on employment cannot be evaluated apart from broader economic conditions and rates of industry growth. The increases in productivity in office work, much of which is done in manufacturing industries and other nonservice sectors, should increase overall productivity. It is likely also to limit the growth of clerical employment. Thus women workers can expect to bear the major cost of introducing a new technology from which society in general expects to benefit. The question is whether women workers will be absorbed by new labor demands.

There are, in fact, two questions to be answered. The first is whether the new technology will result in alternative job opportunities; the second is whether such opportunities will be open to women. Insofar as office work is automated, while clerical positions may grow more slowly the opportunities for support personnel in the automated office should increase. Programmers to design, write, test, and install software, and mechanics to maintain the new office equipment will be required. In addition, highly trained employees capable of analyzing office routine and designing particular computer applications, and for system testing and conversion, will be needed. These, however, are all typically male occupations.

At the other end, it is evident that the production of semiconductor components has resulted in increased employment in this industry.[35] Nationally, women account for 70 percent of the semiconductor industry's production workers. However, they have been "crowded" into the low-paying assembly jobs (at wages which range from $3.75 at entry to $5.50 for three or more years experience), where they constitute three-fourths of the work force; men hold four-fifths of the higher-paying technical and craft positions. Women production workers, who perform routine assembly tasks, are now threatened by the development of automated processing techniques which are already being implemented.

Thus, while the new technology will create opportunities in particular occupations, automation by itself does not promise women improved employment opportunities. Instead, the main opportunities are related to economic growth. Penetration by women of male-dominated occupations is facilitated by tight labor markets and high rates of economic growth. An end to stagflation, therefore, might enable women to benefit from advances in technology.

The full integration of women workers into the economic mainstream can be achieved only in the context of steady growth and full employment.

Temple University

NOTES

1. Ralph E. Smith originated this term.
2. See Jacob Mincer, "Labor Force Participation of Married Women," in H. Gregg Lewis, ed., *Aspects of Labor Economics,* Universities-National Bureau Conference Series 14 (Princeton: Arno Press, 1962). Mincer developed the original framework for analyzing women's labor force participation. Among the major studies applying Mincer's approach, see Glen C. Cain, *Married Women in the Labor Force: An Economic Analysis* (Chicago: University of Chicago Press, 1966); William G. Bowen and T. Aldrich Finegan, *The Economics of Labor Force Participation* (Princeton: Princeton University Press, 1969); and more recently, Glen C. Cain and Martin D. Dooley, "Estimation of a Model of Labor Supply, Fertility, and

Wages of Married Women," *Journal of Political Economy* 84 (August 1976): part 2, pp. S179–99.

3. Measured in 1967 dollars, spendable average weekly earnings of a married worker with three dependents was $82.25 in 1960, $91.67 in 1965, $90.20 in 1970, $83.56 in 1980, and $81.39 in April 1981. (See U.S. Department of Labor, Bureau of Labor Statistics, *Monthly Labor Review,* July 1981, Table 20.)

4. The labor force participation rate of wives increased steadily from 13.8 percent in 1940 to 23.8 percent in 1950 to 27.7 percent in 1955, 30.5 percent in 1960, 34.7 percent in 1965, 40.8 percent in 1970, 45.0 percent in 1975, and 49.4 percent in 1979. (See U.S. Department of Labor, Bureau of Labor Statistics, *Handbook of Labor Statistics,* December 1980, Table 57.)

5. Ibid.

6. U.S. Department of Commerce, Bureau of the Census, *Historical Statistics of the United States, Colonial Times to 1970,* series D49–62.

7. All figures are from Clarence D. Long, *The Labor Force in Wartime America* (New York: National Bureau of Economic Research, 1944), p. 53.

8. *Historical Statistics,* series D49–62.

9. Long, *Labor Force,* p. 70.

10. U.S. Department of Commerce, Bureau of the Census, *Statistical Abstract of the United States: 1974,* Table 550.

11. This argument is developed at length by Valerie Kincade Oppenheimer in *The Female Labor Force in the United States: Demographic and Economic Factors Governing Its Growth and Changing Composition* (Berkeley: University of California, 1970).

12. *Handbook of Labor Statistics,* Table 57.

13. U.S. Department of Labor, Bureau of Labor Statistics, *Length of Working Life for Men and Women, 1970,* Special Labor Force Report 187 (1977).

14. U.S. Department of Commerce, Bureau of the Census, *Current Population Reports,* Series P-23, no. 100, February 1980, Table 9-7. See also Clair Vickery, "Women's Economic Contribution to the Family," in Ralph E. Smith, ed., *The Subtle Revolution: Women at Work* (Washington, D.C.: The Urban Institute, 1979).

15. U.S. Department of Labor, Bureau of Labor Statistics, *Perspectives on Working Women: A Databook,* Bulletin 2080, October 1980, Table 11.

16. *Monthly Labor Review,* Table 20.

17. *Current Population Reports,* Series P-23, no. 100, Table 8-1.

18. *Handbook of Labor Statistics,* Table 3.

19. Ibid., Table 58.

20. *Current Population Reports,* Series P-60, no. 118, Table C, and no. 123, Table A.

21. Beth T. Niemi and Cynthia B. Lloyd, "Female Labor Supply in the Context of Inflation," *American Economic Review* 71 (May 1981): 70–75; and idem, "Money Illusion or Price Illusion: The Effects of Inflation on Female Labor Force Participation," in Nathan Schmuckler and Edward Marcus, eds., *Inflation Through the Ages: Economic, Social, Psychological, and Historical Aspects* (New York: Brooklyn College Press, 1981).

22. For further evidence of this changing employment pattern, and an econometric analysis of its implications, see Eileen Appelbaum, *Back to Work: Determinants of Mature Women's Successful Reentry* (Boston: Auburn House, 1981).

23. U.S. Department of Labor, Employment and Training Administration, *Employment and Training Report of the President, 1980,* Table A-2.

24. *Perspectives on Working Women.*
25. *Handbook of Labor Statistics,* Table 57.
26. U.S. Department of Labor, Women's Bureau, *20 Facts on Women Workers,* December 1980.
27. Richard Easterlin, *Population, Labor Force, and Long Swings in Economic Growth: The American Experience* (New York: National Bureau of Economic Research, 1968); Michael L. Wachter, "Intermediate Swings in Labor Force Participation," *Brookings Papers on Economic Activity* 2 (1977): 545–74.
28. *Current Population Reports,* Series P-23, no. 100, Table 9-7.
29. Ibid., Table 9-8.
30. Data in this section are all from *Employment and Training Report of the President, 1979.*
31. Martin Neil Baily, "Productivity and the Services of Capital and Labor," *Brookings Papers on Economic Activity* 1 (1981): 13.
32. J. Rada, *The Impact of Microelectronics: A Tentative Appraisal of Information Technology* (Geneva: International Labor Office, 1980).
33. Victor A. Vyssotsky, "The Use of Computers for Business Functions," in Michael L. Dertouzos and Joel Moses, eds., *The Computer Age: A Twenty-Year View* (Cambridge, Mass.: M.I.T. Press, 1979).
34. U.S. Department of Labor, Bureau of Labor Statistics, *Industry Wage Surveys: Banking and Insurance, December 1976* (1978).
35. Data are from Michael L. Troutman, "The Semiconductor Labor Market in Silicon Valley," mimeographed (1980).

4

R & D and Labor Productivity: Can Tax Incentives Help?

EILEEN L. COLLINS

Slower productivity growth in the stagflation economy has tended to generate renewed interest in government incentives for research and development (R & D) along the following lines: First, R & D can contribute to productivity growth, which can relieve inflationary pressure. Second, the private sector tends to undertake less than socially optimal R & D because individual firms who perform R & D cannot fully capture its benefits and may be unable to pool the risk associated with some R & D projects. Third, the tendency of the private sector to underinvest is exacerbated in a stagflation economy, for it is harder to predict future prices and market opportunities; this creates uncertainty about the payoff to R & D and the attractiveness of R & D projects. In addition, stagflation can depress business expectations and the perceived payoff to R & D.

Encouraging R & D is one objective of the Economic Recovery Tax Act of 1981, which includes specific incentives for R & D. This essay will assess the contribution an R & D tax incentive might make to diminishing the stagflation problem.

Table 4.1 shows average annual growth rates in real output per hour for all persons employed in the private business sector and in major subsectors. Labor productivity grew at an accelerated rate after World War II, averaging 3.3 percent per year from 1947 to 1966 (compared to roughly two percent per year from 1899 to 1947[1]). Growth slowed to 2.3 percent per year from 1966 to 1973 and to 0.8 percent per year in the later 1970s.

This overall pattern is not necessarily reflected in individual sec-

TABLE 4.1: Average Annual Growth Rate in Real (1972 Dollar) Output* per Hour of All Persons†

	1947–66	1966–73	1973–79	1969–79
Private business sector	3.3	2.3	0.8	1.5
Nonfarm business sector	2.7	2.1	0.6	1.4
Manufacturing	2.7	3.0	2.0	2.7
Durable manufacturing	2.2	2.5	2.0	2.4
Nondurable manufacturing	3.3	3.8	1.9	3.1
Farm	5.4	5.4	3.0	2.9
Mining	4.2	2.0	−4.8	−3.4
Construction	2.7	−1.1	−1.6	−1.9
Transportation	2.2	2.0	1.2	1.9
Communications	5.4	4.8	6.4	5.7
Electric, gas, and sanitary services	6.3	3.7	0.9	1.6
Trade	2.5	2.5	1.1	1.8
Wholesale trade	2.9	3.6	0.4	1.5
Retail trade	2.2	1.7	1.4	1.9
Finance, insurance, and real estate	2.2	0.4	0.8	0.9
Services	1.6	1.5	0.3	1.0

*Output refers to gross domestic product originating in sector in 1972 dollars.
†Hours of all persons refers to all persons engaged in sector, including proprietors and unpaid family labor.
SOURCE: Growth rates for private business sector and nonfarm business sector are based on figures appearing in *Economic Report of the President* (Washington: Government Printing Office, 1981), Table B-38, p. 276. Growth rates for subsectors were supplied by the U.S. Department of Labor's Bureau of Labor Statistics. Although the bureau publishes figures for the manufacturing subsector, figures for other major subsectors are not published because the bureau does not have full confidence in them.

tors. In manufacturing, growth in labor productivity averaged 2.7 percent per year from 1947 to 1966 and 3.0 percent from 1966 to 1973, and dropped to 2.0 percent from 1973 to 1979. In agriculture the figures averaged 5.4 percent per year from 1947 to 1973 and 3.0 percent per year from 1973 to 1979. Communications experienced consistently high productivity rates, averaging 5.4 percent per year from 1947 to 1966, 4.8 percent from 1966 to 1973, and 6.4 percent from 1973 to 1979. Mining and construction experienced *negative* productivity growth during the 1970s; the average annual rate was −1.6 percent in construction and −4.8 percent in mining.

The slowdown was produced by a set of interrelated factors that economists do not fully understand or confirm. Frequently mentioned factors are: slower growth in capital per worker; government regulations requiring the "production" of "unmeasured" products, such as improved environmental quality and worker safety; a shift in the number of workers from manufacturing to the service sector, where measured productivity growth is relatively slower; increased rates of entry of young and female workers, which has increased the proportion of less skilled workers with little or no labor market experience; and a retarded pace of technological change.[2]

Research and development enhances productivity by deepening the pool of knowledge available for invention, adoption, and diffusion of new technology. In an industry that performs R & D, the results can be translated into higher output per unit of input (or per bundle of inputs) or into better products that increase output quality (though this dimension of productivity change is extremely difficult to measure and is not well captured in usual productivity measures). When R & D results in one industry are translated into new or improved capital goods, there are additional productivity gains in capital-using sectors. The contribution of R & D to productivity in the 1960s was found to be positive, significant, and high.[3] Table 4.2 shows R & D expenditures in current and constant dollars for 1953 to 1978. There is some evidence that in the 1970s the contribution has been smaller. While the explanation is not entirely clear, some possible factors are: energy price shocks; swings in capacity utilization; increased uncertainty about future prices that may have inhibited the fruits of R & D from being fully realized; and measurement difficulties.[4]

Nevertheless, it is clear that R & D does enhance productivity growth, though after a lag.[5] Thus, stimulating R & D is considered to be an important component of any program to encourage productivity growth so that direct tax incentives to stimulate R & D have been frequently proposed.

Since 1954 the tax code has explicitly allowed business taxpayers to deduct R & D costs when incurred or to amortize them over five or more years. Capital expenditures for R & D are not eligible for immediate write-off, but they are covered under the tax code's accelerated depreciation and investment tax credit provisions.

Proposed R & D tax changes have generally taken the form of an increased deduction for R & D costs, faster write-off for R & D equipment, or a tax credit for R & D expenditures.[6] The Economic Recovery Tax Act of 1981 includes a hybrid blend of earlier proposals.

The new act provides a tax credit for R & D, retroactive to June 30, 1981, and ending on December 31, 1985. The credit is equal to 25 percent of the *increase* in *eligible* R & D costs above the average for the previous three years. R & D refers to "research and development costs in the experimental or laboratory sense" (the definition now in-

TABLE 4.2: Funds for Performance of Industrial R & D by Year and Source of Funds (Billions of Dollars)

	Current Dollars			Constant 1972 Dollars*		
	Total	Federal	Company†	Total	Federal	Company†
1953	$3.6	$1.4 (39%)	$2.2 (61%)	$6.2	$2.4	$3.7
1954	4.1	1.8 (43%)	2.3 (57%)	6.8	2.9	3.9
1955	4.6	2.2 (47%)	2.5 (53%)	7.6	3.6	4.0
1956	6.6	3.3 (50%)	3.3 (50%)	10.5	5.3	5.2
1957	7.7	4.3 (56%)	3.4 (44%)	11.9	6.7	5.2
1958	8.4	4.8 (57%)	3.6 (43%)	12.7	7.2	5.5
1959	9.6	5.6 (59%)	4.0 (41%)	14.2	8.3	5.9
1960	10.5	6.1 (58%)	4.4 (42%)	15.3	8.9	6.4
1961	10.9	6.2 (57%)	4.7 (43%)	15.7	9.0	6.7
1962	11.5	6.4 (56%)	5.0 (44%)	16.2	9.1	7.1
1963	12.6	7.3 (58%)	5.4 (42%)	17.6	10.2	7.5
1964	13.5	7.7 (57%)	5.8 (43%)	18.6	10.6	8.0
1965	14.2	7.7 (55%)	6.4 (45%)	19.1	10.4	8.7
1966	15.5	8.3 (54%)	7.2 (46%)	20.3	10.9	9.4
1967	16.4	8.4 (51%)	8.0 (49%)	20.7	10.6	10.1
1968	17.4	8.6 (49%)	8.9 (51%)	21.1	10.4	10.7
1969	18.3	8.5 (46%)	9.9 (54%)	21.1	9.7	11.4
1970	18.1	7.8 (43%)	10.3 (57%)	19.8	8.5	11.3
1971	18.3	7.7 (42%)	10.7 (58%)	19.1	8.0	11.1
1972	19.6	8.0 (41%)	11.5 (59%)	19.5	8.0	11.5
1973	21.2	8.1 (38%)	13.1 (62%)	20.1	7.7	12.4
1974	22.9	8.2 (36%)	14.7 (64%)	19.7	7.1	12.6
1975	24.2	8.6 (36%)	15.6 (64%)	19.0	6.8	12.2
1976	27.0	9.6 (35%)	17.4 (65%)	20.1	7.0	13.1
1977	29.9	10.5 (35%)	19.4 (65%)	21.4	7.5	13.9
1978	33.4	11.3 (34%)	22.1 (66%)	22.3	7.5	14.7

*GNP implicit price deflator used to convert to 1972 dollars.
†Company funds include all funds for industrial R & D work performed within facilities except funds provided by the federal government. Excluded are company-financed R & D contracted to outside organizations such as research institutions, universities, and colleges, and other nonprofit organizations.
SOURCE: *National Patterns of R & D Resources* (Washington: National Science Foundation, 1977), Table B-1, p. 22; *Research and Development in Industry 1978* (Washington: National Science Foundation, 1979), Table B-1, p. 9; and National Science Foundation, *Science Indicators 1978* (Washington: Government Printing Office, 1979), Table 4-1, p. 201.

cluded in section 174 of the tax code), except that the act specifically excludes research conducted abroad, research in the social sciences and humanities, and research not paid for by the firm. Eligible costs include wages for researchers, materials costs, and payments for use of equipment (expenditures for direct purchase of plant and equipment are excluded), 65 percent of payments for contract research (e.g., to a research firm or university), and 65 percent of corporate grants made for basic research at universities and certain other organizations. The 65 percent ceiling is intended to approximate the average ratio of wages, supply costs, and equipment leasing costs to total industrial research costs.

Confining the credit to current R & D costs favors R & D projects which are relatively less capital-intensive. Presumably the differential is intended to be counterbalanced by more favorable capital cost recovery provisions for R & D equipment. However, the faster write-off (three rather than five years) is to some degree offset by a smaller investment tax credit (6 percent rather than 10 percent). Whether or not this treatment turns out to be more favorable depends on several factors, including inflation and interest rates and the rate of obsolescence of a firm's R & D equipment.

The act also provides an increased deduction for manufacturers' contributions of scientific equipment to universities, and it suspends for two years the application of Treasury Regulation 1.861-8 to R & D expenditures.[7]

The tax credit could have been tied to the level of R & D (i.e., a "flat-rate" tax credit) rather than just to increases in R & D (i.e., an "incremental" tax credit). A flat-rate credit of x percent for all economic costs of performing R & D would reduce the "net-of-tax cost" of performing R & D by $x/(1-t)$ percent, where t is the effective tax rate on additional income.[8] For example, a 16 percent credit[9] and a 46 percent tax rate would yield a 30 percent reduction in net-of-tax cost.

For an incremental tax credit, $x/(1-t)$ represents the percentage reduction in net-of-tax cost at the *margin*. The percent reduction in *average* net-of-tax cost is smaller and depends on the rate of increase in R & D expenditures. For example, a 16 percent credit for R & D spending above the average for the three previous years, a 46 percent marginal tax rate, and 10 percent per year growth in R & D expenditures, would yield a 5 percent reduction in average net-of-tax cost. The point of an *incremental* credit is to provide a large "carrot" for increases in R & D spending but to withhold "carrots" when there is no increase. An incremental credit is often regarded as "cost-effective" compared to flat-rate credit, fostering a larger increase in R & D per every treasury tax-dollar loss.[10]

A tax incentive's effect will depend on a set of interrelated factors which enter into business decisions about R & D and will vary with the specific firm, industry, and market setting.[11]

There are no published studies that provide empirical estimates of relationships between tax variables, R & D's net-of-tax cost, and the amount or composition of R & D activity. Two studies which have done some preliminary estimates of the responsiveness of R & D to non-tax-induced changes in cost place long-run elasticity at about 0.3[12] and about 0.9.[13] As the authors themselves note, their results are tentative; more refined models are needed to improve estimates of elasticity and to untangle the influence of other variables. Second, it is not clear *a priori* that the responsiveness of R & D will be the same for a tax-induced change as for a market-induced change in net-of-tax cost. Chirinko and Eisner have shown that failure to account for such differences in studies of taxation and investment has resulted in consistent overestimates of tax-incentive effects.[14]

An alternative hypothesis is that some firms may be unwilling or unable to borrow enough to finance additional R & D so that the level of R & D is dependent on internal finance. A sufficiently large tax benefit, by reducing the cash tax drain, can enhance the R & D effort. A survey by Kamien and Schwartz concludes that although the empirical evidence on liquidity or profitability being conducive to innovative activity is slim, cash flow may be an important "threshold" factor.[15]

An implication of this and other work[16] is that a tax incentive's effect on cash flow and net-of-tax cost can influence the level of R & D; but the influence depends on the size and structure of the incentive, the firm's microeconomic circumstances, and the general economic environment.

Firms with insufficient net income to use a nontransferable tax incentive will not benefit. This would exclude many old-line manufacturing firms in the industrial Northeast and Midwest and new innovative ventures as yet unprofitable. Such firms would, however, benefit from a "refundable" tax incentive. "Close cousins" are firms with insufficient cash flow or access to external finance to fund additional R & D even with a tax break.

For firms with small R & D costs relative to total operations, an R & D incentive's effect on total net-of-tax costs and cash flow will be relatively small. Table 4.3 shows 1978 company funds for industrial R & D. Six sectors accounted for 80 percent of the total: nonelectrical machinery (18 percent), electrical equipment (17 percent), chemicals and allied products (15 percent), motor vehicles and equipment (15 percent), aircraft and missiles (8 percent), and professional and scientific instruments (7 percent). For companies that performed R & D, the ratio of company R & D funds to net sales ranged from 2.8 percent in motor vehicles and equipment to 5.4 percent in professional and scientific instruments; the overall ratio was 2.0 percent. Although individual firms

TABLE 4.3: 1978 Funds for Performance of Industrial R & D by Sector and Source of Funds, and Industrial R & D Funds as a Percent of Net Sales in R & D-Performing Manufacturing Companies

	Millions of Dollars			Percent of Net Sales	
	Total	Federal	Company*	Total	Company*
Total	$33,406	$11,301 (34%)	$22,105 (66%)	3.0	2.0
Food and kindred products	431	†	†	0.5	†
Textiles and apparel	87	†	†	0.4	†
Lumber, wood products, and furniture	136	0 (0%)	136 (100%)	0.7	0.7
Paper and allied products	394	†	†	1.0	†
Chemicals and allied products	3,594	361 (10%)	3,233 (90%)	3.6	3.2
Industrial chemicals	1,570	338 (22%)	1,232 (78%)	3.5	2.7
Drugs and medicine	1,281	†	†	6.3	†
Other chemicals	743	†	†	2.2	†
Petroleum and refining	1,071	119 (11%)	952 (89%)	0.7	0.6
Rubber products	504	†	†	1.9	†
Stone, clay, and glass products	331	†	†	1.3	†
Primary metals	546	28 (5%)	518 (95%)	0.6	0.6
Ferrous metals and products	264	5 (2%)	259 (98%)	0.5	0.5
Nonferrous metals and products	282	23 (8%)	259 (92%)	0.9	0.8
Fabricated metal products	397	36 (9%)	361 (91%)	1.1	1.0
Nonelectrical machinery	4,459	582 (13%)	3,876 (87%)	5.0	4.5

Office, computing, and accounting machines	3,126	552 (18%)	2,574 (82%)	11.7	9.6
Other nonelectrical machinery	1,333	30 (2%)	1,302 (98%)	2.1	2.1
Electrical equipment	6,743	2,976 (44%)	3,769 (56%)	6.2	3.5
Radio and TV receiving equipment	54	0 (0%)	54 (100%)	1.1	1.1
Electronic components	834	†	†	6.6	†
Communication equipment	3,252	1,372 (42%)	1,880 (58%)	7.7	4.5
Other electrical equipment	2,603	†	†	5.3	†
Aircraft and missiles	7,680	5,821 (76%)	1,859 (24%)	12.4	3.0
Motor vehicles and equipment	3,783	449 (12%)	3,334 (88%)	3.2	2.8
Other transportation equipment	131	†	†	1.4	†
Professional and scientific instruments	1,689	174 (10%)	1,515 (90%)	6.0	5.4
Scientific and mechanical measuring instruments	452	10 (2%)	442 (98%)	5.8	5.7
Optical, surgical, photographic, and other instruments	1,237	164 (13%)	1,073 (87%)	6.1	5.1
Other manufacturing industries	280	9 (3%)	271 (97%)	0.6	0.6
Nonmanufacturing industries	1,152	547 (47%)	605 (53%)	—	—

*Company funds include all funds for industrial R & D work performed within facilities except funds provided by the federal government. Excluded are company-financed R & D contracted to outside organizations such as research institutions, colleges and universities, and other nonprofit organizations.

†Not separately available, but included in the total.

SOURCE: *National Patterns of Science and Technology Resources 1980* (Washington: National Science Foundation, 1980), Tables 37–41, pp. 43–47.

may devote substantially more to R & D, the industry figures suggest that for many firms an R & D tax benefit will not have much effect on total costs or cash flow.

Incentive effects may be small when R & D cost is not the primary consideration in R & D decisions, for example in concentrated markets where R & D is a substitute for price competition, or when the risk and uncertainty associated with the outcome of some research (in particular, basic and long-range research) may be too large to be bridged by a marginal change in cost.

Finally for specific innovation projects, incentive effects will be larger for innovation projects with relatively high ratios of R & D cost to total project cost. For a sample of thirty-eight innovations in the chemical, machinery, and electronics industries, Mansfield found that R & D accounted for about 40 percent of total innovation cost in the sample of chemical innovations and for about 50 percent for the machinery and electronics innovations, with substantial variation about the mean for each group.[17]

Manifestly, business confidence and robust markets will enhance the effect of a tax incentive; business uncertainty and slack markets will tend to negate it. While high rates of investment encourage innovative activities in the capital goods sector and help to diffuse new technology, slack markets and idle capacity provide little incentive to develop new technology or to make the investments necessary to translate R & D insights into productivity gains. Indeed, the influence of effective tax rates and the state of the economy are likely to overshadow the direct effects of a specific tax incentive.

Translation of R & D results into productivity growth occurs only with a lag and only through subsequent investment in later stages of the innovation process.

This creates a Catch-22 for using R & D tax incentives as a short-run weapon against stagflation. The argument for R & D incentives rests instead on the contribution of R & D to long-run productivity growth and in allaying the tendency of the private sector to *underinvest* in R & D due to individual firm "noncapturability" of returns, and in averting some plausible obstacles to pooling of risks on some R & D projects.

Division of Policy Research and Analysis
National Science Foundation[18]

NOTES

1. Estimate is based on data in John W. Kendrick, *Productivity Trends in the United States* (Princeton: Princeton University Press, 1971), as reproduced in Rolf Piekarz and Eleanor Thomas, "U.S. Productivity Growth: An Assessment of Perceptions and Prescriptions," Table A1, p. 56, in H. R. Clauser, ed., *Progress in Assessing Technological Innovation* (Westport, Conn.: Technomic, 1975).
2. See Edward F. Denison, *Accounting for Slower Economic Growth* (Washington, D.C.: Brookings Institution, 1980); and Martin Feldstein, ed., *The American Economy in Transition* (Chicago: University of Chicago Press, 1980).
3. Rolf Piekarz, ed., *Relationships Between R & D and Economic Growth/Productivity* (Washington, D.C.: National Science Foundation, in press).
4. Zvi Griliches, "R & D and the Productivity Slowdown," *American Economic Review* 70 (May 1980): 343–47.
5. In surveying the sparse evidence about the lag between conception of a research idea and commercial application, Mogee finds estimates range from three to twenty-six years. Mary Ellen Mogee, "The Process of Technological Innovation in Industry: A State-of-Knowledge Review for Congress," in *Research and Innovation: Developing a Dynamic Nation* (Washington, D.C.: Government Printing Office, 1980).
6. Eileen L. Collins, "Tax Incentives for Innovation—Productivity Miracle or Media Hype?" *Journal of Post Keynesian Economics* 4 (Fall 1981): 68–74; and George N. Carlson, "Tax Policy Toward Research and Development," *Technology in Society* 3, no. ½ (1981): 63–86.
7. It has been argued that "861" provides an incentive for American-based multinationals to perform some R & D abroad. Cf. Joseph J. Cordes, "Tax Policies for Encouraging Innovation: A Survey," *Technology in Society* 3, no. ½ (1981): 87–98.
8. Before initiation of any tax credit or benefit, "net-of-tax" cost of performing R & D can be defined as $C(1-t)$, where C represents the economic costs of labor, materials, and equipment for R & D, and t represents the effective marginal tax rate. The reduction in net-of-tax cost created by a tax credit of x percent is xC, and the percentage reduction in net-of-tax cost is $xC/C(1-t)$. If the relevant elasticity, e, were known, the percentage increase in R & D could be estimated as $ex/(1-t)$.
9. If a firm's current R & D costs are 65 percent of total economic costs for R & D, a 25 percent tax credit for current costs would amount to a 16 percent credit on all costs.
10. Cf. Eileen L. Collins, ed., *Tax Policy and Investment in Innovation* (Washington, D.C.: National Science Foundation, in press).
11. Cf. Robert Eisner, "Tax Policy for Investment: Implications for Innovation," and Edwin Mansfield, "Tax Policy and Innovation: Provisions, Proposals, and Needed Research," both in Collins, *Tax Policy.*
12. M. Ishaq Nadiri and M. A. Schankerman, "The Structure of Production, Technological Change and the Rate of Growth of Total Factor Productivity in the Bell System" in T. Cowicy and R. Stevenson, eds., *Productivity Measurement in Regulated Industries* (New York: Academic Press, 1981), as reported by Nadiri in Collins, *Tax Policy.*

13. Lawrence Goldberg, "The Influence of Federal R & D Funding on the Demand for the Returns to Industrial R & D," Center for Naval Analyses paper no. CRC 388, October 1979.
14. Robert S. Chirinko and Robert Eisner, "The Effects of Tax Parameters on the Investment Equations in Macroeconomic Econometric Models," Office of Tax Analysis Paper 47, January 1981 (Washington, D.C.: U.S. Treasury Department, 1981).
15. Morton I. Kamien and Nancy L. Schwartz, "Market Structure and Innovation: A Survey," *Journal of Economic Literature* 13 (March 1975): 1–37.
16. See Richard E. Caves, "Corporate Strategy and Structure," *Journal of Economic Literature* 18 (March 1980): 64–92; Richard R. Nelson, "Research on Productivity Growth and Productivity Differences," *Journal of Economic Literature* 19 (September 1981): 1029–64; and F. M. Scherer, *Industrial Market Structure and Economic Performance* (Chicago: Rand McNally, 1980).
17. Edwin Mansfield, *Research and Innovation in the Modern Corporation* (New York: Norton, 1971).
18. The views expressed are those of the author and are not to be ascribed to the National Science Foundation. The author would like to thank the editors, A. Bean, M. Boylan, J. Cordes, A. Erdilek, D. Jennings, M. Moureau, R. Piekarz, L. Pike, A. Rapoport, and E. Thomas for comments on an earlier draft, and C. Grider for research and secretarial assistance.

5

Reaganomics
and the
Black Community

WILLIAM DARITY, JR.

At the economic level, the small-scale producer and the small-scale owner are close both to the bourgeoisie (through ownership) and to the proletariat, the small-scale owner himself being the actual labourer. They are also opposed to both the bourgeoisie, which progressively crushes them economically, and to the proletariat, as they fear proletarianization and are fiercely attached to (small) property. At the ideological level, this often has the following effects:

(a) Status quo anti-capitalism: against 'big money' and 'great fortunes' but in favour of the status quo, for this group clings to its property and fears proletarianization. This is often associated with an 'egalitarian' aspect, against monopolies and for a return to 'equality of opportunity'; for 'fair' competition on the one hand, and the parliamentary cretinism of equal suffrage on the other. The petty bourgeosie wants change without changing the system. It also aspires to 'participate' in the 'distribution' of political power, without wanting a radical transformation of it.

(b) The myth of the 'ladder': aspirations to social mobility, not the revolutionary transformation of society. With the fear of proletarianization below, and the attraction of the bourgeoisie above, the petty bourgeosie aspires to join the bourgeoisie, by the individual rise of the 'best' and 'most able.' This aspect therefore often takes 'elitist' forms, standing for the renewal of elites, for the replacement of a bourgeoisie 'not doing its job' by the petty bourgeosie, without society changing.

(c) The 'power fetishism' described by Lenin. Because of its economic isolation (which also gives rise to 'petty-bourgeois individualism'), and because of its economic closeness and antagonism to both bourgeoisie and proletariat, the petty bourgeosie believes in the 'neutral' State above classes. It expects the State to nurture it and arrest its decline. This often leads to 'statolatry': the petty bourgeosie identifies itself with the State, whose neutrality it supposes to be akin to its own, since it sees itself as a 'neutral' class between the bourgeoisie and the working class, and therefore a pillar of the State—'its' State. It aspires to be the 'arbitrator' of society, because, as Marx says, it would like the whole of society to become petty-bourgeois.

Nicos Poulantzas, *Fascism and Dictatorship*, London, 1974, p. 241.

Black America is in disarray materially, spiritually, and ideologically. The tendency toward chaotic disintegration of the black community is particularly apparent in current concerns over the emergence of a permanent "underclass" that is disproportionately black and eking out survival on government-funded transfer programs and illegal activities.[1] Blacks themselves have come to question prospects for their survival as a race—even calling into question whether blacks still are viewed as necessary by the society at large.[2] In the background lies the continued fear that public policy directed toward the black community is nothing less than genocidal in character. Blacks, especially low-income blacks, long have perceived such ostensibly "humane" programs as family planning measures as a means for systematically reducing black numbers.[3]

The tendency toward the present disarray is not attributable to Ronald Reagan's administration. The destruction of black family life, the collapse of the education of black children, and the increasingly visible division of the black community into distinct social classes are all trends that accelerated well before the Reagan presidency. Paradoxically, acceleration of these trends has been associated with the post–World War II era, a period in which the greatest national attention was drawn to the design of policies alleged to uplift black Americans, particularly the liberal "civil rights" agenda. Those policies unfortunately tended to contribute to the current disintegration of black life in America.

In principle the Reagan administration has been left with a re-markable opportunity to chart a new policy direction. Unfortunately "Reaganomics" represents a return to policy notions more backward than the practices implicit in "civil rights." Either direction—Reagan's

neoconservatism or the liberal programs enacted prior to his administration—offers little hope for the black masses. Black Americans are
confronted with a prisoner's dilemma. The only way out of the bind
is to challenge the very nature of cultural and political domination in
American society, for as long as black aspirations are limited to notions
of success within the existing class structure, black America is doomed
to make tenuous its own prospects for survival.

EQUALITY: THE CONVENTIONAL ELIXIR
FOR RACIAL PROGRESS

The objective that has structured the design of public policy initiatives alleged to bring about "black progress" in the post–World War
II era has been "equality." Racial equality has been the ideological and
rhetorical cornerstone of the civil rights movement. This objective has
led to the operation of a Jackie Robinson principle, which asserts that
blacks should enter every sphere of American life from which they
have been excluded historically and that all blacks should cheer whenever another black enters a field that was formerly the exclusive do-
main of whites. A black presence in a previously white environment
becomes an instant *cause célèbre*.

The initial focus of racial equality was attainment of "equality" in
the political-legal sphere. This phase of the civil rights movement pursued voting rights, housing desegregation, open access to public accommodations, affirmative action, and school desegregation. Although
these specific programs had economic implications, their overriding intent was to give blacks full citizenship. Now some prominent blacks
actively involved in the earlier phase can be heard declaring that the
new effort must hunt down bigger game: economic rights or income
equality. For example, Andrew Young has said: "We struggled in the
50's to integrate the schools and the buses. We struggled in the 60's
to integrate the lunch counters and the ballot boxes. And we've got to
struggle in the 80's to integrate the money."[4]

There are at least two interpretations of economic or income equality: (1) equality of results and (2) equality of opportunity.[5] Equality of
results would mean that the mean and variance of black incomes would
parallel that of the whites. Of course, equality of results could be
achieved by moving the white profile of accomplishment downward toward the black profile, but no one has advocated this route except in

jest. Equality of opportunity means all persons face the same rules of the game. In this sense, *on average* any black would face the same life chances at money-making as any white.

Equal opportunity can imply unequal results. Assuming no racial differences in ability, arguably, there could be racial differences in career preferences under a regime with equal life chances for all groups. Even if rules are the same, both groups' members may not begin at the same starting point. Correspondingly, equal results may require unequal opportunity. If the starting points differ, one might give those who start behind extra points to compensate for their handicap.

Proponents of racial economic equality have not always sorted out which of these two interpretations they have in mind. Regardless, proponents generally have settled on the position that economic equality requires adequate black *representation* in all occupations. Concretely, this would mean having a larger share of blacks as corporate managers, lawyers, doctors, construction workers, truckers, and so on. This would ostensibly move the nation closer to the day when race is no longer a factor in American life.

Visionaries of equal results dream of 11 to 12 percent of all corporate managers being black, distributed across all ranks in like proportion. Visionaries of equal opportunity anticipate a world where any black MBA would have as good a chance as a white MBA of comparable skill and motivation to become a corporate board member. Black and white would share the same opportunity *to compete.*

On the surface the pursuit of equality appears uncontroversial and laudable. But surface looks can be deceiving. As Derrick Bell once observed, "the remedy can be the repression."[6] Unfortunately this seems to characterize the case of the chase after equality. To examine why the "remedy is the repression" requires a systematic framework for analysis of the condition of blacks in the United States. Such a framework is sketched in the section of the essay that follows.

THE CLASS CHARACTER OF AMERICAN SOCIETY

It is inadequate to conceive of the United States as a "capitalist society" any longer. Instead, it is increasingly a managerial society where control over knowledge and information, that is, over ideas rather than finance, has become the fundamental source of power. There is a technocratic aura in the new age absent at the height of capital's dominance of national life in the late 19th and early 20th centuries. The new age witnesses professionalization of careers involving supervision and management of human lives.

The coming of managerial society has been achieved by the rise of a *managerial class* which consists primarily of the *social* managers, the *manufacturers or producers of public policy.* Their vehicle for autonomous action—independent of the direct control of capital—has been the central government.

Dominance of the managerial class has become so visible today that scholars as disparate as Daniel Bell[7] and the late Nicos Poulantzas[8] depict its rise. Bell refers to a transition toward "postindustrial" society, while Poulantzas refers to the growing strength of a "new petite bourgeoisie"—the class of technicians.

James Burnham argued in the 1940s that the rise of the social managers already had occurred in response to the Great Depression of the 1930s.[9] Capitalists had fostered the development of new professional occupations to provide a new cadre of workers to supervise the working class both inside and outside the factory at the turn of the century.[10] What the capitalists did not anticipate was the possibility that some of their progeny would come to view themselves as advocates for the working class, providing a lubricant for the New Deal. Rather than accede to a working class revolution in the 1930s, capital had to accept a partial defeat in the form of the ascension of the social managers. The social managers brought a New Deal. Capital opted to survive under the restraints brought by the managerial revolution rather than die under a proletarian revolution. The managers promised a "neutral" government that would provide skillful arbitrage to keep capital and labor in a healthy pattern of cooperation, but it would be, in the last instance, the *manager's government.*

With the managerial revolution, macroeconomic stabilization policy also gained full legitimacy. It became the norm for central governments to use fiscal and monetary control measures to supervise aggregate economic performance. It also became the norm to extend an array of transfer programs to assist the poor and jobless. The macro-interventionist thrust of the managerial revolution meant, eventually, a corresponding transformation of the nature of business cycles. The classic pattern that business cycles took evident in the work of Wesley Clair Mitchell would be hard to discern with consistency in the postwar era.[11] The demise of the original Phillips curve trade-off between inflation and unemployment must be associated with the growing importance of macro-stabilization and the transformation of labor market conditions between the 1930s and the present. Moreover, no post-World War II recession ever has paralleled the severity of the Great Depression. Although mainstream economists are still torn between two views on the source of the Great Depression, they seem to agree that it cannot happen again:

> ... What caused it? Could it have been avoided? Can it happen again? ... The first question is still hotly debated. ... There are, essentially two hypotheses about the cause of the initial downturn and the deepening of the decline in activity. These are, respectively, (1) an autonomous decline in aggregate demand and (2) a monetary contraction. ... There is a general verdict to the second question: The Great Depression could have been avoided if there had been prompt, strong, expansive monetary and fiscal policy, the economy would have suffered a recession but not the trauma it did. On the third question, could it happen again, there is agreement that it could not, except, of course, in the event of truly perverse policies. But these are less likely now than they were then.[12]

These "perverse policies" are less likely apparently because of the care and feeding of the economy administered by the managerial class.

Moreover such an assessment is probably correct. The managerial economy flounders but never seems to plunge into full-scale depressions. It teeters along a path increasingly characterized by slow real growth but somehow avoids dropping over the edge. As long as the managerial class retains its position as "neutral" arbiter it is possible that depression can be avoided indefinitely.

However, the position of strength of the managerial class has been eroded in large part by the current economic crisis—the first *managerial* crisis. The managerial revolution left untouched an ultimate reservoir of capital's class strength—the capacity to determine the performance of the economy by the decision to invest. With the investment decision still in private hands the new class, whose authority is essentially public, still remains dependent on capital's actions. Capital's refusal to invest at a rate sufficient to sustain at least a 2 to 3 percent annual rate of real economic growth is a factor that has made it increasingly difficult for the managers to maintain their rule.

The Reagan presidency represents a resurgence of the capitalist class—the reassertion of big business politics in pure form. Its "solutions" are an attempt to resurrect labor market conditions that predated the New Deal by using recessions to discipline the labor force.

To reverse the historic New Deal accommodations to the working class, capital must first blunt the manager's instrument for independent activity: the central government.

Given the preceding, it is useful to recognize three great social classes in modern America—managerial, capitalist, and working class. From the perspectives of the managers, both capital *and* the working class must be contained for the social good. Of course, the managers themselves necessarily define the social good. Idealization of "pluralist democracy" represents the essence of managerial thinking on conflict containment.

Capital, in contrast, wants to place its progeny in a subordinate position—to eradicate the social manager's neutrality—with the long-term aim of restoring a fully capitalist character to American society. The working class, stung by the patronizing character of managerial policy and disenchanted with managerial "liberalism," voted for Ronald Reagan, who with big business support is mounting a capitalist counterrevolution.

THE CLASS CHARACTER OF THE BLACK COMMUNITY

Comparable class divisions exist within the black community, and these are particularly pronounced because of the small size of the black elite containing (1) a black managerial class acting as a subordinate adjunct to the larger white managerial class, including the "new" black petite bourgeoisie, engaged in supervising the black masses, and (2) black businessmen—small-scale entrepreneurs or the "old" black petite bourgeoisie. The two groups comprise 5 to 7 percent of the black population.

It is notable that the black managers largely administer programs aimed at the black population but have little involvement in the design of the programs. Clearly they have no voice on "non-black issues." The emphasis in describing black businessmen should be on the word "small." There are no black-owned corporations listed among the Fortune 500. Working class blacks constitute the overwhelming majority of the black population, with the most deprived and desperate fraction consituting the black "underclass."

The black elite probably is sincere in its belief that its personal progress will pull other "less fortunate" blacks along. Patricia Roberts Harris applauded Du Bois' "talented tenth" in her recent paean to the black "middle class."[13] So when the talented tenth speaks—or more accurately the talented one-fifteenth—it claims to speak for all blacks. But the *class* position of the black elite severs it from the black masses.

When the black elite professes to speak for all blacks, racial equality is preached as a goal.[14] Contemporary efforts to promote racial equality have included balancing and busing, fair housing laws, and affirmative action as policies advanced as though they reflect the desires and wishes of all blacks. But do all blacks share black elite priorities? A negative answer often seems warranted.

• A recent poll taken in Washington, D.C. (a city with a black population in excess of 70 percent) revealed that the majority of respondents disagreed with the "equal results" premise of affirmative action. Lower-income blacks registered the strongest opposition to giving blacks special treatment to compensate for past discrimination. But blacks with middle incomes registered the least opposition to white entry into predominantly black neighborhoods.[15]

• In the mid-1960s in the District of Columbia, a massive grass-roots effort to restore quality education to the city's public schools led to the petitioning of Congress. The effort ultimately was destroyed by white and black social managers who gave the city a desegregation plan rather than good schools.

• The issue in the Miami rebellion during the summer of 1980 was justice from the legal system despite black leaders' claims that the issue was jobs. While Andrew Young now declares that the old civil rights struggle aimed at legal equality has ended in victory, this is not the message from below, where the black underclass goes to jail in disproportionately high numbers. It certainly is not the message from Liberty City in Miami.[16]

• The alienation of the black masses is reinforced by their dismissal of the importance of voting. Voter turnout declined sharply in the 1970s. In contrast, black government employees, who administer public service programs, have maintained high voting rates.[17]

• In concrete terms the programs endorsed by the black elite have improved their own economic position while leaving the black masses demoralized. Some programs may have actually furthered the deterioration of the condition of the black underclass—in particular, social welfare programs adminstered by black social managers have rendered the "underclass" intensely dependent on government largesse.[18]

Despite the humanitarian overlay to the black managers' rhetoric, they basically feel that the black working class—or an "underclass"—is stupid, perhaps uneducable, and incapable of making decisions for themselves. The black managers care, but their caring is too often condescending. The black managers should know better since the great symbol of their own progress—affirmative action—has been used to denigrate their accomplishments (e.g., "You're only in this job *because* you're black").

Journalist Joel Dreyfuss, in defense of the black "middle class," has argued that they are the only authentic advocates for the poor.[19] Dreyfuss retains the view that the black social managers perform a valuable function on behalf of the needy who, once again, must be presumed unable to speak for themselves. Dreyfuss' protestations to the contrary, the black managers' impassioned commitment to social welfare programs does often appear "self-serving," given their class' status links to maintenance of those programs.

REAGANOMICS: A SOLUTION TO THE CURRENT CRISIS?

The renewed appeal of "conservatism" to working class whites, and even some working class blacks, stems from the fallout resulting from liberalism (or neutralism). Speaking from capital's perspective, the new conservatives articulate the need for social change that strikes a note consistent with many working class sentiments: (1) the rejection of cultural "permissiveness," (2) the importance of quality education—especially teaching of "fundamentals," (3) the restoration of traditional family life, and (4) a renewed sense of order and moral decency. Of course, simultaneously the new conservatives advocate a set of business-oriented policies that further endanger the already fragile condition of the black underclass, for example, the repeal of various income support programs.

The intentions of the neoconservatives are not pure by any means. Neoconservative advocacy of better schools and stronger families is motivated by the desire to ensure the availability of disciplined, healthy, and well-trained productive workers. It constitutes a complete rejection of the managerial flirtation with educational and social radicalism in the 1960s.

Whereas the Carter administration began the retreat into austerity,[20] it had not embraced the full range of capitalist policies for correcting the U.S. economic crisis. Reaganomics seeks to advance a program rooted in capital's own self-image, issuing all the familiar themes Marx clustered under the rubric of "vulgar political economy." Specifically, the new administration promises (1) to reduce the scale of federal government, especially by engineering a contraction in numerous social programs, (2) to shift the composition of aggregate national income from wages to profits, and (3) correspondingly, to shift the composition of our gross national product from consumption to investment, in large part by tax breaks to spur *personal* savings.

Bruce Bartlett's new book *"Reaganomics": Supply-Side Economics in Action,*[21] blessed with Representative Jack Kemp's imprimatur, gives full vent to the "new" ideology. Bartlett seeks to anchor the Reagan program in "classical economics" down to a perfunctory invocation of Say's Law. Production is characterized as driven by individual desires to consume rather than the corporate pursuit of profit. Savings is viewed as the determinant of investment, *reversing* Keynes' insight. Additional familiar themes that emerge under the spell of big business ideology include a renewed stress on militarism and defense spending, the salving role of free market activity, extensive deregulation, and even the desirability of restoring the gold standard. Balanced budgets were the Reagan religion until unruly facts compelled some shedding of the dogma.

The diminution in the scale of the federal government simultaneously involves drastic reduction in an array of transfer payments that assures income to those without work and erodes the power base for the managerial class. The proposal to replace welfare with "workfare" has as its intent to press the poor into the labor market at low wages. Concerns expressed by Robert Buckley of the Department of Housing and Urban Development about how the consumer price index overcompensates for inflation really reflect a desire to curb inflation-adjusted transfer programs in a roundabout assault on the lower end of the wage standard.

There has been a drumbeat attack on disability and social security payments. Thus the handicapped and aged are being pressed into the active labor force as well.

The cutting edge of the charge against social security has been led by Harvard professor and National Bureau of Economic Research (NBER) president Martin Feldstein. Feldstein's claims that the social security system reduced personal savings, and hence capital accumulation were first popularized in a 1974 article in the University of Chicago's *Journal of Political Economy.*[22]

Feldstein's ideologically motivated empirical results are still taken seriously, despite a critical mistake in Feldstein's computer program, an error that won Feldstein some polite chastisement from Moses Abramovitz:

> The large effect shown in Feldstein's original much-noticed time-series analsis (1974) has been thrown into doubt by the discovery of a flaw in his computer program. In a forthcoming NBER working paper, he now finds a smaller but still significant effect. Such time-series estimates remain uncertain because it is hard to measure expected Social Security benefits and hard to separate the effects of Social Security wealth on saving from those of other variables during periods of relative stability, as in samples covering the postwar years alone. The conclusion that Social Security benefits work to reduce saving, however, is supported by other studies, based on samples of individual households and on cross-country evidence, to which Feldstein refers in his new working paper.[23]

Less polite was Peter Stone's caustic labeling of Feldstein as the "econometrician of the month."[24] Nevertheless, Michael Darby makes similar claims about how social security has impeded the growth rate.[25]

In a recent *American Economic Review* article, one of Feldstein's protégés, Lawrence Summers, has produced "evidence" that shifting taxation from capital income to consumption will have pronounced growth-generating effects.[26] Summers' work, in an analysis centered in steady state growth, reveals once more all the essentials of capital's own declarations about its process of economic development. Immediately, this obscures the unstable character of the economy. He utilizes a deterministic life-cycle model of consumption which precludes individual bankruptcies and individual bequests to offspring. In Summers' fantasy, personal savings are portrayed as the mainspring of funds for investment. The Darby-Feldstein-Summers world is the epitome of the self-adjusting economy venerated in bourgeois ideology.

It is, of course, the independence of private investment from personal savings that is the crucial issue. It ignores the flexibility afforded corporate capital by its own retained earnings and the capitalists's capacity, regardless of the volume of personal savings, to turn finance away from production toward sheer stock market adventurism. Keynes abhorred the tendency toward "speculation" instead of "enterprise."[27] Marx noted the same phenomenon nearly fifty years earlier. Capitalists, at will, chose to slough their finance into speculative activities:

> Our capitalist, who is at home in vulgar economics, may perhaps say that he advanced his money with the intention of making more money out of it. The road to hell is paved with good intentions, and

he might just as well have intended to make money without producing at all. . . .

Thus from 1844 to 1847 he withdrew part of his capital from productive employment in order to throw it away in railway specula-
tions; and so also during the American Civil War, he closed the factory
and turned the workers onto the street in order to gamble on the Liv-
erpool cotton exchange.[28]

Stagnation is the result of a "capital strike," but, unlike labor, when
capital receives additional concessions it still need not complete its end
of the bargain. Capital as a class can hold out far longer than labor.
Labor must eat; capital can speculate.

The Reagan "supply-siders" mask the true origins of the current
slowdown in growth to justify a program best suited to capital's interests. But Reaganomics has not been able to push forward (backward?)
without encountering contradictions. The attempt to limit inflation by
unemployment has involved the use of monetary restraints by the Federal Reserve Board. This has, however, led to complaints from business
about the high price of credit and to protestations of inhibitions on the
incentive to invest. Thus a heated and surprising debate arises between
the "supply-siders" and the "monetarists."

The culprit in the dispute is the peculiar feature of the current economic slowdown that reveals its uniquely managerial character—the
coexistence of stagnation and inflation. The consensus that the inflation rate must be reduced by monetary policy confronts the tax-cutting
supply-siders with a dilemma. To balance the budget while reducing
taxes, they find that they even must consider cutting defense spending—especially if they are disturbed by the interest rate policy of the
Federal Reserve. Moreover, the Wall Streeters, who do not even exist
in conventional supply-side models, are the unconvinced skeptics.[29]

Now, there is groping for a panacea in a move to restore the gold
standard to induce an inflation-curing "confidence" in the currency.
William Fellner, not unsympathetic to much of Reaganomics, has observed that gold-mining has displayed low rates of productivity increase in recent years.[30] An effective gold standard might well be deflationary on a depression scale unless money wages can be forced down
faster than commodity prices fall. One way or the other, the target of
Reaganomics is to lower the pace of *nominal* wages to reduce *real*
wages, in a thinly disguised plan to reduce nonlabor sources of income
which, in real terms, *have declined* during the long inflation.[31]

Reaganomics seeks to restore the capitalist economy on capitalist
terms. A recession without income cushions is the path that it charts

as a necessary prelude to expansion. Candor about its premises would risk working-class political support.

SOWELLNOMICS: A SOLUTION FOR THE BLACK PROBLEM?

Concurrent with Reaganomics is Sowellnomics, the economics of Thomas Sowell, as the "new" solution to black economic inequality. Sowellnomics asserts that the trickle-down drippings of the imminent supply-side upswing plus individual initiative will carry blacks forward. Sowell's contention is that government intervention in the marketplace has set up barriers to black enterprise and that many programs, like affirmative action, degrade black achievement.[32] Sowellnomics is the economics of the bootstrap.

Its one meritorious feature is that it is not condescending in its assessment of black ability. But it is a vision as bankrupt as managerial liberalism. Sowell dreams of a shift in the leadership of the black community away from an education-cultural elite toward a financial-business elite. Education is valued primarily if it produces more black success stories in the corporate world. But Sowell is no more willing to surrender the floor to the black masses than the traditional "leadership."

Sowellnomics displays no grasp of the continued importance of discrimination, or its source of sustenance, in the class relations of contemporary society.[33] Historically, workers already in place have sought to prevent workers from other ethnic or racial groups from supplanting them in the workplace. It has been no different for whites confronting blacks moving from Southern agriculture into Northern industrial labor markets during the postwar era. The same resistances also are evident in the control over rules of access exercised by the members of the managerial class. Blacks are more consistently the outcast group—more consistently the "surplus" population—than virtually any other ethnic group in the United States. Sowell refuses to see these resistances as real or important, viewing them as at most another hurdle to be leaped by individual talent and perseverance.

It is clear that both factions of the black elite want "equality," but the black managers espousing liberalism look forward to a new age in mangerial society. The petit bourgeois black capitalists look backward to the dying age, seeking "equality" within bourgeois society. In both cases the idealized outcome is the ascendancy of a small few, while the black masses sink deeper into despair.

Racial equality as a goal serves both elements of the black elite in maintaining their position at the "top" of the black community. The black managerial path venerates the attainment of a pure meritocracy based upon selection by sheer individual quality. But there is no immutable standard for judging human quality. Should it be left to the whims of those in command of society? To challenge the meritocratic ideal is to challenge the thrust of managerial society—to refuse to accept its tendency to sort people between desirables and undesirables. After all, for some to have merit some others must not have merit; some must remain outside salvation.

The bourgeois or capitalist path shares in the meritocratic impulse, but with a narrower focus in that it idealizes attainment of a wealth hierarchy among blacks, parallel to that among whites. But for some to become capitalists, others must be workers who must remain among the "unelect."

ARE BLACK PEOPLE NECESSARY?

To be deemed "undesirable" under managerial society is to be deemed unnecessary, or at least to be of questionable value. A recent paper by Gary Orren and E. J. Dionne implies that blacks matter for one reason alone: They are expected to vote for the new managerial agenda (aptly termed "the *next* New Deal") if they can be convinced to turn out.[34] But otherwise, what purpose do blacks serve in managerial society? Entertainers (singers and athletes)? Objects of social science research? Objects for human experimentation? But what is their intrinsic necessity?

Dreyfuss already has worried that evidence of the black managerial failure to control the black masses could spell doom:

> At one time, middle class blacks were viewed as a buffer between the black poor and the white majority. Blacks who succeeded were held up as models for the poor to emulate.
> But white disillusionment with the black middle class came to a head during last summer's Miami riots when it was realized that middle class blacks have little control over the black poor and make no impact on urban problems such as crime and punishment.[35]

Already some black social managers are claiming some of their brethren are beyond hope and will have to be left behind. John Mack, president of the Los Angeles Urban League, has been quoted as saying:

> I really believe that the major focus has to be on the ones who are still salvageable; on the younger ones . . . those who have not become so hardened and so caught up in their own hopelessness that no amount of effort or resource can make a difference. That's something that represents a shift in my own personal philosophy. . . .
>
> We cannot be all things to all people, and we have to face the fact that we do have some who are beyond salvation. I think they're still human beings, maybe a few of them can be reached and dealt with here and there, but I think we have to still deal with those who dare to have a glimmer of hope. . . .
>
> We are a race of people who are equal to anyone else, but within that framework we have some winners, and we have some losers.
>
> We have to go with the winners.[36]

Mack does not explain how one is to judge who are the winners and who are the losers. His comments are nonetheless revealing. They demonstrate that some black managers are themselves relegating members of the underclass into the category of lost population, not realizing that the managers' own reason for being is cast into doubt at the same time.

Capitalist society, however, gives blacks an affirmative but conditional answer to the question of whether blacks are necessary. Under capitalism, one is necessary if one will work. Reaganomics and Sowell-nomics even offer a fig leaf of sorts by suggesting that past policies created work disincentives for blacks.

The Reagan administration will work to eliminate those disincentives, and all will be forgiven if blacks respond "properly" to the "new" labor market conditions, involving a regime of lower wages, an absence of income supports, and a drastic reduction in in-kind support—after already having been devastated by the impact of managerial liberalism. By August 1981, the black jobless rate had reached 15 percent and the black youth unemployment rate was close to 50 percent.[37]

The black elite will see its status pierced by the new administration's programs, for it is particularly vulnerable. The Congressional Budget Office (1981) issued a report in July predicting that the Reagan administration's proposed budget cuts would eliminate 15,500 permanent full-time federal employees by the end of 1981. Black U.S. employees happen to be disproportionately located in administrative roles in social welfare programs slated for abolition.[38] Rearguard actions to protect their class position included the efforts of former assistant secretary of labor, Ernest Green, to dole out last-minute contracts that would reach black managers during President Carter's last days in office.[39] But many black managers will find themselves relegated to the working class. Some may drop as far as the underclass.

Black businessmen, while sympathetic toward the refurbished laissez-faire ideology, will still be faced with the conditions that have kept them on the fringes of American corporate life. With the demise of affirmative-action style programs, they now will lack even the billion dollars set aside in minority contracts.[40]

Thus the pursuit of "equality" has plunged blacks into an abyss between a rock and a hard place. After being crippled by policies that emerged in the post-World War II era alleged to produce black progress, Reaganomics now invites blacks to compete *equally* with all other citizens. The black elite, in their concern for their own development, have left blacks as a whole dangerously vulnerable in the light of capital's demands for rugged individualism and managerialism's demands for technical expertise and long-range planning.

Thus, it is not too early to raise the question of whether blacks *can survive* Reaganomics. The answer lies in whether blacks can develop an ideology independent of the thinking of the dominant classes. It depends upon whether blacks repudiate equality—with its implicit acceptance of the prevailing rules of the game—as the goal of the black struggle; a new ideology must necessarily be inclusive in character, rather than exclusive. It depends in part upon whether the black elite can find the wherewithal to surrender pretensions of "eliteness" and let the struggle be defined from below. Otherwise, intraracial class distance will widen and an ominous day will draw closer, "when," as Rudolf Bahro has warned in a different context, "contact with those below is broken [and] the hour of rebellion is not far off."[41]

But this matter can be resolved only by blacks themselves. In the end, Reaganomics or any "-nomics" will pale in importance relative to the resolution of the self-determined destiny of black America. Black people alone can decide how necessary they are in modern American life, hopefully by constructing the new road beyond hell and high water.

University of Texas at Austin

NOTES

1. On the black "underclass," see William Wilson, *The Declining Significance of Race: Blacks and Changing American Institutions,* 2d ed. (Chicago: University of Chicago Press, 1980); and David Glasgow, *The Black Underclass: Poverty, Unemployment, and Entrapment of Ghetto Youth* (San Francisco: Jossey-Bass, 1981).

2. Representative of these fears is an editorial that appeared in the Howard University student newspaper written by Kofi Quali, "Fear of Not Being an Asset Threatens Black Existence," *The Hilltop,* November 5, 1976. Quali reacted to congressional testimony by Nobel Laureate Linus Pauling where Pauling had declared that 150 million is the optimum population for the United States. Quali wondered if the 70 million persons required to be eliminated to reach Pauling's optimum would be overwhelmingly black and Native American.

3. See, e.g., William Darity, Castellano Turner, and H. Jean Thibeaux, "An Exploratory Study on Barriers to Family Planning: Race Consciousness and Fears of Black Genocide as a Basis," *Excerpta Medica,* International Congress Series no. 246 (1971): 20–32.

4. As quoted by Juan Williams, "The Black Elite," *Washington Post Magazine,* January 4, 1981.

5. For a fascinating discussion of the differences between the two concepts of equality, see Daniel Bell, *The Coming of Post-Industrial Society: A Venture in Social Forecasting* (New York: Basic Books, 1976), pp. 408–56.

6. Derrick Bell in a speech to the Minority Section of the American Association of Legal Scholars, San Antonio, Texas, January 1981.

7. Daniel Bell, *Post-Industrial Society.*

8. Nicos Poulantzas, *Classes in Contemporary Capitalism* (London, 1975; American edition, New York: Schocken Books, 1978).

9. James Burnham, *The Managerial Revolution* (New York: John Day, 1941).

10. See Barbara and John Ehrenreich, "The Professional-Managerial Class," in Pat Walker, ed., *Between Labor and Capital* (Boston: South End Press, 1975).

11. Wesley Clair Mitchell, *Business Cycles* (1913; reprint ed., New York: Franklin, Burt, Pub., 1970).

12. See Rudiger Dornbusch and Stanley Fischer, *Macroeconomics* (New York: McGraw-Hill Book Co., 1980), p. 311.

13. Patricia R. Harris, "Who Speaks for Black People?" *Washington Post,* February 18, 1981, p. A19.

14. Marian Wright Edelman's *pro forma* cataloging of black-white and rich-poor disparities among children with an accompanying plea for foundation support epitomizes the black elite style of "service" to the underclass ("The Status of Children in America: How Foundations Can Help Build a Fairer Society," *Grants Magazine* 3 [March 1980]: 4–12).

15. See Courtland Milloy and Barry Sussman, "Post Poll Finds D.C. Opinions Split by Race," *Washington Post,* January 11, 1981, pp. A1, A6.

16. See Kenneth Walker, "Miami Blacks Tell Why Fury Gripped the Ghetto," *Washington Star,* May 20, 1980, p. A1.

17. Steven P. Erie, "Public Policy and Black Economic Polarization," *Policy Analysis* 6 (Summer 1980): 305–18.

18. See Richard Joseph's excellent discussion on this point in "Black Depen-

dency: The Real Challenge," *First World* 2, no. 4 (1980): 12–13. Charles Brown, on EEOC and OFCC data, suggests that to the extent that federal enforcement of affirmative action has been effective, it has aided blacks "concentrated at the upper end of the skill distribution" ("The Federal Attack on Labor Market Discrimination: The Mouse That Roared?" National Bureau of Economic Research Work Paper no. 669 [Cambridge, Mass., 1981]). The greatest beneficiaries from affirmative-action enforcement appear to have been white women; see Judy Simmons, "Struggle for the Executive Suite: Black vs. White Women," *Black Enterprise* 11 (September 1980): 24–27.

19. Joel Dreyfuss, "New Assault on Black America," *The Daily Texan*, October 20, 1980, p. 4.

20. See K. H. Bacon, "Political Ramifications Loom Large in Plan to Spur the Economy," *Wall Street Journal*, August 29, 1980, pp. 1, 4.

21. Bruce Bartlett, *"Reaganomics": Supply-Side Economics in Action* (Westport, Conn.: Greenwood Press, 1981).

22. Martin Feldstein, "Social Security, Induced Retirement, and Aggregate Capital Accumulation," *Journal of Political Economy* 82 (September/October 1974): 905–26.

23. Moses Abramovitz, "Welfare Quandaries and Productivity Concerns," *American Economic Review* 71 (March 1981): 7, n. 15.

24. Peter Stone, "Econometrician of the Month?" *Working Papers for a New Society* 7 (November/December 1980): 9–10.

25. Michael R. Darby, *The Effects of Social Security on Income and the Capital Stock* (Washington, D.C.: American Enterprise Institute, 1979).

26. L. H. Summers, "Capital Taxation and Accumulation in a Life-Cycle Growth Model," *American Economic Review* 71 (September 1981): 533–44. Ironically, Summers' "supply-side" model on tax incidence assumes that as the population grows (in the steady state) an increasing percentage of the population is younger. This assumption would invalidate the circumstances that led to the current crisis in funding Social Security! But what else would one expect from models designed to support predetermined policy positions?

27. J. M. Keynes, *The General Theory of Employment, Interest and Money* (London: MacMillan, 1936).

28. Karl Marx, *Capital, Volume I* (New York: Random House, 1977), p. 298 and note 15.

29. A "monetarist" at the San Francisco Fed, Michael Keran, has recently argued that the persistence of high interest rates is attributable to the failure of the participants in money markets to believe that the Federal Reserve Board will maintain its efforts to restrain credit creation. In contrast, monetarists themselves believe that the Fed will *not* "monetize" the federal deficit (see "Economic Diary," *Business Week*, Sept. 21, 1981, p. 20). This is a case of "heterogeneous" expectations. One wonders what this implies for the economics of the so-called "New Classical School" (rational expectations).

30. See "A Return to the Gold Standard," *Business Week*, Sept. 21, 1981, p. 118. The supply-siders as "vulgar" Ricardians seem to find themselves stumbling toward a search for an invariable standard of value! Somehow they seem to think their search ends on the back of black laborers in South African mines.

31. See, e.g., the careful study on the fall in the real purchasing power of AFDC payments and food stamps during the 1970s by Richard A. Kasten and

John E. Todd, "Transfer Recipients and the Poor During the 1970s," paper prepared for the Second Research Conference of the Association of Public Policy Analysis and Management, October 24–25, 1980.

32. See "How Supply Siders Would Help Minorities," *Business Week,* December 22, 1980, p. 78.

33. For the classic discussion on this thesis, see O. C. Cox, *Caste, Class, and Race* (New York: Monthly Review Press, 1970), esp. chaps. 18, 19.

34. Gary Orren and E. J. Dionne, "The Next New Deal," *Working Papers for a New Society* 8 (May/June 1981): 25–35.

35. Dreyfuss, *loc. cit.*

36. Cf. Richard E. Meyer, "Black Leaders Call for Action to Relieve Desperation," *Los Angeles Times,* July 12, 1981.

37. Cf. John Berry, "Blacks' Jobless Rate Hits Record 15 Pct.; Price Rise Moderate," *Washington Post,* September 5, 1981, pp. A1, A3.

38. Cf. Karlyn Barker, "For Black U.S. Employees, Topic Is Survival," *Washington Post,* August 27, 1981, p. A3.

39. Cf. Howie Kurz, "GAO: Carter Labor Dept. Spent Millions on Last-Minute Contracts," *Washington Post,* September 3, 1981, p. A3.

40. Cf. Martha M. Hamilton, "The End of Minority Programs by SBA Seen Possible," *Washington Post,* May 19, 1981, pp. F1–2.

41. Rudolf Bahro, *The Alternative in Eastern Europe* (London: New Left Books, 1978), p. 78.

PART THREE

MONETARY
AND
FINANCIAL ASPECTS

INTRODUCTION

ROBERT A. DEGEN

The major theme of Lacy Hunt's essay is an exoneration of the Reagan administration from responsibility for the 1981 recession. About 80 percent of the essay is devoted to accounting for our present economic slump; the remainder strongly suggests that a brighter future lies ahead "later in 1982 and 1983."

A defective monetary policy is fifth among seven causes listed to explain the recession. It is viewed as a complicating factor, whereas wrongheaded federal expenditure and tax policies head the list of pre-Reagan pitfalls and false trails: (1) Federal expenditures rose rapidly from 1976 to 1980, bringing inflation and distortions to the economy. (2) Federal tax revenues rose rapidly from 1977 to 1981, obstructing the private sector. (3) The rise in the tax rate reduced the personal savings rate contributing to the rise in interest rates. (4) The rise in the tax rate reduced incentives leading to unprecedented declines in productivity, falling profits, and inflation. (5) The money stock grew much too rapidly during the second half of 1980 and too slowly during the middle of 1981. (6) The automobile industry collapsed, largely due to the overpricing of its products. (7) The removal of interest rate ceilings on deposits in banks and thrifts, together with the introduction of financial instruments that pay market rates of interest, cut off the flow of funds to the housing industry.

What does Hunt see for the future? Reagan's policies are succeeding in cutting the growth rate of federal spending and in reducing tax rates. If the Federal Reserve cooperates by stabilizing money growth, the new fiscal policies can work their curative powers, with inflation ebbing, personal savings rising, productivity improving, and the economy recovering.

Thus Hunt looks at Reaganomics and finds it good. He indicates no apprehension over the massive federal deficits, lofty interest rates, or the surge in unemployment. The social, psychological, and environmental effects of the policies are outside the scope of his essay. No alternative course is considered—the words "incomes policy" are not to be found. Once the "serious downturn" of late 1981 has passed, we may expect sustainable progress.

Paul Davidson's starting point: The accepted view of the United States today is that it has great unmet needs and the real resources to meet them, but it is not allowed to realize its potential because of the shackles of tight money to contain inflation. Over the years, restrictive policies have resulted in a succession of recessions, each justified as a sacrifice necessary to end inflation, yet the core rate of inflation has successively risen.

Monetarism, having captured the financial centers, central banks, and government treasuries, tends to hobble the economies it is meant to serve. Just as the orthodox pre-1929 neoclassical economic theory blinded policymakers as they approached the abyss of the Great Depression, the new orthodoxy threatens to lead capitalism into a fresh disaster.

Davidson sees two basic methods of controlling incomes inflation: (1) traditional conservative neoclassicism (monetarism) and (2) Post Keynesianism. To Davidson, the conservative approach is either brutal or fanciful, or both. The economy may be impoverished by it—the British Thatcherism is a case in point. American rational expectations theorists suggested that inflation would subside by the mere anticipation of a tight monetary policy and a taut fiscal policy. Then again, the Laffer tax cuts were sold as a means of ending stagflation.

What is to be done? Post Keynesianism is waiting in the wings. Davidson thinks it is high time to put "nineteenth-century economic Darwinism" behind us and to develop new institutions to "provide a fair and efficient income distribution." Specifically, he advocates a National Policy to Coordinate Income Claims to be implemented by a tax-based incomes policy.

Is Davidson's prescription likely to be adopted? The idea that an incomes policy is a necessary complement to monetary policy seems to be on the margin of becoming orthodox. When, for example, financier Felix Rohatyn writes that "inflation will not come down sufficiently as long as wage and price behavior continues to operate independently of market forces" and explicitly advocates the addition of a tax-based incomes policy to the agenda of the Democratic party, the concept can hardly be said to lack influential friends outside academe. Keynes, it will be recalled, spoke of the "gradual encroachment of ideas" in the field of economic and political philosophy.

Hyman P. Minsky enlightens all of us with his magisterial theme of the *fragility* of the capitalist financial network in posing the question of why our economy has escaped another Great Depression. He gives as his reason the ultimate cliff-hanger rescue in Federal Reserve monetary accommodation by way of a suspension of its money pressures in following the venerable Bagehot dictum to act as a "lender of last resort" in conjunction with a federal fiscal policy stance that leaned heavily to deficit finance. Deficits, to Minsky who extracts from Kalecki's analysis, have shoaled up *profits*. Under the Reagan administration a great test is brewing over whether a tax-deficit posture, which favors profits, is not in conflict, and indeed in mortal combat, with a tight money clamp. Minsky is pessimistic, even alarmed, at a dismal outcome for the capitalistic system. He estimates a latent fear of a depression shadow over the land from the contrary tugs.

These interesting and relevant essays grapple with the great and grave issues that affect all of us. The systems of ideas they represent provide a clear choice of outlook and policy—perhaps even a paradigm's worth of difference. There is more at stake than a squabble between economists. The economic world will be shaken or go on to new material progress.

University of the South

6

The Causes of the 1981-82 Recession

LACY H. HUNT

As the dimensions of the most recent recession have become more distinct, and as the jobless totals have risen, the factors that caused the downturn should be examined. A number of strident voices are blaming current conditions upon the failure of the Reagan economic program. But is this view really correct, or is the present recession a result of longer-term problems that have built up over more than just this year? My view is that this recession stems from seven major longer-term developments, not from current economic policies.

THE SURGE IN GOVERNMENT SPENDING

First, there was the surge in government spending between 1976 and 1980. This resulted in a dramatic acceleration in inflation that in turn led to numerous distortions and imbalances in the U.S. economic system. Total federal outlays were $369.2 billion in fiscal 1976, an 8.2 percent increase over 1975. By 1980, federal expenditures had jumped by more than $200 billion, or by 17.3 percent over 1979. Thus, the rate of increase in federal spending more than doubled between 1976 and 1980.

Government spending is far more inflationary than private spending. When an individual is paid to produce goods in the private sector, income, wages, and spending go up, but there is a commensurate increase in supply. However, when someone is paid to do a government job, or when there is a transfer of income from the government, income, wages, and spending rise but the supply of consumable goods and services does not increase. Hence, more money is chasing the same supply of goods—the basic cause of inflation.

The inflationary impact of the surge in federal outlays can be seen in all three of the widely followed measures of inflation. In 1976, the consumer price index (CPI) rose by 5.7 percent, but by 1980 the rate of increase was 13.5 percent. Over this same period, the producer price index (PPI) accelerated from a 4.4 percent increase in 1976 to a 13.5 percent rate in 1980, and the consumption deflator went from 5.2 percent to 10.2 percent. Thus over these four years, the consumption deflator accelerated two times while the CPI more than doubled and the PPI more than tripled! Over this same period, the rate of growth in federal spending also more than doubled, suggesting that this acceleration in federal spending is closely related to inflation.

FAILURE OF FEDERAL TAX POLICY

Second, there was a serious failure in federal tax policy from 1977 until the summer of 1981. In 1976, federal tax revenues from all sources were $309.3 billion. Then, there were double-digit increases in federal tax revenues for every year from 1977 to 1981. It took two hundred years to bring federal revenues to the annual rate of $300 billion, and then only five years more to add the second $300 billion. In fiscal 1976, Treasury revenues constituted 18.53 percent of current dollar gross national product (GNP). But as individuals were pushed into higher tax brackets through "bracket creep," and as Congress instituted the windfall profits tax on oil and related products and legislated social security increases, Treasury revenues relative to GNP rose to 21.3 percent in fiscal 1981. This bulge in federal tax revenues greatly weakened the private sector of the economy. Out of every $100.00 generated in the private sector, there was $2.77 less for private use in 1981 than in 1976, which meant less spending for housing, automobiles, and capital spending.

DECLINE IN SAVING

Third, the rise in the tax rate, coupled with the surge in inflation, resulted in a significant decline in the savings rate. As the inflation rate and tax rate went up sharply, the typical family tried to maintain its standard of living by spending more of their disposable income. The savings rate averaged 6.9 percent in 1976 but by 1981, it had fallen to 5.3 percent. During this same period, the effective tax rate on earned family income, which includes both personal taxes and social security contributions, went up dramatically, from 15.7 percent in 1976 to 18.1 percent in 1981. In other words, as the effective tax rate rose by 2.4 percent, the savings rate declined by 1.6 percentage points. This drop in the savings rate, in turn, had negative repercussions. Investment in plant and equipment is financed by the resources that are provided to the economy from those consumers who do not spend all their current disposable income. With corporations competing with the Treasury for increasingly scarce savings dollars and with investors demanding a rate of return greater than the inflation rate, interest rates escalated to extremely high levels.

DISMAL PRODUCTIVITY

Fourth, the growth in the tax rate over the postwar period served to undermine productivity growth after 1977. One of the basic tenets of economics is that a rising standard of living requires increasing gains in productivity, and these higher taxes discouraged the incentive for work, particularly for the hard-pressed middle class. For the first time in U.S. economic history, there were three consecutive yearly declines in productivity—1978, 1979, and 1980. The decline in productivity reinforced inflationary pressures by raising labor costs, which in turn contributed to the drop in after-tax profits from $182.9 billion in the first quarter of 1980 to $118.0 billion in the first quarter of 1982. With profits down, the corporate cash deficit rose at the same time as firms' dollar financing needs moved up with inflation.

MONETARY INSTABILITY

The fifth cause of the most recent recession is that monetary authorities pursued destabilizing policies. Monetary policy has generally overaccommodated the surge in Treasury expenditures. After moving to an extremely expansive monetary growth in the final six months of 1980, the Federal Reserve switched to overly restrictive monetary growth in the middle part of 1981. In the last six months of 1980, M1-B + RPs + .2 MMFs grew at a 19.3 percent annual rate, the fastest rate for any six-month period. (While the thrust of monetary forces can be calculated in a number of different ways, we prefer a measure that indicates the basic M1 money stock—currency, checking accounts, and NOW accounts—plus repurchase agreements—RPs—and 20 percent of the money market mutual funds—MMFs. This statistic could be a better reflection of transaction balances since RPs are essentially interest-bearing corporate checking accounts and, to a certain extent, MMFs are used by households as interest-bearing checking accounts.) This surge in monetary growth, which revived the fading economic recovery late in 1980 and early in 1981, led to considerable additional borrowing in the private sector, which meant further leveraging of an already over-extended corporate America. Thus, the Federal Reserve further aggravated an already imbalanced situation.

After having swung the pendulum too far in one direction, the Federal Reserve then reacted too far in the other direction. From April through October 1981, M1-B + RPs + .2 MMFs grew at less than a 6.9 percent annual rate. This massive and unprecedented 13-percentage-point deceleration in monetary growth was too pronounced for an economy with extreme inflationary pressures, weak productivity growth, and a decimated private sector. We estimate that an annual growth rate of about 8.0 percent using our formula and about 5.0 percent for the basic M1 measure used by the Federal Reserve is required to keep this economy on a positive direction. In other words, about 8.0 percent is required in order to finance the long-range expansion of the economy, increases in the labor force, and gains in productivity.

THE AUTOMOTIVE DIFFICULTIES

A sixth factor contributing to the current recession is the difficulties of the automobile industry. In 1978, domestic manufacturers sold 9.2 million cars in the U.S. market. This dropped to 8.2 million in 1979, to 6.6 million in 1980, and to 6.3 million for 1981. Sales this year are expected to decline further to an estimated 6.1 million units. The drop in sales in the automotive market was partly related to the acceleration in inflation which resulted in the undermining of consumer confidence, the dramatic swings in monetary growth, and the escalation of interest rates. However, these low sales levels are largely a result of policy failures in Detroit. In October 1981, the average hourly earnings of nonsupervisory production workers on all private nonagricultural payrolls were $7.41. Including fringe benefits, total compensation was somewhere in the vicinity of $10.00. However, domestic auto manufacturers incurred wage and compensation costs of $20.00 an hour, *twice* the national average. Since it is the $10.00 per hour workers who are the potential purchasers of these cars, the demand would naturally be quite limited. In short, it is safe to say, the American-made car has become significantly overpriced, a good estimate is that the U.S. product is at least $1,500 too expensive, and perhaps as much as $3,000 too expensive.

REMOVAL OF REGULATION Q

Finally, the removal of Regulation Q interest-rate ceilings also contributed to this recession. Regulation Q is the Federal Reserve regulation that controls the interest rates that commercial banks and other institutions may pay on their deposits to the banking public. In 1978, with the introduction of the six-month money market certificates, savers began to earn a rate on their banking deposits that was more commensurate with a fair market return. This trend accelerated with the introduction of NOW accounts (interest-bearing checking accounts), 30-month small savers certificates, and the rapid growth of money market mutual funds. With the banking industry placed in a situation where its liabilities float with market rates, the ability of financial institutions to make fixed 30-year traditional home mortgages has been substantially, perhaps permanently, altered. Commercial banks are paid to manage the margin between interest rates on their assets and liabilities. They are not paid to take major interest rate risks associated with holding fixed rate 30-year assets. If consumers are going to earn the market rate on their deposits, financial intermediaries will have to charge something over that market rate in order to stay in business.

Regulation Q was in essence an imposed subsidy to the housing industry and its removal resulted in a dramatic decline in housing starts from 2.0 million units in 1978, to 1.7, 1.3 and 1.1 million for 1979, 1980, and 1981, respectively. The phase-out of Regulation Q implies that the housing industry in the future will be substantially different from what it was before 1978.

RECESSION OVERVIEW

The most recent recession is a result of the policy failures of earlier years and the imbalances and structural changes that ensued. The economy developed an unstable inflationary bias as a result of increases in federal spending. The lesson of economic history is that high and rising inflation is the precursor of recession. The escalation in federal tax rates reduced the ability of the typical family to save. The reduction in the savings rate meant that sufficient funds were not available for capital formation, which, in turn, accelerated the deterioration in U.S. productivity and weakened the basis for any sustained increase in the standard of living. Complicating these matters was a highly destabilizing Federal Reserve policy. Finally, there were the serious problems that developed in the automotive and the housing industries.

THE 1982/83 BUDGET PROBLEM

The U.S. Congress is now in the midst of a major policy debate that could have long-lasting significance. Economic frustration and dissatisfaction are running high. The economy faces potentially extreme budget deficits over the next four years. Correction of these deficits will require many painful decisions, most of which are not politically expedient. From October 1981 to March 1982, federal outlays gained 11.0 percent above the year earlier level. In the first six months of fiscal 1982, federal revenues advanced 11.1 percent from the year earlier, while the overall economy was up by only 7.3 percent. Thus, the thrust of the President's tax program has hardly begun. The tax reductions to date have yet to offset the effects of bracket creep and previously legislated tax increases. Growth in government spending is down from the breakneck pace of 1980, but even with all the presumed budget cuts, outlays have continued to advance at a double digit pace. The deficit in the current fiscal year will rise to approximately $110 billion, versus $57.9 billion last year.

The budget picture for 1983 is far more uncertain even though the nonbinding budget resolution has placed the 1983 deficit at $104 billion. Without enactment of new taxes or reduction of existing spending programs, the budget deficit for next year would be in the vicinity of $184 billion. We have assumed the political process will eventually lead to a $147 billion deficit for 1983. A combination of $37 billion of tax increases and expenditure cuts would be needed to be enacted to reach our figures.

These budget and expenditure figures suggest five considerations.

First, the budget deficit is merely a symbol and symptom, not a fundamental cause of our government's fiscal problem. Second, the basic cause of the current predicament is the unbridled growth of federal spending. Apparently, there is no political power that is able to stop the sharp surge in federal spending even though the President is committed to that objective and he presumably has a political mandate to carry out that plan. Third, interest rates are high, not because of the deficit, but because of the rapid surge of federal spending. Fourth, the government is going to take an increasing share of output. This means that the government could absorb any potential rise in economic activity, thus denying prosperity to the private sector. Fifth, the past deficits are an important cause of current deficits. Due to the nearly $1.08 trillion federal debt now outstanding, the government will spend $90 billion paying interest this year, and $110 billion in 1983. If the past deficits had not been there, the budget would nearly be balanced.

Why is the current budget dispute of such critical importance to U.S. economic performance? An answer is suggested by the post-war trend found in national income and federal, state, and local revenues from 1947 to 1981. National income includes both corporate and personal or family income. The governmental revenues exclude any double counting for grants in aid to state and local governments from the federal government. In 1947, governmental revenues accounted for 29.2% of national income. By 1976, the ratio was up to 39.0 percent and in 1981 another post-war period record of 40.7 percent was set. We know of no economy that has prospered with a tax burden that is so high. The tax situation is resulting in terrible inequities and considerable resentment against the tax system. Tax avoidance is increasing as the underground economy mushrooms and as use of tax shelters spreads. The working middle class that is unable to hide income is facing an increasingly disproportionate burden of taxes. More importantly, the rising tax burden leaves increasingly fewer of the country's available resources to be ploughed into capital investment, housing, cars, and other consumer goods. Hence, raising taxes to cover the deficit is the wrong solution to the problem. A small reduction in the large Treasury deficit, accompanied by substantially higher taxes, will have such a limited impact on interest rates that any short-term gratification will pale in comparison with the further deterioration to the basis for prosperous U.S. long-term economic growth.

CONCLUSION

The U.S. economy has been through its eighth post-war recession. As a consequence of the downturn and some slowdown in federal spending, the inflation rate has been cut sharply. The reduction in inflation has led to a gain in real disposable income over the course of the 1981–82 recession. This is highly unusual. Moreover, further increases in real income should occur when the July 1 tax cut takes effect. However, interest rates have remained stubbornly high, leaving many of the interest-sensitive sectors of the economy at very low levels of activity. Unfortunately, the interest rate problem is not likely to be resolved until Congress can demonstrate a credible control over federal spending.

Fidelity Bank, Philadelphia

7

Monetarism
and Reaganomics

PAUL DAVIDSON

Despite the prolonged existence of idle plant and heavy unemployment among a literate, trained labor force, the United States seems unable to mobilize these resources to rebuild our decaying cities, to revitalize mass transit, to regenerate clear air and waterways, and so on. Why are we so impotent? Conventional wisdom suggests that any mobilization of idle resources for a war on such things as decay, pollution, poverty will require either additional government expenditures or private-sector tax cuts. This means huge deficits financed by increasing the quantity of money which, monetarists claim, can only fuel the fires of inflation. Until we tame the dragon of inflation, we are told, these projects—no matter how desirable—must wait. Conventional wisdom says we must stoically accept tight money and stringent constraint on governmental spending for many years (the long run?) if inflation is to be stopped.

Five times since World War II, the United States has evoked the conventional restrictive monetary approach and restraints on government spending to fight inflation. Each time a recession followed the medicine; each slowdown was worse than the one preceding it. Moreover, even when the rate of price increase slowed in a recessionary pause, the expansion that followed brought an even higher underlying rate of inflation than the previous period of growth. In other words, tight money and recession were a temporary palliative, while the inflationary temperature jogged its long-term upward trend.

The philosopher Santayana once said, "Those who do not study history are destined to repeat its errors." Are our policymakers in Washington so foolish that they have not learned the lessons of history and are therefore dooming us to repeat its errors? I think not. Policymakers are trapped by pre-Keynesian economic theories which have little applicability to a modern entrepreneurial economy. Politicians know that tight money and fiscal policies cannot succeed; nevertheless, "worldly wisdom teaches that it is better for reputation to fail conventionally than to succeed unconventionally."[1] And, for politicians, reputation is everything.

These practical men cannot be blamed entirely for the possibility of economic collapse that awaits us. Conventional economic theory, as espoused by Nobel prize winners in economics, has not provided our politicians with any other course.

Adherence to monetarist policies for handling inflation, which now appear to dominate the thinking of the central banks and Western governments, will ultimately result in the breakdown of the capitalist system of financing productive activities by private sector entrepreneurs and/or state and local governments. In the last decade, the monetarist brinksmanship of the Federal Reserve has brought the economy close to the precipice (e.g., the Penn Central, Lockheed, and New York City financial crises). Only at the last moment, when decision-makers felt financial collapse was imminent, did they "temporarily" abandon monetarist strictures to institute ad hoc practical medicines to avoid disaster. Fortunately our economic system is strong enough to withstand many "macho" monetarist episodes, but the cumulative effect is to make a permanent solution more difficult. It may already be too late to institute such reforms until the second great economic collapse of the twentieth century is upon us.

Yet history is warning us. At the end of the 1920s, when the quantity theory and the benefits of unfettered market activity dominated economists' writings and provided rationalization for the acts of central bankers and politicians, one after another of the capitalist economies collapsed. It took the revolutionary ideas of Keynes on the workings of a developed monetary economy to provide the guidelines for saving capitalism.

It is instructive to note that pre–Great Depression neoclassical analysis united a supply-side concept—Say's Law of Markets ("Supply creates its own demand")—with the quantity theory of money (which emphasizes limiting the money supply to prevent inflation) and the gold standard to establish full employment without inflation. Exactly one week before the stock market crash the world-famous monetarist precursor of Milton Friedman, Irving Fisher of Yale, announced that the U.S. economy was marching along a "permanently high plateau" of economic prosperity. No doubt future historians will note Arthur

Laffer, Robert Lucas, Arthur Burns, and Friedman in a similar lemming leadership role today![2]

It is difficult to identify a unique economic, or econometric model, that can symbolize monetarism. One prominent monetarist, David Laidler, has written, "Like beauty, 'monetarism' tends to be in the eye of the beholder."[3] Having over the years analyzed various theoretical deficiencies in monetarist theory,[4] I believe monetarists have adopted Milton Friedman's pragmatic debating philosophy, namely, "It is very hard to hit a moving target." Hence, every time a logical or practical deficiency of monetarism is publicly exposed, a new mutant rears its head.

Consequently, at best, one can only attempt to identify various "unchanging" propositions as monetarist and then check these propositions against Federal Reserve statements and policies under the Reagan administration to see if the Fed is following a truly monetarist drift. We can thereafter evaluate whether the policies and goals are logically compatible (a) with monetarist theory and (b) with real world phenomena.

The four basic identifiable propositions of monetarism are:

1. Inflation is always a monetary phenomenon.

2. There is a conceptual *ex ante* difference between the real and nominal rates of interest.

3. Control of money supply growth at a rate compatible with the long-run growth of real output (exogenously determined by growth in labor force and technology) will impel a real world economy growing at its long-run real rate at market clearing prices without inflation.

4. A Monetarist approach to the demand for money involves a belief that "fluctuations in the quantity of money are *the dominant cause* of fluctuations in money income."[5]

No one could seriously argue with the first principle enunciated above, for in the absence of a monetary system there could not be any phenomenon known as inflation. Nevertheless, it is my view that propositions 2, 3, and 4 are logically incorrect[6] and/or inappropriate to real-world entrepreneurial economies as we know them. (By an entrepreneurial economy I mean an economic system that organizes production and exchange activities on the basis of *forward money contracts*.) Yet these propositions are fundamental to the monetarist tack which Paul Volcker and the Board of Governors have adopted ever since late 1979, when they smelled the victory of monetarism in the political wind. No wonder recent monetarist policy has been the disaster which now threatens the viability of basic financial institutions in our real world entrepreneurial system.

Volcker, in testimony before congressional committees, public speeches, and so on, reiterates the "technical aspects of monetary policy and our numerical targets for the various monetary aggregates," as if inflation can be harnessed *if and only if* the Federal Reserve would "avoid excessive growth in money and credit."[7] Apparently Volcker, under the watchful eye of Beryl Sprinkel and the Shadow Open Market Committee, like Margaret Thatcher in the United Kingdom, would be willing to tolerate unemployment rates of 12 percent plus tidal waves of business bankruptcies as the necessary medicine that must be swallowed to achieve the long-run cure for our inflation malaise. After all, Volcker's job and pension are secure, and the Federal Reserve, as a nonprofit organization, need not fear going bankrupt. Unfortunately, only when their jobs are in jeopardy do politicians abandon the puritanical medicine of monetarism—as President Richard Nixon and Prime Minister Edward Heath did in the early 1970s and as President Ronald Reagan and Prime Minister Thatcher are likely to do by 1983. By then, however, heavy damage and ugly scars will remain as a recurrent reminder of monetarist sawbones hacking away at capitalism's body.

In fact, those in Washington who are worrying about the employment of Republican Congressmen and Senators after November 1982, such as Treasury Secretary Donald Regan and Council of Economic Advisors Chairperson Murray Weidenbaum, have already complained publicly that perhaps the Federal Reserve has already been too successful in its monetarist operation on the U.S. economy. Weidenbaum, in an address to the walking wounded of the National Association of Savings Banks, was quoted by Leonard Silk in the *New York Times,* September 16, 1981, as declaring that an increase in the annual rate of growth of the money supply "should not be viewed as alarming, even though individual month-to-month increases may appear at first blush to be excessive to the untrained observer." Obviously, excessive growth of the money supply, like true beauty, is only to be revealed to the trained observer! What we need, apparently, is a Pavlovian training for market observers. But who gets to ring the bell?

There are only two basic (with many variants) competing anti–incomes inflation policies being advocated—one by neoclassical theory, one by Post Keynesian analysis. The traditional conservative analysis calls for restrictive monetary and fiscal policy—what Friedman calls "bullet-biting"—which so impoverishes the economy that it cannot be held up for economic blackmail by powerful subgroups who are attempting to gain more of the national product for themselves. Thatcherism is symptomatic of this painful medicine offered to the unions in the United Kingdom. Monetarist Mach II, alias rational expectations theorists, however, have held out the hope that just the threat of such a painful medicine will be sufficient to achieve a painless remedy to incomes inflation in the United States. These "supply-side" nostrum peddlers suggest that inflation can be stopped by merely announcing that the Reagan administration will have a tight monetary and fiscal policy and, like Margaret Thatcher, permit people to price themselves out of the market if they insist on raising wages and profit margins. If the unions and management believe Reagan, Regan, and Stockman, it is claimed, then "rational expectations" will prevail as everyone recognizes that everyone else will stop asking for inflationary wage and profit margin increases, and inflation will stop dead in its tracks without the punishing depression of Thatcherism. (If you believe in this scenario, you probably believe in the Good Tooth Fairy.)

What is so odd about the current political-economic scene in Washington is the entertainment as gospel of the inane utterances of supply-side gurus such as Laffer well after evidence has proved his previous locutions false. In the upside-down world of Reaganomics and the financial press, nothing succeeds like failure—everyone is too polite to remark that these supply-side impresarios are without clothes. (Apparently, blunt truths on official mandarins are hazardous to reporters. Readership is titillated by a serialization of fictional events which always rescue the economic damsel in distress—as in the fabled "Perils of Pauline." Limit the financial press to checking the official assertions against the unfolding facts, diagnosing the theories, and publications such as *Business Week* could scarcely survive even as a biennial issue, let alone a weekly!)

Recall that in the spring of 1981 the Laffer curve assured one and all that a reduction in marginal tax rates (even without any cut in government spending) would significantly reduce, even eliminate, the pending deficits of 1982, 1983, and 1984, while simultaneously stimulating enough gross national product activity to end stagflation—despite a lack of supporting evidence. Never mind the fact that upon coming into office in May 1979, Margaret Thatcher immediately slashed the higher marginal tax rates of the wealthy (by even more than was contemplated in the original Kemp-Roth bill) and plunged the United Kingdom into the worst depression since the 1930s while her government deficits ballooned. Late 1981 saw Budget Director David Stockman confessing to the wild supply-sider deficit assertions as utterly lacking in original substantiation, as a $100 billion deficit mocked the promises of the Reagan people for 1982.

Summer is often dubbed the season of "crazies" by reporters, and therefore it is possible to explain the Reagan budget and tax victories in Congress in July 1981. But the autumn (1981) cool shows the economy still ticking historically high inflation rates while activity tumbles as a result of the Federal Reserve's tight money policy and Reagan's budget attempts to "get the government off our backs." For the minor slowdown in the inflation rate since President Reagan took office, we must certainly remember to thank the Organization of Petroleum Exporting Countries (OPEC), as it pauses to catch its breath after its whirlwind increase in oil prices in 1979–80, rather than the Reaganomic budget which became effective only on October 1, 1981 and scarcely could have accomplished the inflation slowdown last spring (1981). Moreover, high nominal interest rates (and historically high real rates) still plague the economy despite monetary dogma which asserts that a *constant* real rate should have led to falling nominal rates as actual inflation declines and rational expectations conditioned by Reagan congressional victories reduced the inflation premium in nominal rates even further.

But in 1981 autumn's early light it is evident that enormous deficits loom ahead despite the airy Laffer curve and that nominal interest rates will not decline until the Federal Reserve actively increases bank reserves sufficiently, no matter what the public's (rational?) expectations on future inflation. If I were a subscriber to a belief of "rational" behavior on the part of independent economic and political decision-making agents, I would think that recent events which indicated continuing and *increasing* deficits, and high nominal interest rates, would be sufficient for the marketplace of ideas to bury the Laffer curve theorists and the real versus nominal monetarists in the Rube Goldberg cemetery for crackpot inventions.

Instead, supposedly serious economic publications such as *Business Week* (e.g., September 21, 1981, pp. 114–20) continue to peddle and provide an aura of pseudo-credibility to the latest gibberings of the Laffers, namely, the need to reinstitute a gold standard to stabilize the purchasing power of money so as, according to Laffer, to "dramatically change inflationary expectations." Apparently, the greater the previous error in your prognosis, the more *Business Week* assigns current credibility, and therefore the greater fees the gurus can command from the lecture circuit. Apparently, "failing conventionally" does, as Keynes suggested many years ago, pass the market test—especially if your failures are wrapped in a trickle-down format designed to redistribute more income to the most wealthy in the resulting impoverished community.

Monetarism Mach II, in its rational expectations armor, instantaneously market clearing twaddle, and bombastic mathematical pretensions demonstrates how economists are able to foist a horrendous superstructure based on wholly absurd assumptions on the gullible economics profession while pandering to the lecture market circuit (normally bankrolled by wealthy special-interest groups). Lucas monetarists and Laffer supply-siders join curiously in the rational expectation hypothesis that active monetarist (and fiscal) policy lacks ability to stabilize jobs and output. If the public swallows this pap with its "rigorous" mathematical wrappings as high thought, then the Federal Reserve is relieved of all responsibility if it fails to stabilize employment or to stop inflation or the resulting skewness in income inequality. Ah, then the golden vision of a pure gold standard can be promised as the miracle cure in lieu of the Federal Reserve monetary authority, whose activities merely exacerbate our problems!

In the real world of entrepreneurial economies, however, as Friedman notes, returning to the gold standard is not a painless way of controlling inflation. *Business Week* (September 21, 1981, p. 115) quotes Friedman as stating: "In order to stabilize prices you will have to go through a recession. That has been the experience of most countries that have stopped inflation. If it is not politically possible to accept that cure without a gold standard, it will not be possible to do it with a gold standard."

In sum, then, Monetarism Mach II, including its occasionally deviant but equally conservative rational expectations and supply-side wings, insists that if government announces an antiinflationary policy—in some memory of Senator George Atken's spoof policy on Vietnam—and simultaneously rewards the wealthy first, then each of us will adopt a congenial "rational expectations" to trust your neighborhood plumber, oil company, landlord, and so on not to raise his price if you do not raise yours. Friedman, in his Monetarism Mach I model, maintained a more familiar nineteenth-century "liberal" approach—an approach more properly labeled "economic Darwinism." For the more traditional Friedman monetarists, once inflation has become widespread the cure for those whose inordinate wage and price demands are symptoms of the inflationary disease must come through economic deprivation, starvation, and even economic death via bankruptcy!

Friedman's statement, however, does imply that the ultimate cure for inflation rests on a political basis. Hence, enlightened twentieth-century social democratic nations should recognize that there are viable political alternatives to Friedman's nineteenth-century economic Darwinism, or the Laffer-Lucas twentieth-century version of Alice in Walrasland. One plausible alternative would involve a National Policy to Coordinate Income Claims (NPCIC) to assure each agent that there will be an equality of sacrifice when economic events are unfavorable and an equality in sharing of gains when our economy is prosperous. In other words, the economy must develop a policy to supplant the current Darwinian free market struggle for income shares which is the primary cause of our current inflation problems; the present arrangement is not endemic to entrepreneurial systems. Just as society encourages fair and efficient traffic flows by a judicial system which extracts penalties (related to the severity of the offense) for drivers who violate well-defined traffic laws, so we must develop institutions to provide a fair and efficient income shake to make sure that the aggregation of our individual income claims does not total more than 100 percent of available real income. If the public was educated to the need for and objectives of a well-designed legal system for coordinating income claims, there could be overall compliance by a law-abiding people. Hence, the creation of an institution to carry out a fair NPCIC (such as a well-designed tax-based incomes policy) would immediately create an environment where success—without significant deprivation—could be assured.

No civilized nation leaves the decision about which side of the road to drive on to individual free choice, to see who is "chicken" as autos approach each other and each driver tries to intimidate the other in determining who is "king of the road." Yet "free marketeers" abide a similar process of intimidation and dominance for determining the distribution of income, under the guise of free market libertarianism. But just as war is too important to be left to the generals, income distribution is too important to be left to the god of unfettered markets to resolve. One would have hoped that the worship of Social Darwinistic determination of the distribution of income would have been long abandoned when we learned that cooperation under society's laws of contract—rather than plunder—was a better design for dominating transactions in a civilized society.

Adoption of a NPCIC does *not* mean that income must be distrib-

uted equally. There are social, economic, and psychological justifica-
tions for significant inequalities of income and wealth. The task is to
manage human nature and the desire for income, not to transmute
these desires. Enterprise and the production of desirable goods and services are the props of society, and most citizens would recognize that
those who contribute most are deserving of a somewhat larger share
and that each one's share is determined by some equitable and clear
rules of the game, allowing for anyone who feels aggrieved by the current rules to have a day in court. If instead the rules of the game for
the distribution of income are such that each *expects* the other to grab
as much as he can without consideration of others, and therefore *expectations* are generated that there may not be enough to go around, then
a mortal blow will be thrust at our entrepreneurial society because it
would damage the psychological expectational equilibrium tolerating
the societal acceptance of unequal economic rewards within the available output of a zero sum society.

Why then do most politicians and businessmen appear to support
economically restrictive monetarist policies in their public oratory,
rather than a permanent incomes policy? First, they are never told and
they are never clear that the object of the restrictive policies is to involve
business firms in losses and our people in unemployment. If they were
told this and they still chose restrictive policies, they would have for-
feited their right to complain when these results ensue; they would be
voted out as either the impoverished electorate or the bankruptcy
courts removed them from office. Instead, restrictive policies are always
presented as if only *others*—painted as more greedy than your own
group—will suffer! Second, and more important, with the development
of industrial markets and the percolation of the democratic ethos
through society, each group believes that it can, and has the right to, insulate itself against the market forces unleashed by restrictive policies
and thereby to shift the burden to others. As Kenneth Galbraith has
forcefully argued, with the growth of industrial society and democracy
people have learned that they can, and should, attempt to control their
own destinies.[8] If you can gain control of your income, then your fate is
largely in your own hands. Galbraith indicates that there are three
ways people can attempt to control their own income: (1) develop a
unique marketable qualification, that is, establish a monopoly position;
(2) organize with others who have similar market capacities in order to
exercise some joint monopoly control; and finally, if market power still
eludes such groups, (3) organize and employ political activities to tilt
government policy toward augmenting your income. Thus, "poor" farm-

ers, poor people, senior citizens, rich and poor corporations, educational institutions, labor unions, and so on, each in turn march on Washington, and a lobbying industry grows and enriches itself.

These developments are permanent; we cannot return to the nineteenth century, when the ordinary person accepted his income as part of his kismet, beyond his control, believing that poverty on earth could be redressed by heavenly rewards. Today we must employ the democratic processes to work out a "social contract" which permits the equitable sharing of an economic pie that is growing at its maximum potential.

In an economy when strong social and political forces have already gained control of the money costs of production, the power over the domestic price level has passed beyond the levers of the central bank, or the Office of Budget Management. The firm of Reagan, Regan, and Stockman can attempt to unleash recessionary forces to put "labor" back in its place, that is, to induce future changes in money wages relative to productivity so as to soften the future inflationary process. Even if such oppressive measures turn out successful, Reagan, Regan, and Stockman cannot control the pace or the route of the journey to the new era of "noninflationary expectations." The path will be long and dreary, and our mainly enterprise economy, if it survives, will be the poorer for the experience. Luck alone cannot prevail for very long against the exactions of OPEC, internationally, and the uncoordinated domestic demands of unions, firms, and ordinary citizens for bigger shares of the gross national product.

Monetary policy and Reagan, Regan, and Stockman, with or without the always-subject-to-change vagaries of "supply-side economics," are singularly ill-adapted for preventing domestic incomes inflation, for they cannot directly influence the major costs of production of reproducible goods. On this premise there is no viable set of options for any modern capitalist society which relies upon cooperation among the factors of production for its national production. As the private flow of long-duration money contracts breaks down and each group demands more rapid income increases, and we leapfrog over one another on our treadmill to higher money incomes, our society must either collapse or enter into a social contract to reestablish the "rules of the capitalist game"—a game in which sticky money wages and price contracts over a long future are at the core.

In keeping with the game analogy, it should be noted that President Jimmy Carter had likened the current incomes-inflation problem to a crowd at a sporting event—all standing on tiptoe to get a better view. The result is no better view, but instead aching leg muscles for all, with survival for the tallest. All would be better off if there was a permanent rule, equitably enforced, requiring everyone to sit down. Any temporary rule or any restrictive policy which reduced the tempo of the game *might* provide temporary relief as the crowd relaxed, but the throngs would be on their feet again at the next flurry of activity.

Why is a permanent incomes policy (or PIP) feared? For three reasons: (1) the uncertainty associated with anything new, (2) PIP may subsidize inefficiency (in others) by penalizing the productive and the skilled (i.e., me), and (3) by permanently freezing relative prices, resource misallocation creating greater economic losses than would otherwise occur.

The third fear is not well founded since (a) restrictive policies create worse economic losses and incite social conflicts and (b) incomes policies can be designed to permit relative price changes and/or resource reallocation as desired. The first and second fears contain substance; hence policy solutions must not only be developed upon correct economic analysis, but must also be designed in a form that is politically acceptable and encourages compliance. Economists can provide politicians with guidelines for being "good," but it will also require the services of political scientists, social psychologists, and opinion research specialists to tell politicians how to be clever.

In sum, then, in twentieth-century entrepreneurial economies, central banks no longer have the power to control the price level (if they ever had). Unions, oligopolies, multinational corporations, international cartels, governments, and other groups who have positions of strong economic and political power share responsibility for our stagflation malaise.[9] Monetary policy cannot directly affect this distribution of power which, without any constrained legal rules in the capitalist game, is free to make excessive and incompatible claims on the gross income of modern economies. A democratically determined incomes policy, which coordinates claims to the maximum potential output of society, is the only *civilized* solution to this second great crisis of capitalism. It is in the vested interest of all groups to support such a policy, for as Benjamin Franklin noted, in an interconnected interdependent society "We must all hang together or we will all hang separately."

Rutgers University

NOTES

1. John M. Keynes, *The General Theory of Employment, Interest and Money* (New York: Harcourt, 1936), p. 58.
2. Since the latter two are associated with Rutgers University (Friedman as an undergraduate mathematics major was introduced to economics by Arthur Burns, who was his instructor at Rutgers), Post Keynesians at Rutgers today bear an extra burden in trying to set economic theory and policy right!
3. David Laidler, "Monetarism: An Interpretation and an Assessment," *Economic Journal* 91 (1981): 1.
4. Cf. Paul Davidson, *Money and the Real World* (London: Macmillan, 1972; 2d ed., 1978); "A Keynesian View of Friedman's Theoretical Framework for Monetary Analysis," in R. J. Gordon, ed., *Milton Friedman's Monetary Framework: A Debate with His Critics* (Chicago: University of Chicago Press, 1974); "The Dual-Faceted Nature of the Keynesian Revolution: The Role of Money and Money Wages in Determining Unemployment and Production Flow Prices," *Journal of Post Keynesian Economics* 2 (Spring 1980): 291–307. "Post Keynesian Economics: Solving the Crisis in Economic Theory," (1980): 151–73; *The Public Interest,* special issue; Paul Davidson and Sidney Weintraub, "Money as Cause and Effect," *Economic Journal* 83 (December 1973): 1117–32.
5. Laidler, "Monetarism." Italics added.
6. In an appendix omitted in final publication, I demonstrated that proposition 2 is logically flawed. Propositions 3 and 4 have been demonstrated to be faulty in Davidson, *Money and the Real World;* Davidson and Weintraub, "Money as Cause and Effect"; and Davidson, "The Dual-Faceted Nature."
7. Paul A. Volcker, "Prepared Statement Before U. S. Committee on Banking, Finance and Urban Affairs," House of Representatives, July 21, 1981, p. 13.
8. John K. Galbraith, "On Post Keynesian Economics," *Journal of Post Keynesian Economics* 1 (Fall 1978): 8–11.
9. Monetary policy cannot and should not exogenously "control" some arbitrary and vague aggregate known as "the" money supply. An endogenous money supply is a necessary institutional arrangement to ease financing of economic growth. Monetary policy can and should affect the spot prices of bonds (the rate of interest) and other liquid assets (e.g., foreign exchange, commercial paper) in such a way as to avoid any potential shortages of liquidity which threaten the growth of real output and employment. See the works cited in note 6.

8

Pitfalls Due to
Financial Fragility

HYMAN P. MINSKY

The most important economic event of the thirty-five years since World War II is something that as yet has not happened: We have not had a deep and long depression. In the light of the history of the American republic prior to World War II, not having one or more deep depressions over a thirty-five-year period is a radically new phenomenon.

THE MAJOR NON-EVENT

Somehow the economic and financial institutions, combined with the economic policy regime of the years since 1946, succeeded in fulfilling this major aim of the economic reforms of the Roosevelt era. It is important to acknowledge this success these days for two things are happening. The evolution of the financial structure over the years since the end of World War II, and more particularly since the credit crunch of 1966, has made the economy more susceptible to the type of financial crisis that almost always was part of the historical scenario for a deep depression. In addition, a serious attempt to reconstruct institutions and revolutionize policy is taking place; the ostensible objective of this effort is to eliminate the inflationary thrust that has been evident over the last fifteen years and to modify institutional arrangements and tax structures that, it is asserted, are barriers to efficiency and growth. In terms of economic and human loss a big depression will cost far more than the inflation, or the resource use inefficiency that the combination of high taxes and government regulations may impose. The question that has to be asked is whether the changes being legislated and imposed by administrative edict make a deep depression more likely by weakening our protective shields against a deep depression.

The era since 1948 rather neatly breaks into two parts. The first part, from approximately 1948 through 1966, was an era of tranquil progress within on the whole remarkable price stability. The second part begins in 1966 and continues to today. It is characterized by increasing financial turbulence, cycles with widening amplitudes, stepwise accelerating inflation, and chronically higher unemployment rates. Although the label "stagflation" may be applied to the era since 1966, we must recognize that this stagflation is also characterized by greater turbulence than the preceding "growth" era. In particular—and this is critical for the view being put forth—there were credit crunches and threats of financial crises in 1967, 1970, 1974-75, and 1980 that evoked special lender-of-last-resort interventions by the Federal Reserve and other government and private institutions, even as there were no such crunches, thrusts, and interventions in the prior tranquil years. See Table 8.1.

Given the emphasis on inflation in today's policy measures, it is significant that the inflation rate during the era of tranquil progress averaged 2.08 percent per year and that the inflation rate over the second, the turbulent, period averaged 6.17 percent per year, almost three times as high. It is this inflation rate—together with significantly higher unemployment rates—that triggered the wave of discontent behind today's legislated restructuring of the economy.

The success of 1948–66 was both striking and unexpected. The common expectation at the end of World War II was that the economy would soon sink into a high unemployment trap such as ruled in the second half of the 1930s. It is important, therefore, for us to understand what was "right" about the economic structure at the end of World War II, and why the era of tranquillity ended and was replaced by an

TABLE 8.1:   Implicit GNP Price Deflators, 1948/66 and 1966/80

	1948	1966	1980
Price deflator (1972=100)	52.98	76.76	177.45

	1948–66		1966–80
Average annual rate of growth of price deflator	2.08%		6.17%

SOURCE: *Economic Report of the President* (1980), Table B5, p. 239.

era of turbulence. Why was a regime of essentially noninflationary growth replaced by an era of inflationary cycles?

STABILIZATION PITFALLS

My original subtitle was "Pitfalls of Stabilization Policy in Our Economy." Therefore, we have to understand my meaning of "our economy." Our economy is a capitalist economy which uses complex, expensive capital assets and has a sophisticated, intricate, and ever evolving financial system. The essential characteristics that make an economy "capitalist" are privately "owned" so that the income (profits) earned by capital becomes, in all or in part, private income, and capital assets have a market determined value (price) and this value becomes private wealth. The financial system exists because the ostensible (proximate) owners of expensive capital assets need to finance their ownership by raising funds by issuing some set of negotiable instruments. In dealing with a capitalist economy, we are involved in trying to understand how an integrated production, trading, and wealth-owning system, with a structure of financial claims and commitments, operates through real world irreversible time. In such an economy it is impossible to separate the processes that determine particular outputs, prices and incomes from the financial transactions that determine the commitments of asset holders and the investments that are taking place. Thus the "methodology" of standard economic theory, by which a "nonmonetary" exchange and producing economy is studied in order to derive propositions relevant to our economy, cannot lead to valid propositions for our economy for, without financing relations, capital asset prices are indeterminate. The relation between capital asset prices *and* current output prices is a main factor that determines investment, and investment determines the markups on labor costs that can be realized in prices. Thus relative prices cannot be determined without knowledge of investment's share in output. In particular, the ratio of investment to output determines the real wage, which is the relative price that is most significant politically and socially.

Stabilization policy normally refers to monetary and fiscal measures undertaken to achieve some policy goal. Pitfalls awaiting policy are: (1) the way in which successful functioning of the economy—whether or not due to policy—changes the response to policy measures, i.e., the behavior of the system, as well as the efficacy of policy changes, and (2) the side effects of policy measures. The stable performance of the economy over the tranquil first period (1948–66) led to the emergence of the fragile financial structure that has characterized the more recent years, creating a policy pitfall. Similarly the ways in which monetary and fiscal responses to inflation lead to the emergence of credit crunches, and the way in which "lender of last resort" and budget deficit response to credit crunches leads, with a lag, to inflation, are pitfalls of policy.

Policy measures reflect a theory of the way the economic system functions. Unexpected side effects reveal the inadequacy of theory. The behavior of the economy since 1966 should be taken as strong evidence that those economic theories which do not explain how the potential for Debt deflation/Deep depressions are "normal functioning" results of the economic process are inadequate. This means that both establishment Keynesianism and monetarism, in either their traditional, naïve, or technically sophisticated rational expectations form, will not do.

STABILIZATION QUESTIONS

The questions in stabilization policy may well be (1) What is to be stabilized? (2) In the in real world can the objective be achieved? and (3) Can the effectiveness of policy measures change as the structural and institutional characteristics of the economy change? If the answer to the second question is conditional on the stabilization goal, and the answer to the third question is yes, then stabilization policy must always adapt to changing environments. It will be necessary to continuously modify policy rules to allow for the impact of institutional and structural changes.

What is it that stabilization policy attempts to stabilize? The candidates for "stabilization" include the gold/dollars exchange ratio, prices, employment, economic growth, and profits.

Under an international or a unilateral gold standard the policy rule for the central bank is to keep the price of gold in dollars within a narrow predetermined range. As bank liabilities serve as money, the objective of policy becomes to keep bank liabilities in some market-determined ratio to the gold stock, so that bank money and gold coins exchange at par. Otherwise there will be a "drain of gold," from the banks or the central bank. Banks have to be able to reverse this drain;

they must have some power to force the transacting units of the economy to "deliver gold" to the banks.

One of the paradoxes of banking is that a banker has to be rich, even as profitability dictates that the banker has to be fully invested. Being rich therefore does not mean that a banker needs cash in hand; it does mean that the banker is able to force "cash" to flow in his direction without having to pay too great a price in income or wealth.

As Richard H. Sayers showed in his monumentally significant (though neglected) study, *Bank of England Operations 1890–1914* (1936), the Bank of England succeeded in working an international gold standard without inducing serious instability within Britain, because the operations that led to gold drains and gains by the Bank of England centered mainly around the pace of long term (mainly debt) financing in Britain by overseas units. Britain's capital account, rather than the level of activity and prices in Britain, was the slack variable that carried the adjustment burden. As a result, the Bank of England was able to maintain parity between the various currencies and the British pound and between the pound and gold without greatly upsetting Britain's income, employment, and the flow of trade.

CENTRAL BANK IMPACTS

The effects of various central bank operations upon domestic activity were discovered when actions to protect or disperse gold holdings were taken in environments in which the special investment financing conditions that ruled in the twenty-five years prior to World War I (which Sayers analyzed) no longer ruled. It can be argued that prior to World War I it was Britain that was on a gold standard and that the rest of the world was on a sterling standard. Once the gold standard rules for central bank behavior were implemented in an environment which did not conform to the financial and balance of payment relations of 1890–1914, it was discovered that the quest for external, that is, exchange rate, stability imposed politically unacceptable costs in domestic price and employment instability. In the interwar period the "return to gold" was costly in terms of domestic stability; as a result, it did not last long. Britain went "on gold" in 1925 and "off gold" in 1931.

The post-World War II era of tranquillity reinforces the view that fixed exchange rates can rule only as a transitory situation in which a special kind of dominance by a financial and economic center exists. As long as the United States could finance a part of its overseas investment by short-term debt issued abroad without causing the holders of such debt to want to cash in their dollar assets, the Bretton Woods System of temporarily fixed exchanges (based upon the dollar as the fixed point) was "viable." Once the liquidity so imposed upon the rest of the world led to significant excess liquidity, with inflationary pressures in the "dependent" countries, the "gold standard without gold" of Bretton Woods was no longer conducive to stable expansion.[1]

Perhaps the major lessons to be learned from both the gold standard and the Bretton Woods era is that the validity of a "policy regime" or "stabilization" objective is conditional upon the institutional structure that prevails. This implies that success, if achieved, is transitory, as long as institutional evolution is permitted to take place.

LIMITS TO STABILIZATION

When one emphasizes pitfalls in stabilization policy, the concern is mainly with unwanted and perhaps unforeseen consequences of efforts to stabilize the economy. Stabilization policy, even as it succeeds in stabilizing some target of policy, may destabilize other dimensions of the economy which feed back upon and affect the ability of policy to achieve the desired stabilization objective. It is such "roundabout processes" that explain the problems with stabilization policy today. Experience since the end of World War II is evidence for the transitory success of any policy regime. In truth, as the structure of relations within institutions changes in response to the opportunities that arise in any stable regime, "stability in and of itself induces destabilizing changes."

To return to the question of "what stabilization policy stabilizes," the aim in the years immediately after World War II was full employment. The enormous increase in government debt and in money during World War II, as well as the felt need to keep the enormous government debt from declining in value, meant that the ratio of money and near monies to income and to the value of nonmonetary assets was very large indeed in the late 1940s and the 1950s. Yet there was no serious inflation in the years up to the mid-1960s. The inflation that broke out when the Korean War began is ample evidence that the ability to finance rapid inflation was in place, but the asset acquisition, liability-emission behaviors needed to transform ample liquidity into inflation were missing. The failure of serious inflation to appear in the first twenty years after World War II shows that monetary abundance and monetary growth are not, in and of themselves, sufficient to cause a rapid inflation. Responsible fiscal policy, which means that there is a willingness to tax to finance spending and contain inflation, in the context of a government that is big by prewar standards (although significantly smaller than today's government), can lead to an era of tranquil expansion without significant inflation, in spite of a very high money/income ratio. Monetarists must explain why accelerating inflation was not a problem in this first epoch after World War II even though the money supply was very large and potentially very elastic.

In the Kennedy administration the main objective of economic policy shifted to economic growth. The basic difference between full employment and economic growth as the objective for stabilization policy is that the full employment goal is neutral with respect to the composition of aggregate demand. Consumption demand is just as good in generating employment as investment demand, whereas if economic growth is the goal the policy instruments are used to develop incentives to investment. Ever since the mid-1960s accelerated economic growth has been a major goal of stabilization policy. Perhaps, in a subtle way, the measures undertaken to spur growth actually *retard* growth, induce unemployment, and lead to inflation. These perversities come about because the investments which result from policy inducements are not efficient in generating useful output.

MODERN INFLATION

Inflation became a serious problem in the late 1960s. After World War II and prior to 1968 the year to year changes in the consumer price index exceeded 3.0 percent only in the "first" post-price control year 1948, in the year the Korean War broke out (1951), and in 1957 (when the rate was a modest 3.7 percent). In the years since 1968 the inflation rate fell below 4 percent only in 1972—the year of price controls—and exceeded 10 percent in 1974, 1979, and 1980.

Economic policy measures aimed to control this inflation for the best part of the 1970s. Not only have monetary and fiscal policy measures been aimed at reducing inflation, but both price controls and wage-price guidelines have been used. Perhaps the reason that antiin-

flation policy has not succeeded is that the theories (and the policy prescriptions that follow from the theories) of the economic policy advising
establishment have basically misspecified the way our economy now
behaves.

Inflation became a serious problem only after the credit crunch of
1966. The liquidity squeeze of 1969—70 temporarily lowered the inflation rate but inflation soon exceeded the 1966–69 rates. Similarly the
Franklin National/Real Estate Investment Trust crisis of 1974–75 led
to some abatement of inflation, but in the late 1970s inflation raged
at a rate well above that of 1970–74. The hypothesis that the stagflation
of 1966 to date is related to the appearance of "credit crunches," and
to the policy interactions that follow these crunches, seems to conform
with this experience.

We live in an economy in which borrowing and lending on the basis
of margins of safety are used to finance both the ownership of durable
capital assets and output as it is being produced. Banks are the central organization in the business lending that takes place. Even business access to the open market by way of commercial paper depends
upon the issuer having "backup" lines of credit at banks. Banks, in
turn, finance their lending by a variety of liabilities including demand deposits (which are bank liabilities), which serve as the primary "money" of our economy. Thus, in our economy, money is
mainly the result of bank acquisition of assets. Peering through the
veil of the bank balance sheets, we perceive that the "owner" of a
bank deposit is financing a variety of activities, but, in truth, deposits
mainly finance business. Looking "through the balance sheet," we
can also perceive that the units being financed have signed contracts
to deliver money, i.e., deposits at banks, to banks when the loan ma-
tures. When loans are repaid, money in the hands of the nonbank
public is decreased. The lending and then the repayment of bank
debts involve the creation and then the destruction of money; the destruction occurs when the borrower repays "money plus interest" to
the bank. Any particular rate of growth of the money supply is thus
the result of two flows which involve the creation and the destruction
of debts and money.

Banks are in the business of lending. They seek to accommodate
customers and their sales people instruct business and households in
the use of debt. If bank funds are restricted by central bank policy, financing competition will lead both to higher interest rates and to the
development of new modes of financing banks and business. But higher
interest rates on bank liabilities and on business borrowing imply

lower prices for outstanding assets (whose market prices are the capitalized value of future interest or profits).

The adaptability and flexibility of the financial structure mean that increased demand for financing can be accommodated. This means that the financed demand for the inputs to investment output can exceed the supply of such inputs at existing prices, i.e., inflationary demands can be financed. Efforts by the Federal Reserve to offset such accommodation cause higher interest rates—which can compromise the asset values and safety margins of borrowers. A credit crunch results when financing demands outrun the supplies of funds so that the liquidity and solvency of business units and financial markets are threatened. Often, the "break" occurs when units have to "make position" by tapping some "unusual" or "backup" source. The use of government securities to make position by money market commercial banks in 1966, the collapse of Penn Central and the need for banks to refinance Chrysler from the commercial paper market in 1970, the refinancing of the Franklin National Bank by the Federal Reserve together with the forcing of the REITs out of the commercial paper market and into the banks in 1974–75, and the refinancing of Chrysler (again) and the Hunts in 1980 are examples of "flash points" and embryonic financial crises since the middle 1960s.

Although monetarists emphasize the aggregate money supply and the Federal Reserve as the ultimate "regulator" or "controller" of the money supply, the Federal Reserve was created to be a lender of last resort. The function of a lender of last resort is to refinance organizations and markets whose continued normal operations are deemed necessary if the economy is to avoid deep depressions, whenever these units cannot be financed on commercial terms. The typical problem of a refinancing crisis occurs when the "normal" liabilities cannot be issued either because the borrower cannot meet the market terms (not only in interest payments and protection for repayment of principal but also on the various coverages that are specified in the "words" of a financial contract) or because a market that has been counted on is not working normally. When this occurs, assets have to be sold or the borrowing unit cannot fulfill obligations to the prior lenders who may seek to withdraw their funds in a "run." Such failure of borrowers to perform in any significant market means that throughout the credit markets a more skeptical view of permissible liability structures and income prospects begins to rule: A shift in the expectational climate which Keynes folded into the concept of liquidity preference has taken place.

Such a shift in preferences that makes liquidity more highly prized makes the terms of debt financing of investment and of the ownership of capital and financial assets more onerous. This leads to a sell-off of inventories and to cutbacks in investment, driving the economy towards a recession/depression. Without the concessionary refinancing provided by the Federal Reserve, the various deposit insurance organizations, Treasury guarantees and consortia of private institutions (that are usually orchestrated by the Federal Reserve), the economy could easily become a victim of the downward spiraling interaction that Irving Fisher in 1933 characterized as a "debt deflation."

There is a maze of payment commitments on financial contracts in our type of economy which can be validated only if gross capital income—what we can call profits—is sustained. What then determines the flow of profits in our economy?

If we assume a simple (Kalecki) model in which *all* of workers' wages are spent on consumption, and *all* capitalist profits are saved (and no government or foreign sector), then gross capital income is equal to investment. This simple formula, Profits Equal Investment, tells us that if financial stringency leads to a decline in financed investment activity, then the flow of funds available to validate the debt structures of business will erode; this will reinforce the financial stringency. If the debt-deflation process—a critical element in the development of deep depressions—is to be aborted, the profit flows and thus the debt servicing capacity of business must be sustained even as private investment decreases.

If a government that spends and taxes is introduced into the model—so that we now have consumption, investment, and government—then the gross *after* tax capital income equals investment *plus* the government deficit. If government is small relative to investment, then a rise in the deficit cannot offset a decline in investment. If government is large relative to investment, then a rise in the government deficit can offset the investment swing.

Thus in 1929 Gross National Product was $103.4 billion, gross private investment was 16.2 percent of the GNP and Federal government expenditures were 2.5 percent of GNP. In 1966 GNP was $756.0 billion, gross private investment was 16.6 percent and the Federal government was 18.9 percent of GNP. As Table 8.2 shows, gross investment as a percent of GNP has been relatively stable over the years since 1966, even as federal government expenditures, as a ratio to GNP, have risen from 18.9 percent to 22.9 percent in the turbulent years 1966 through 1980.

TABLE 8.2:   GNP, Investment, and Federal Government Spending (Current Dollars)

	Gross National Product	Gross Private Investment		Federal Government Expenditures	
	$ (billions)	$ (billions)	% of GNP	$ (billions)	% of GNP
1929	103.4	16.2	15.7	2.6	2.5
1966	756.0	125.7	16.6	143.6	18.9
1970	992.7	144.2	14.5	204.3	20.6
1974	1434.2	228.7	15.9	299.3	20.9
1979	2413.9	415.8	17.2	509.2	21.1
1980	2627.4	395.1	15.0	601.2	22.9

SOURCE: *Economic Report of the President* (1981) Table B1, p. 233.

The much higher ratio of government to GNP in the post-World War II era allowed changing deficits to offset the effect on profits of a decline (or a rise) in investment; big government provides a major underpinning to business profits. If business profits are sustained and increased even as private investment tumbles, two things happen: (1) The cash flows to validate business debts are sustained, so that orderly debt liquidation can take place and (2) business remains profitable so that the optimism of businessmen and bankers is soon rekindled. As a result the liquidity-crisis-induced shift in demand is quickly reversed.

We now can understand why we have not had a deep depression. Business profits have been sustained by increased government deficits in the aftermath of each crunch we have identified. This is the hidden facet of the big government and huge deficits of the past fifteen years; they have sustained and then increased profits in the recessions. Although stabilization policy of the post-war years has had income, employment, and prices as its ostensible goals, the essential effect of policy was to sustain profits even when private demand fell in the aftermath of financial crunches and crises.

There are two quite separate elements in the technique that was used since 1966 to stabilize our big-government capitalism that is vulnerable to credit crunches and has the potential for deep enduring depressions. One element is the lender-of-last resort intervention which refinances financial institutions, markets, and business units that are in distress on concessionary terms. This intervention attenuates the repercussions of distress in some markets upon other aspects of finance; this removes the potential "domino effect." The other element is the government deficit, which sustains business profits even as output, employment, and investment fall.

The policy mix of Deficit-No and Lender of Last Resort-No in Table 8.3 represents the response in the Hoover administration. Between 1929 and 1933 the Federal Reserve so feared inflation that it largely stood aside and did not refinance failing financial institutions in the various crises within the major crisis. At the same time the government, wedded to fiscal orthodoxy, tried to maintain a balanced budget even as income slumped from the 1929 peak.

The Yes/Yes square represents the policy mix used in 1966–81, when the Federal Reserve (and other dependent and cooperating institutions) reacted to financial market crunches with various innovative refinancing measures even as the Federal Government ran a large deficit during the associated recessions.

The other two squares, namely Deficit-Yes, Lender of Last Resort-No and Deficit No, Lender of Last Resort Yes, are as yet untried combinations. The refinancing and income concessions to savings and loan associations and the presumed efforts of the Reagan administration to achieve a balanced budget in spite of the massive decrease in tax schedules make it likely that we may test the Deficit-No/Lender of Last Resort-Yes strategy. If the government persists in trying to balance the budget even as tax revenues decline due to a fall in investment, income, and employment, then the resultant decline in profits will swell the number of organizations that require concessionary refinancing. Although large deficits will occur in spite of the administra-

TABLE 8.3:   Policy Combinations
Lender of Last Resort

		Yes	No	
D Y		D: Yes	D: Yes	D-Deficit
E e				
F s		L: Yes	L: No	L-Lender of Last Resort
I				
C N		D: No	D: No	
I o				
T		L: Yes	L: No	

tion's desires, a Deficit No, Lender of Last Resort-Yes policy mix can lead to a deep and long recession.

The Deficit-Yes, Lender of Last Resort-No strategy does not promise bliss but it may well be the best we can do if getting off of the 1966–82 treadmill is the goal. The strategy allows the Hunts and Chryslers, and even a multi-billion dollar bank or savings and loan association to fail. Furthermore, if financial institutions fail the depository insurance organizations should stick to the letter of the law in making good on deposits. The objective of a Lender of Last Resort-No, Deficit-Yes strategy is to induce balance sheet conservatism by allowing significant failures and losses to occur even as policy aims to maintain the overall cash flows to business. By making liquidity and safe balance sheets valuable, such a policy mix will restrain the portfolio experimentation that leads to financial fragility and demand-generated inflations.

Both the Lender of Last Resort No, Deficit Yes and Lender of Last Resort-Yes, Deficit-No strategies need *not* be absolutist. A pragmatic central bank, which is cooperating in a Lender of Last Resort-No, Deficit-Yes strategy, would stand aside for a time while bankruptcies take place, even as it is ready to intervene to prevent repercussions from initial failures from touching off a string of induced failures. Similarly, if a Lender of Last Resort-Yes, Deficit-No strategy leads to a string of bankruptcies as profit flows decline, a nonideological government will stop trying to "balance" the budget and move consciously to deficit.

The overall topic of every essay is stagflation. I have sketched why periodically we have come to the brink of a financial crisis and a deep depression and explained how a fully realized deep depression has been aborted. Although this period of flirting with disaster and the years characterized as "stagflation" are identical, the links between the periodic threat, and rescue, from financial crisis and depression and the deteriorating inflation and unemployment picture have not been drawn.

In an economy with overlapping contracts and supply prices that are based on costs, inflation has its momentum. Prices and the change in prices can be broken down into unit labor costs and markups per unit of output. Markups on labor costs in consumer goods depend upon the *weight of demands that are not financed by those incomes that are earned in the production of consumer goods.* In simplified models, this is the ratio of total wages and transfer payments to total wages in consumer goods production. In our economy a fall in income and employment leads to a sharp rise in transfer payments to persons. These transfer payments are quickly transformed into a demand for consumer goods. If, as in 1975, profits are sustained, or even increased, when output is down and the economy is in recession, the average markup must rise. This is so for it is the markup on labor costs that carries profits. But if the markup on unit labor costs rises, then the unit price must increase.

In a world with cost of living clauses in wage contracts, and with government transfer payment schemes that are indexed, if wages and transfer payments continue to rise in a recession even as unemployment increases, then both labor costs and the markup will increase. This persistence of inflation will be especially marked if the government deficit is so large as to allow total business profits to increase during a recession. Rising business profits guarantee that a quick economic recovery will take place. However, this recovery will take place in a context of balance sheets which remain fragile and a continuing high rate of inflation. With some upswing of private investment, both income and prices will rise as unemployment falls: but the increased pace of inflation will foster central bank and Treasury actions to "fight" inflation. The wage/price relations in an economy where profits are sustained by deficits are such that during a recovery inflation accelerates; this induces constraining monetary and fiscal measures despite the existence of considerable slack. Constraint is imposed with more unemployment than existed when constraint was imposed the "last time around," in the previous cycle. The stagflation phenomenon, in which inflation and unemployment are positively associated in a step-wise sense, is a normal result in a big-government capitalism in which depressions are stopped from running their full price- and production-deflating course by profit-sustaining government deficits.

We can conclude that stagflation is what results when over some fifteen years, policy, in the form of lender-of-last-resort interventions and government deficits, is used to prevent a debt deflation and an associated deep depression. Instability is a robust characteristic of a capitalist economy for it has survived radical changes in institutions and balance sheet structures. However, what results from instability has changed. Prior to World War II instability led to minor inflations and deep enduring recessions/depressions, in recent years instability has led to serious inflations and short-lived recessions. The processes that led to serious depressions in the past are now *not* allowed to fully function. Combined with active government interventions the relations that make for instability now lead us to stagflation. The inflation of the 1970s was not wholly obscene; it had a redeeming social virtue for it was a result of the interventions that prevented deep depressions.

Past policy failed not because the economics of Keynes was "wrong" but rather because it was "right." The so-called Keynesian economists of the policy advising establishment ignore financial relations. Monetarists, with their emphasis upon one financial variable, money, which they have trouble identifying in the real world economy, go beyond the "Keynesians" who ignored financial relations, for monetarists deny the significance of financial relations. The view that financial instability is exogenous—or "externally imposed"—is an essential theorem of monetarism.

We fared poorly in the 1970s because policy reflected a set of theories which ignored the rich set of financial interactions that make debt deflations and stagflations normal results. If we are to do better, policy and the legislated aspects of the economy's structure will have to be reconstituted to reflect an understanding of what makes financial relations fragile and how the fragility is brought about. Policy must attenuate the tendency for fragile financial relations to emerge.

The best policy guideline at the present critical juncture is for the Federal Reserve to constrain its intervention as a lender of last resort, so as to induce financial conservatism, even as the government runs deficits, so as to sustain business profitability. With business profitable, income and jobs are also sustained. Stabilization policy will do better only as it is recognized that the policy objectives are to sustain profits and constrain liability experimentation by bankers and businessmen by removing the safety net of premature lender-of-last-resort interventions.

Federal Reserve policy with respect to lender-of-last-resort interventions seems to reflect a belief that the financial/economic structure is now so fragile that any significant refinancing problem can lead to a large scale collapse in asset values. In truth the financial system is not so fragile that any significant failure to perform on financial contracts will trigger an uncontrollable debt-deflation. However, the likelihood that an uncontrollable debt-deflation is set off by a particular failure depends upon the size of the failing unit. The very largest banks, other financial institutions, and corporations are now of such size that it is well nigh certain that the Federal Reserve or the Treasury will intervene to protect the holders of their liabilities. For a Lender of Last Resort-No, Deficit-Yes strategy to be feasible it may be necessary to limit the size of private organizations so that the Federal Reserve could stand aside and allow the liabilities of even the largest private organization to go into default. One corollary of the argument that has been advanced is that policy with respect to the organization of business and industry determines whether or not a Lender of Last Resort-No, Deficit-Yes strategy can be tried. A quite radical restructuring of finance and industry, so as to increase the weight of the smaller private units in the economy, may be necessary before the Federal Reserve and the Treasury can guide our economy to a closer approximation to full employment at stable prices than we can realize now.

Washington University

NOTE

1. These comments on the limitations of gold and the gold standard are prompted by the current push for a return to the gold standard. Unfortunately, the protagonists as well as the opponents of the return to gold know little of what they speak. Their frame of reference is all too often the literature of economics rather than an appreciation of the experience of the gold standard in its heyday.

PART FOUR

MONEY WAGES, CONTROLS, AND ENERGY

INTRODUCTION

SAMUEL A. MORLEY

The orthodox stabilization remedies for inflation are ineffective for three reasons: our commitment to full employment and unemployment compensation, the growth of sectors of the economy able to set their own prices, and pessimistic expectations about the continuation of inflation. All these make inflation rates resistant to recession and contractionary monetary and fiscal policy enduring, costly, and inefficient. Charles Rockwood sees incomes policies as a viable alternative strategy. He disputes the notion that wage and price controls "never" worked in the past. He thinks they *can* work, but only when accompanied by at least restraining monetary and fiscal policy. In designing an incomes program, the trick is to choose one in which the cost of regulation is small relative to the antiinflation benefit it is able to achieve. Rockwood briefly considers two such systems, Lerner's Market Anti-Inflation Plan (MAP) and the Wallich-Weintraub Tax Incentive Plan (TIP).

The MAP plan is based on the issuance of saleable wage-increase permits across firms. Firms would retain the flexibility to raise wages at any rate they wished, but on average, wages would rise only at the desired rate set by the government. The Wallich-Weintraub plan would apply the federal tax rate for corporations granting excessive wage increases.

Laurence S. Seidman directly confronts the differential treatment of wages and profits by arguing that the core of a new economic program should be a symmetrical wage-price TIP on large corporations. Without a TIP program, monetarism will condemn the economy to stagnation. Proponents of TIP have persuasively argued that, in theory, money wage growth is the decisive lever; reduce it, and price inflation will subside automatically. Nevertheless, political reality requires that a TIP appear to be symmetrical and therefore fair. It is therefore necessary to extend the original TIP to prices as well as wages. Seidman believes that the cost of this extension has been exaggerated, particularly if the program is limited, as he suggests, to the largest two thousand corporations. Given this restriction, it is not clear that measurement of the average price increase is more difficult than measurement of the average wage increase; both have a quality problem. Monetarist opponents of TIP plans always refer to the administrative costs of enforcement and the efficiency costs of market intervention. The great advantage of TIP is that the market solution is retained. Administrative costs are not as likely to be as high as trying to bring inflation under control by monetary restraint.

Even if TIP succeeds in reducing inflation without recession, there will be a need for two complementary policies. To raise productivity and wages, we must allocate a greater share of income to saving and investment. Seidman proposes that we replace our progressive personal income tax with a progressive tax on consumption. This would surely be a more equitable supply-side tax reform than the 25 percent across-the-board tax rate reduction enacted in the United States in 1981. In addition, Seidman proposes that we give targeted tax cuts in low-income, high-unemployment areas of the economy.

Robert Kuenne examines the price increases of the Organization of Petroleum Exporting Countries (OPEC) as a factor in our recent stagflation and offers some interesting conjectures on the future of OPEC and future price increases. He finds that oil price increases explain surprisingly little of either our inflation or our recessions between 1974 and 1979. However, he does not think that current price reduction and division within OPEC intimate that the organization is likely to fragment. The current oil glut is likely to be temporary because it is primarily a result of the one-time adjustment to higher oil prices in the United States since decontrol, the severe worldwide recession, and a drawdown of inventories. If and when the economy returns to full employment, we are likely to return to a world in which OPEC again will be able to hike prices, in real terms, by 4 to 5 percent per year. Though OPEC will not go away, the macroeconomic impacts of relative energy prices should be manageable.

In an entirely different contribution, Sidney Weintraub, an originator of TIP theory and policy, argues that collective bargaining in its present form has become an obsolete institutional practice. This follows from his view that unions are inherently *unable* to control the relevant strategic variables. It should be stressed that his view is not that unions are obsolete but that the unrestrained wage bargaining is outmoded. Unions participate in many other valuable functions that make them an indispensable and desirable institution in our democratic economy.

Vanderbilt University

9

A TIP for
the Stagflation Era

(and Other Complementary Policies)

LAURENCE S. SEIDMAN

The public has become so accustomed to failure, political as well as economic, that the slightest advance engenders gratitude and triggers expressions of elation. The inflation rate declines minimally below the double-digit range, and voices are heard declaring prices under control. The unemployment rate drops trivially toward 7 percent, and sirens blare that full employment is virtually restored. A president manages to persuade Congress to enact his economic program, and his political success is eagerly confused by the media with economic results.

The current mood notwithstanding, it remains unfortunately requisite to plan beyond Reaganomics. When monetarism and tax cuts have had their trial and been found wanting, a new approach to stagflation will be required. It is the indispensable task to begin developing the new economic strategy.

In my view, the central element of the new approach must be a tax-based incomes policy (TIP) to restrain the wage and price increases of large corporations. First proposed in 1971 by Sidney Weintraub and Henry Wallich, TIP has gradually entered the mainstream of policy debate. When Reaganomics proves inadequate, its time will finally arrive. Yet in order to make it a political reality, one obstacle that has hindered its adoption from its conception must be removed. It is on this aspect of TIP that I will focus this essay.

The origin of this obstacle is ironic. The central insight motivating TIP is the crucial role of the money wage in the macroeconomy. No one has done more to illuminate this role than Sidney Weintraub. His writings have emphasized the futility of analyzing movements in the price level while ignoring movements in money wages. In my view, he has persuasively demonstrated that the crucial distinction among analysts of inflation is whether they apprehend or ignore money wage growth.

It is therefore not surprising that a monetarist is puzzled by the proposal to deter large corporations from granting excessive wage increases. Believing that inflation is solely a "monetary phenomenon," the monetarist is confused by a proposal aimed at money wage growth. It is also not surprising that, having focused on the pivotal role of money wages in macroeconomic theory, Weintraub would propose a tax incentive to discourage excessive wage increases.

I am persuaded that Weintraub, and the many other economists who share his theoretical perspective, are right to argue that money wage inertia is the crux of our inflation problem. I am also convinced that if a TIP on wage increases slows wage inflation it will automatically slow price inflation. But this brings us to the central political problem confronting TIP.

As a participant in the TIP debate, I am persuaded that the public in general and labor in particular will not perceive a TIP limited to wage increases as *equitable*. Assurances that prices will automatically follow costs will not succeed in allaying fears. Equally important, stressing wage increases solely appears to blame workers for inflation. No matter how vigorously Weintraub or Seidman or any other supporter of TIP denies this implication, the perception remains.

The time has come, then, for TIP advocates to remove the political obstacle that deprives TIP of the support it would otherwise receive. This can be done by making TIP completely symmetrical on price and wage increases of large corporations. To do so is not to abandon the view that wage growth is the prime mover, the crux of the problem. It is only to recognize the practical reality that only a symmetrical price and wage TIP can win the support necessary not only for enactment but also for operational success.

What is lost by making price increases, like wage increases, subject to TIP? Weintraub has argued that price increases are much more difficult to corral administratively than wage increases, and that the extension of TIP to price increases would significantly complicate TIP's feasibility. In this essay I want to challenge that assumption. Both in principle and in practice, measuring the average price increase of a large firm may not be a higher hurdle than measuring the average wage increase.

In extending the original TIP to price increases, it will be essential to reaffirm two features of the original TIP. First, practical administration requires limiting TIP to the largest corporations—perhaps two thousand—that constitute roughly half the gross national product (GNP) and about three-fourths of industrial activity, and set the wage-price pattern for the economy. Second, the tax *penalty* on the large corporation for violating either the wage standard or the price standard must be the key element in any TIP "package." A tax reward for good behavior can supplement the tax penalty for inflationary behavior; it cannot supplant it no matter how attractive "rewards" appear to the politically timid.

Although a symmetrical wage-price TIP is the key feature of the policy that must replace Reaganomics, it is not the only element. There are two handmaiden policies that I regard as essential complements to TIP. First, to promote growth and productivity without sacrificing equity, the income tax should be reformed into a progressive personal consumption (expenditure) tax that makes saving and investment tax-deductible. Second, to reduce unemployment and raise real wages in low-income areas, enterprise zones utilizing targeted tax cuts should be created. In all aspects the incentive-deterrent nature of taxes constitutes the underlying philosophy. (The Reagan, or Kemp-Roth, tax bill shares this attribute.)

By bringing down inflation without engineering a tight-money recession, TIP will promote growth. Nevertheless, once TIP permits the economy to be run at full capacity, two important issues will remain. First, how much of the GNP should be devoted to capital formation and how much to consumption? Second, how should new capital be allocated among alternative uses?

Economic history teaches that capital accumulation has been associated with rising labor productivity, real wages, and living standards. Why is the average worker in the United States today more prosperous than his counterpart in 1900? Or his counterpart in a developing country today? Surely the central reason is that the average U.S. worker today is equipped with more physical and human capital. Capital formation has been the "antipoverty program" of economic history.

What policies can be adopted today to raise the real wage that a young low-skilled worker will earn in 1990? I want to describe briefly two: the progressive personal consumption tax, which will raise the capital stock available in 1990 to all workers; and enterprise zones, which will raise the share of that new capital available to workers from low-income areas.

The personal consumption (expenditure) tax has long attracted the interest of economists. The principle (practical administration aside) of taxing a person according to his consumption rather than his income has received support from distinguished economists, including John Stuart Mill, Alfred Marshall, Irving Fisher, A. C. Pigou, and Nicholas Kaldor. Until recently, however, feasibility has been doubted.

Two studies, however, have reopened the question of feasibility. The U.S. Treasury's *Blueprints for Basic Tax Reform* (1977) and the United Kingdom's *The Structure and Reform of Direct Taxation* (Meade Commission Report) (1978), both concluded that conversion of the income tax to a personal consumption tax would be both operational and desirable. Each taxpayer adds his cash inflow from earnings and the sale of assets, but then subtracts saving and investment before applying the tax rates. A new debate has sprung up over the merits— theoretical and practical—of the two tax bases, the conclusion being that there is no longer a consensus that the income tax is simpler to implement. The pros and cons of each tax have once again become relevant.

The first question that arises is: Won't a consumption tax be less progressive than an income tax, because the affluent can afford to save a greater fraction of their income? The answer would be yes if the income tax tables remain unchanged. But why should they be? If tax rates on the consumption of the affluent are properly adjusted, then the same share of total tax revenue can be secured from this class.[1] A personal consumption tax can be made as progressive as desired by adjusting the tax tables.

A second response is Keynes' "paradox of thrift": If households try to save a greater fraction of their income, this need not result in greater actual capital formation if an increase in investment demand is not forthcoming. Recognizing the paradox of thrift should cause not an opposition to greater saving but only an insistence that complementary policies stimulate investment demand. Once an economy is at full employment, two things are required for greater capital formation: greater saving and greater investment demand. Neither one alone is satisfactory. One function of TIP is to free monetary policy to stimulate investment demand; tax incentives for business investment may also prove useful to overcome the paradox of thrift.

A third reaction is: Why should the current generation sacrifice consumption to improve the standard of living of the next generation, which will be richer than we are? This familiar argument implicitly regards each generation as a single social class with members of identical income. However, the merit of a progressive consumption tax is that it will cut the consumption of today's affluent so that the low-skilled worker of 1990 enjoys a higher standard of living. It is simply not true that such a worker in 1990 would be richer than today's affluent who make the sacrifice.

Finally, it is argued that it is unfair to levy different taxes on two persons of identical income solely because they differ in their propensity to save. Years ago, in his *The Expenditure Tax* (1955), Kaldor explained that current consumption may be a better measure of permanent income than current income and therefore a fairer tax base. I would attach another response. Although the affluent saver may be as self-interested as the affluent consumer, he unintentionally contributes more to the earning ability of the future low-skilled worker so that the social consequence of behavior justifies differential tax treatment.[2]

While conversion of the income tax to a personal consumption tax will provide a larger capital stock for the whole economy in 1990, it is desirable to adopt another element to assure that a larger share of that capital raises the productivity of workers who reside in low-income areas. Enterprise zones come to mind.

Enterprise zone legislation has been co-sponsored in the House by Democrat Robert Garcia of the South Bronx, and Republican Jack Kemp. Although Kemp's fondness for citing John F. Kennedy's tax cut is by now well known, he has for some reason neglected to pay homage to Robert Kennedy. Yet it was Robert Kennedy in 1967 who introduced urban enterprise zone legislation. In *To Seek a Newer World,* Kennedy wrote:

> To ignore the potential contribution of private enterprise is to fight the war on poverty with a single platoon, while great armies are left to stand aside. . . . In my judgment, the lack of private enterprise participation is the principal cause of our failure to solve the problem of employment in urban poverty areas. . . . The most effective way to encourage new enterprise in urban poverty areas is through tax incentives.[3]

The key to the zone strategy is to set the tax rate on capital income earned in the zone (i.e., designated low-income areas) significantly below the tax rate on capital income earned in the rest of the economy. This differential tax treatment should encourage firms to locate in the zone and investors to finance intrazone production.

Objection to a differential tax rate is that it results in an inefficient allocation of capital. Economists argue from this premise that if aid to zone residents is desirable it would be better to use *direct* income transfers rather than "distort" the geographical allocation of capital.

These "free-marketeers" are, however, disposed to think—or are acting as if they believe—that income transfers are a substitute for higher real wages. Suppose enterprise zone incentives would raise the productivity of a low-skilled zone resident so that he earns $12,000 instead of $8,000. Is it really equivalent to leave his productivity and earnings at $8,000 but give him a government transfer of $4,000?

Most low-skilled zone residents would surely prefer the $12,000 of earnings, no doubt believing they are entitled to what they earn from an employer but dubious about a transfer from the government. Moreover, the transfer is less reliable, depending on the generosity of taxpayers. These taxpayers surely do not regard the two options as equivalent. Many would oppose transfers to able-bodied adults but would respect the right of any person to the wage he earns at his workplace.

To increase the rate at which our society reduces poverty through capital accumulation, it is therefore necessary to go beyond TIP to a progressive consumption tax and to enterprise zones. TIP, however, is essential to their success. As long as monetarism, in its pathetic, dreary battle against inflation, deprives the economy of adequate aggregate demand, the consumption tax and enterprise zones will be overwhelmed by recession. The remainder of this essay will therefore concentrate on the design of a symmetrical wage-price TIP.

The essential difference between TIP and monetarism is the certainty of the penalty at the time management and labor at a given firm set wages and prices. The monetarist view holds that a determined stance by the Federal Reserve will make it evident to the price and wage setters, at the time of decision, that failure to cut the increases will result in a fall in sales, profits, and jobs. Anticipating this promised penalty in monetary wrath, wage and price increases will be cut, thereby escaping the unpleasant recession scenario. Such *hypothecated* "rational expectations" enable monetarism to cure inflation without recession (in imagination), as its advocates insist.

But will actual managers, union leaders, and employees respond this way? At the moment of decision, the future penalty under monetarism is uncertain, for it does not depend simply on the behavior of the Federal Reserve. It rests peculiarly on the link between a tight money policy and the fate of a particular firm, and it is well known that firms are affected differently by monetary policy. Some will survive nicely even if they fail to cut wage and price increases; others will be battered even if they cut their increases in advance. The claim that tight money is "neutral" is an academic myth.

The penalty that monetarism threatens is in the *future*. "Perfect foresight" models notwithstanding, a distinguishing feature of the future is that it cannot in the present be known with certainty. Is it realistic to believe that if sales are strong today firms will nevertheless cut wage and price increases because the Federal Reserve promises to make things worse next year?

The aim of TIP is to make the penalty for exceeding the wage or price standard *absolutely* certain and unequivocal at the time the decision is contemplated. Instead of depending on the future behavior of the Federal Reserve and the economy, the tax penalty for the corporation will be sealed by its own decision. Future behavior of the economy or any policymaker will be largely irrelevant.

An example will illustrate. Today pay increases average about 9 percent; productivity increases, say 1 percent; prices jump 8 percent. Suppose the TIP amendment to the corporate income tax law established an initial wage guidepost of 5 percent and a price guidepost of 4 percent (in practice, a different price guidepost might be established for each major economic sector). Because the purpose of TIP is not to raise revenue, assume the base corporate tax rate for all corporations (covered and not covered by TIP) is reduced to 36 percent (from its current 46 percent) when TIP is introduced.

If a large corporation covered by TIP matches the guideposts, raising its average wage 5 percent and its average price 4 percent, it will enjoy the same 36 percent tax rate as uncovered firms. If it instead exceeds the wage guidepost by 1 percent, its tax rate for that year would rise 5 percent; if it also exceeds the price guidepost by 1 percent, its tax rate would rise another 5 percent. Thus the large corporation that sets a (6 percent, 5 percent) wage-price combination would face a 46 percent tax rate; (7 percent, 6 percent) would result in a 56 percent tax rate; and persisting in today's (9 percent, 8 percent) combination would result in a 76 percent tax rate.

If TIP succeeds in moderating wage increases to 5 percent, and price increases to 4 percent, then Congress should *lower* the guideposts. Eventually the price guidepost should be set at 0 percent and the wage guidepost made equal to expected productivity growth (1 percent in this example, but hopefully 2 or 3 percent if policies such as the consumption tax raise productivity growth).

While the contrast with monetarism is apparent, it is equally important to recognize the difference between TIP and wage-price controls. The TIP penalty is intended to be "stiff, but not prohibitive." It should be strong enough to induce most large corporations to grant smaller wage and price increases than they otherwise would have, yet it should not be so rigid that no firm can afford a minor violation of the guideposts.

A TIP penalty of this intermediate magnitude provides automatic *flexibility*. If a corporation faces a sharp increase in product demand, and thus a severe labor shortage, it is free to exceed the guideposts and accept the penalty with equanimity. In contrast to the situation under controls, the firm will not require approval from a pay board or price commission to act. Wage and price decisions remain *with* each firm. In particular, the result of any collective bargaining agreement would automatically be valid under TIP; the firm would of course be required to accept the tax consequences. Wage bargains would properly be over intrafirm pay scales.

TIP is therefore compatible with decentralized wage and price decision-making. Like other elements of the corporate income tax, TIP would alter the incentives on the firm: Firms would be free to pursue their own self-interest and make their own decisions without government approval. Automatically, market forces would continue to affect relative wage and price adjustments in the economy. In this important respect, TIP differs fundamentally from controls.

Like controls, TIP will require each covered firm to measure its wage and price increase. Government auditors—under TIP, located in the Internal Revenue Service—would review the calculations of a *sample* of firms so compliance and administrative costs would be similar (but far lower than the army of enforcers under controls).

Monetarist opponents of TIP are fond of alluding to these administrative and compliance costs, as well as allocative efficiency costs, because TIP may slow the speed of adjustment of relative wages and prices. They are unmoved by the provision that TIP be limited to the largest two thousand corporations to reduce these costs. They enjoy reciting the "damage" such "distortions" will create.

There is a myopic lack of perspective in the monetarist obsession with the "distortions" of TIP. To listen to a monetarist, one would think that the monetarist policy is free of inefficiency and havoc. Yet nothing could be further from the truth. What could be more inefficient than Friedman's several years of "transition" to full employment, during which a significant fraction of potential GNP is implicitly destroyed by the "transitional" recession? Somehow it is inefficient to impel compliance and administrative costs, but it is sub-

limely efficient to sacrifice jobs and GNP through a "necessary" recession. As James Tobin once observed, "it takes a heap of Harberger
[consumer well-being] triangles to fill an Okun [production] gap."

Perhaps the central objection to the extension of TIP from wages
to prices is the "quality problem." From one year to the next the typical
large corporation varies the quality and features on at least some of
its products. The intention of a price TIP is to measure the genuine
price increase on products of unchanged quality. Annual quality variation, therefore, presents an obstacle to implementing a price TIP.

It has been assumed by many TIP proponents that the quality problem is much more severe for prices than for wages. Yet it need not be
clearly true. In fact, the most serious "quality problem" may pertain
to labor.

Certain products are unequivocally unchanged from one year to
the next. Steel of a particular specification is one example. In contrast,
no worker is the "same" in two adjacent years. The worker's human
capital has altered as a result of on-the-job experience and aging, even
if he remains within the same occupational category. It is always possible to pretend that all man-hours are the same and to compute the
wage by dividing the total wage bill by total man-hours. As Weintraub
and Wallich clearly recognized in their initial TIP paper, such a compu-
tation cannot eliminate the input-quality problem. They offered some
practical methods of computing the wage increase under TIP, fully
aware that the quality problem for labor exists and cannot be perfectly
solved, but this need not prevent the satisfactory implementation of
a wage TIP.

Similarly, many products are altered from one year to the next.
But in contrast to labor, at least an important fraction of a large corporation's products are unaltered. In this sense the quality problem is
less severe for prices. It would be sensible, under a price TIP, to use
a sample of products and to heavily weight the sample with products
identical in the two adjacent years (the procedure followed by the Carter administration's Council on Wage and Price Stability).

Measuring price increases when products change is a familiar problem to the government agencies responsible for collecting price index
data. Various methods have been devised to yield good estimates. For
example, when specific features are added they can be separately
priced. The experience of the Bureau of Labor Statistics could be invoked to instruct corporations on permissible methods of computing
the price increase in these cases.

Obviously each corporation's estimate of its "genuine" price increase will be imperfect. It will therefore be possible for a corporation with a genuine average price increase of 7 percent to report perhaps 6 percent and defend itself satisfactorily under audit. The inevitable discrepancy between the "genuine" and "reported" price increase warrants two observations.

First, it is curious how some critics of TIP quickly conclude that such discrepancies render the policy unfeasible. Yet, having dismissed TIP as "impractical," these "practical" men will then turn their attention to some other aspect of tax policy that they do regard as tolerable, such as accelerated depreciation. Open-minded observers, in contrast, should maintain perspective. Slippage is not unknown in other parts of the tax code. If so severe and perfect a standard of feasibility had been applied in the past, the corporate and personal income taxes would never have been broached, much less enacted.

Second, it is crucial to recognize that such slippage in no way undermines the incentive effect of the price TIP. Suppose management knows that it can report 6 percent if its true price increase is 7 percent. It will also know it can report 5 percent if its true increase is 6 percent. Thus the incentive to *cut* its genuine price increase by 1 percent is unimpaired.

To summarize: The "quality problem," while formidable, is not a sufficient reason to reject a price TIP. It is comparable for wages and prices. Imperfections in measurement will not undermine the strength of either incentive. Further aspects of a price TIP are therefore worth exploring.

One immediate advantage of complementing the wage TIP with a symmetrical price TIP is that it should largely solve "the shifting problem." In response to the proposal of a wage TIP, it was often asked, Won't a large corporation ignore TIP, grant the same wage increase, and "pass on" the tax with a price increase, shifting the TIP burden to consumers? Even under a wage TIP, arguments can be made that shifting would be imperfect, so that a wage TIP would succeed in reducing pay increases. A price TIP makes the shifting scenario less likely. The firm that contemplates such a response would be taxed first on its excessive wage increase, and second on its excessive price increase. It would therefore be doubly penalized for ignoring TIP. If the penalties are sufficiently stiff, few firms could afford such a response.

One potential problem with a price TIP is that it seems "unfair" to penalize a firm that raises its sales price solely because the price of inputs purchased from other firms has risen. Every incomes policy of the controls variety has wrestled with this "cost pass-through" problem. Often, ad hoc adjustments are made in extreme cases, while retaining sales price as the appropriate price concept. One approach to this problem would be to substitute "value-added price" for sales price as the determinant of tax liability, for this automatically deducts the effect of price increases of inputs purchased from other firms.[4]

It follows that value-added price would consist primarily of unit labor cost and partly of unit profit and tax costs. Some may see a price TIP as fully supplanting a wage TIP, rather than complementing it. This would no doubt be attractive to the politically timid, who would be more comfortable presenting the TIP proposal to representatives of labor.

Such replacement, however, would ignore a vital psychological aspect of the problem. While management would recognize that an excessive wage increase would push up value-added price and its TIP penalty, workers could persuade themselves that management is bluffing, that management could still avoid a TIP penalty by squeezing its profit. It is essential that management be able to point to an explicit wage-TIP, so that workers recognize that management faces a stiff penalty if it grants an excessive wage increase. For TIP to work effectively, both management and workers must easily grasp the unambiguous consequences of an excessive pay increase, so miscalculation and resentment are minimized.

Another obstacle to a price TIP concerns the use of a single price guidepost for the whole economy. In a given year, across major economic sectors, the variation of price increases around its mean generally exceeds the variation of wage increases around its mean. One explanation is that while considerations of equity, and labor mobility, tend to narrow the variance of wage increases, variation in productivity growth across sectors results in variation in cost, and therefore price increases.

Instead of a single price guidepost for the whole economy, it thus seems desirable to vary the guidepost across sectors according to the average productivity growth in the sector. For example, suppose the wage guidepost is 5 percent, average productivity growth is 1 percent, so the average price guidepost is 4 percent. If Sector X has productivity growth of 3 percent in year t, then its price guidepost would be 2 percent for that year; if Sector Y has productivity growth of -1 percent, then its price guidepost would be 6 percent for that year.

Several aspects of sector price guideposts should be emphasized. First, no corporation would measure its own productivity increase. The sector price guideposts would be given to corporations on their tax return. They would be based on official Commerce Department productivity data. Second, a sector would contain sufficient firms so that no firm would be able to influence its price guidepost by varying its own productivity.

Even with sector price guideposts and a value-added price concept, the wage-price-productivity relation holds more closely over a several-year period than in any single year. It may therefore be desirable to base TIP on the average wage and price increase given by a corporation over the previous three years, rather than one year. This would limit the importance of short-term fluctuations and aberrations.

Finally, it is probably desirable to cut the tax rate of a corporation that sets its average price increase below the guidepost; the price TIP should be a symmetrical penalty-reward TIP. In the case of wages, such symmetry is probably not advisable. Representatives of labor would no doubt object to literally rewarding corporations for below-average wage increases. A reward for below-average price increases would not elicit comparable objection and would assure that each corporation always has an incentive, induced by TIP, to reduce its price increase still further, even if it is already below the guidepost.

Reaganomics should be enjoyed now by its architects, before its failures make such rejoicing no longer possible. Thus it is not too soon for critics of the monetarist–tax cut fashion to propose a successor. In my view, the core of a fresh economic policy should be a symmetrical price-wage TIP on large corporations, complemented by transforming the income tax into a progressive personal consumption (expenditure) tax, and by the creation of enterprise zones.

Even if TIP succeeds in reducing inflation without recession, there will be a need for two complementary policies. To raise the productivity and real wage of the low-skilled worker of 1990 and beyond, today's economy must allocate more resources to investment and less to consumption, so that the capital stock of 1990 is thereby increased. The burden of today's sacrifice of consumption should be distributed progressively. Reform of the income tax into a progressive personal consumption tax would accomplish this. Simultaneously, monetary policy and investment tax incentives must stimulate investment demand. To assure workers in low-income areas a larger fraction of the new capital, enterprise zones could attract capital regionally through special tax incentives.

TIP, however, holds the key. Without it, monetarism will condemn the economy to stagnation. The time has come to remove the principal political obstacle to TIP: its apparent asymmetric treatment of wages and prices. Proponents of TIP, such as Weintraub, have persuasively argued that, in theory, money wage growth is the decisive lever; reduce it, and price inflation will subside automatically. Moreover, in the arena of macroeconomic theory, it is not possible to overemphasize the role of money wages. I share Weintraub's view that the neglect of money wages is the most serious pervasive error in macroeconomics, with disastrous consequences for practical policy recommendations.[5]

Nevertheless, political reality requires a symmetrical TIP that is fair to all parties. It is therefore necessary to extend the original TIP to prices as well as wages, for the cost of extending TIP to prices has been exaggerated. It is most important to follow the advice of the original Weintraub-Wallich TIP proposal that TIP be limited to the largest corporations—perhaps two thousand. Given this restriction, measurement of the average price increase should not be more difficult than measuring the average wage increase; both have a "quality problem." Like other aspects of a TIP, problems should prove manageable, or no more vexatious than implementing other facets of the tax code.

Supporters of TIP have in the past committed a tactical error in allowing those hostile to any kind of incomes policy to contend that a price TIP is impractical, so that only a wage TIP should even be discussed. In so doing, they have been titillated in watching the political process reject a wage TIP as supposedly unbalanced and inequitable to labor.

This tactical mistake can be reversed. A symmetrical price-wage TIP will continue to be opposed by those who reject anything that smacks of novelty. Symmetry, however, will open an appeal to a large public, including labor. The time for symmetry is now.

University of Delaware

NOTES

1. Cf. Laurence S. Seidman, "A Personal Consumption Tax: Can It Break the Capital Formation Deadlock?" *Business Review* (Federal Reserve Bank of Philadelphia), January 1981.
2. Cf. Laurence S. Seidman, "A Personal Consumption Tax and Social Welfare," *Challenge* 23 (September/October 1980): 10–16.
3. Robert F. Kennedy, *To Seek a Newer World* (Garden City, N.Y.: Doubleday & Co., 1967), p. 4.
4. Value-added price is computed as follows. Current dollar expense on inputs from other firms is subtracted from current dollar sales to obtain current

dollar value-added. Current dollar expense is deflated by a price index to get constant dollar expense; current dollar sales is similarly deflated to get constant dollar sales; the difference between constant dollar sales and expense is constant dollar value added. When current dollar value added is divided by constant dollar value added, the result is value-added price. These computational steps could be given on a tax return, and would no doubt be comparable to the steps required to compute accelerated depreciation. The use of value-added price would enable policymakers to explain, accurately, that a corporation is not penalized for passing on these input costs.

5. Cf. Sidney Weintraub, *Capitalism's Inflation and Unemployment Crisis* (Reading, Mass.: Addison-Wesley, 1978).

10

The Dismal Science of Stagflation Control

CHARLES E. ROCKWOOD

INTRODUCTION

The United States now faces stronger, more deeply rooted inflationary forces than ever before. Conservative monetary and fiscal policy alone, or even supplemented by supply-side economics, cannot root out these persistent and pervasive inflation forces without enormous economic cost. That being the case, there is a need to continue to consider additional programs and policies. But when the list of supplementary policies is investigated it proves to be a very short one. Therefore, we cannot afford to discard wage-price controls as a policy option, particularly since the harmful nature of their side effects is greatly exaggerated and their potentially helpful contribution to inflation moderation much overlooked.

THE NATURE OF THE INFLATION PROBLEM

Three major events have led to the condition where the United States now faces a more virulent strain of inflation than in the past.

First, greater stress on full employment as a policy goal, together with a more relaxed attitude toward government expansion even when not fully financed by tax revenue, represents a fundamental change in macroeconomic policy with strong implications for inflation expectations. The roots of this change go back to the Employment Act of 1946 and before. But prior to the adoption of a flexible exchange-rate regime for the dollar, a major constraint on expansionary macroeconomic policy was the need to maintain some monetary and fiscal restraint in order not to worsen the balance of payments unduly. Once the dollar was allowed to float, under the Nixon administration, that motive no longer held for the United States. Since then government deficits, money stock growth, and the inflation rate have accelerated, as have inflation expectations. Public pessimism about the probable success of antiinflation programs has increased, and as a consequence the output, employment, and political consequences of inflation eradication have become much stronger.

Second, the strengthening of unemployment compensation plans and the growth of public assistance programs, together with an increased number of two-income families, have provided a financial safety net for many workers. This has enabled individuals and the groups that represent them to take job actions that would have been much less thinkable in an earlier period. The financial consequences of adventurous microeconomic behavior are softened. As a result the belligerence with which wage demands are pursued or wage cuts resisted is strengthened, which again makes inflation eradication much more difficult.

Third, the concentrated sector of the economy has been able to isolate itself from the pressure of market forces to a substantial degree. Since nearly 50 percent of national income in this country originates in the concentrated sector, as defined to include regulated and unregulated industries plus government, this is a major factor. To be sure, an expanded volume of international trade has reintroduced market pressures in some markets, but it also has brought about some increase in economic instability that has prompted some expansionary monetary and fiscal behavior, with attendant inflation consequences.

This, then, is that new more virulent strain of inflation with which policy must try to cope. It is inflation born of the economic security found in a depression-protected, partially welfare-state, concentrated-sector-dominated, post-Keynesian world. It is, in short, the bad that comes with a great deal of good. To suggest that this country should return to a period of atomistic competition regardless of the efficiency consequences of such a change, to a period when workers were not protected against unemployment and when they had very little power in the work environment, and to a period when the nation was plagued with depressions with such regularity that they were thought to be an economic law of nature, is surely to throw out far too much that is desirable for precious little gain.

SOLUTIONS TO INFLATION

The orthodox solutions to the new inflation are clearly inadequate, as all but their staunchest proponents recognize.

MONETARY AND FISCAL POLICY

Restrictive monetary and fiscal policy carries with it a cost in terms of output and employment loss that the public seems unwilling to accept and economic common sense decries. As expressed by Okun's Law, this loss would be in the vicinity of 10 percent of a year's output for each percentage point decline in the basic inflation rate.[1] It is to be hoped that Okun's Law would not persist without amendment should these policy instruments be employed gradually to reduce the basic inflation rate from over 10 percent to 3 or 4 percent. Whether this proved to be the case would depend upon the expectations that a policy of gradualism generated.

In one extreme case, the U.S. Army of Occupation in early postwar Japan was able to halt a major inflationary movement through implementation of a very restrictive monetary and fiscal policy program without serious adverse output and employment effects. Presumably the occupation forces were as successful as they were because the public expectations generated conformed closely to the policy's actual intent. The Japanese people had been led to expect that they would have to suffer great atrocities as a result of their defeat, and the Army of Occupation gave them conservative monetary and fiscal policy.[2]

On the other hand, a policy of restraint that did not influence expectations at all would have failed to deal with the major inflation problem of today: inflationary expectations. And certainly the modern world from Israel to Brazil, from the United Kingdom to the United States, is replete with examples of episodes when attempts to introduce conservative monetary and fiscal policy were defeated by the failure of the public to believe that the authorities would, could, or should hold the line.

SUPPLY-SIDE ECONOMICS

Promotion of improved economic efficiency as an alternative for, or supplement to, restrictive monetary and fiscal policy is a superficially appealing method for dealing with the inflation problem. This is because improved economic efficiency provides more economic goods (products and/or leisure) at the same time that it helps deal with the inflation problem. And there is no real doubt that improved economic efficiency can provide at least temporary aid in inflation control. According to Christopher Caton and Christopher Probyn, a 1 percent increase in productivity, with about a four-year lag, will reduce inflation by about 2 percentage points.[3]

Unfortunately the magnitude of productivity gain needed for inflation control in the current context would be several times current rates. This might not even be possible, but at a minimum it would be very difficult to achieve. Unlike monetary and fiscal policy, supply-side economics cannot be regulated with just a stroke of the policy pen.

Perhaps even more important, increased productivity gain could easily promote early inflation control at the expense of making later inflation control more difficult. This is because increased productivity can lead to heightened expectations about real wage and profit gains. And unrealistic expectations about productivity gains lead to the same type of economic-control problems as persistent expectations of inflation. In each case these expectations must be corrected through restrictive monetary and fiscal policy measures or ratified by improved productivity gain.

KILLING THE SNAKE

Most troublesome of all in the fight against inflation is the likelihood that, once eradicated, inflation pressures will reemerge given sufficient time. Inflation brought to heel by monetary and fiscal policy will not stay under control. The battle will have to be fought again and again, with attendant output and employment losses each time. And, as mentioned, inflationary wage and price decisions made possible through improved economic efficiency gains will likely be followed by even more gluttonous wage and profit decisions in subsequent periods.

It is human nature to want more than it is possible to have. An economic system that is managed without a method for controlling unbounded desires will be doomed to repeat again and again its dosage of antiinflation medicine, however difficult it may be for the doctor to provide or for the patient to endure. The basic point is that our society quite properly has chosen not to use ruthless and merciless economic punishment to control excessive wage and price decisions. So a new and more virulent inflation strain has emerged, one that cannot be controlled satisfactorily by the old methods. At this point, either we find additional strategies for inflation control or we face a history of unsatis-factory battle. That search for other means should include consider-ation of wage and price controls as an antiinflationary device.

COSTS AND BENEFITS OF PAST INCOMES POLICIES

EFFECTIVENESS OF CONTROLS

The popular notion that wage-price controls as an antiinflationary device do not work is incorrect. They do not always work. If they work, they will do so for only a limited time.

To be effective, wage-price controls need to be properly structured. The form of the controls matters. The economic environment also must be supportive for wage-price controls to be at all successful. If, for exam-ple, controls are introduced in an atmosphere of expansionary mone-tary and fiscal policy, they will break down very quickly. Should this happen the economy will have borne the not inconsiderable cost of a controls episode and reaped none of the benefits. Monetary and fiscal policy is more than powerful enough to override wage-price controls. And as has been known at least since Roman times,[4] in an unfavorable economic environment the strongest of enforcement regimes will not be sufficient to maintain control effectiveness.

Nonetheless, subject to these caveats the controls can work. The econometric evidence, while somewhat mixed, supports that general contention.[5] It tells us that some control episodes have been associated with a modest downward shift in wage-price behavior from what other-wise would have been expected. Wage-price controls cannot effectively control excess demand inflation or inflation that is caused by exogenous shocks, but they can make a contribution to the control of inflation ex-pectations.

It is important to note, however, that past control regimes gener-ally have not dealt effectively with the need for adjustment of relative product and factor prices. This means that as the need for relative price change intensifies over time, as a result of shifts in product demand, import product prices, labor needs and availability, and so on, control prices become less and less appropriate. This use of rigid controls leads to ever more intensive market pressure for control breakdown. This breakdown process is made worse by the fact that controls can never be introduced at a point when relative prices are in equilibrium. Factor and product price changes are sequential, not simultaneous. This means that, whenever controls are suddenly imposed on an economy, some prices will be frozen after just having been adjusted for inflation and relative price changes, others will have been frozen just prior to such adjustments. Both the problem that controls become dated and the problem that controls cannot freeze prices at an equilibrium point are major limitations of wage and price restraints that ultimately contribute to a regulatory breakdown. But the point remains that controls can work, for a time.

The econometric evidence that controls have sometimes been helpful in inflation moderation provides indirect support of the conclusion that expectations can be influenced by this means. A survey of Nixon control phases I and II by Joel Popkin at the University of Michigan Survey Research Center provides additional, direct evidence on the point.[6] He showed that from February 1971 to May 1972 the percentage of consumers expecting prices to rise by 5 percent or more in the coming year dropped from 41 percent to 30 percent.

As I have argued on other occasions, for controls to make an effective contribution to the reduction of expectational inflation they need to be used as a temporary device to reinforce conservative monetary and fiscal policy.[7] Introduction of the controls should be delayed until a program of restrictive monetary and fiscal policy has been in place long enough for the economy to feel pinched. At that point wage-price controls should be introduced. The public, in effect, is then being directed by law not to take economic actions contrary to the kind of environment the monetary and fiscal authorities are creating. In such an application, wage-price controls reinforce sensible economic actions. In this way controls aid conservative monetary and fiscal policy by reducing the political pressures that tend to build against such policy, and public confidence in a controls policy is reinforced because the policy is supportive of private self-interest. This is in contrast to a number of past applications of wage-price controls where those who complied with the controls program aided the inflation fight, but at the expense of their private best interest.

COST OF CONTROLS

The notion that wage-price controls cannot be worth the cost because they are expensive to administer and represent an unwarranted interference with the free interplay of market forces needs considerable amendment.

In one sense, if control episodes are associated with a rise in output, then one might argue that they were worth it from the economic stand-point. Certainly the burden of proof would be on the other side, particularly as the alternative of restrictive monetary and fiscal policy is so costly in terms of output foregone. But if by cost one means administrative cost, then the cost of wage-price controls depends greatly upon how they are structured. If the control program contemplated is some form of jawboning such as President Gerald Ford instituted under his WIN program, the cost of controls would not be enough to warrant consideration, and the program probably would not be very effective. If, at the other extreme, the control program were as elaborate as our World War II controls, then by an earlier estimation (1979) I calculate that the cost would amount to perhaps 0.5 percent of the gross national product. This is a lot of money, but a modest sum in comparision with the cost of the restrictive monetary and fiscal policy alternative and presumably also with the alternative of allowing inflation to continue unchecked.

Clearly the cost of a wage-price control program is an important matter. Economic efficiency is always a desirable goal, and some control programs could be quite expensive. But controls can be structured in such a way that cost is not an effective argument for no controls at all.

POTENTIAL FORM AND STRUCTURE FOR FUTURE CONTROLS

Historically, wage-price controls as an antiinflation device have been advocated for all sectors of the economy as a matter of fairness. The administration of the controls has then been placed in the hands of some federal government entity. This policy has saddled past control programs with an unnecessarily large, highly centralized administrative burden, which has surely added to the cost of the controls and to public resentment of them. The very comprehensive nature of the administrative charge to the controls authority has undoubtedly led also to the simplemindedness of past control rules, and that too almost certainly has added to public resentment of them. Thus the structure of past control regimes has contributed to their lack of acceptance.

There is a need to develop a controls program that is evenhanded in its treatment of capital and labor and thereby enhances public acceptance, as well as one that both minimizes the administrative task and makes some allowance for unusual market circumstances. In this respect, incentive-based incomes policies such as Abba Lerner's Market Anti-Inflation Plan (MAP)[8] and the Wallich-Weintraub Tax-based Incomes Policy (TIP),[9] while still imperfect, represent exciting new approaches to this problem.

The attractive feature of the Lerner plan is its provision for the issuance of wage increase permits which, if not needed by the firm to which they are issued, may be resold to a firm that has a greater need. This approach has the desirable feature of relying on private markets to determine which firms have the most compelling need for a wage adjustment. The plan as proposed calls for the entire economy including government to be regulated, but this is not an essential feature. If it was decided that only some sectors needed to be controlled, the plan could be limited accordingly. The more serious difficulties with the Lerner plan are the complexity of the calculations required and its perverse treatment of productivity change.

The Lerner MAP requires that the cost of input factors be limited to their cost for the previous year plus an adjustment for the average gain in national productivity of, say, 2 percent. If in a particular case that limit is to be exceeded, additional MAP credit would have to be purchased from a firm that had a surplus. In making MAP credit calculations, factor cost is defined as all costs. In the case of labor, cost would include the value of any fringe benefits.

Under MAP a firm would be free to adjust the quantity of its inputs or its input mix, but its MAP credit calculations would be affected. If inputs were released, the associated MAP credits also would be lost. If inputs were added, the gain in MAP credits would not necessarily be equal to the cost of the new inputs. New entrants to the labor or capital markets could be paid whatever the firm thought appropriate and carry MAP credit based upon this payment. Input factors hired from some other firm or employment, however, would already carry MAP credit based on their previous use or cost. Thus a firm could hire a worker for more than he had been earning previously, or purchase a machine for more than the previous owner's user cost, only at the expense of reduced payments to other input factors.

Finally, under MAP, if labor and management jointly were experiencing productivity gains above the national average they would be required to buy additional MAP credit or reduce prices. Firms with less than average productivity gains would be required to raise prices or sell MAP credit. Thus MAP sends out inappropriate market signals to productive firms.

The Wallich-Weintraub plan (TIP), as an alternative to Lerner's

MAP, would allow only noninflationary wage adjustments as a deductible cost for federal income tax purposes. The Wallich-Weintraub proposal includes the suggestion that the TIP rule be applied only to the largest firms. Limiting application of the program to the largest one thousand firms would still encompass 55 percent of the gross business product. Limiting the program to the largest two thousand firms would encompass about 85 percent of the gross business product. The proposal calls for enforcement by the Internal Revenue Service.

The attractive features of the Wallich-Weintraub TIP are the automatic nature of the tax penalty it would place on "inflationary" wage adjustments and its economy of administration. Criticisms of TIP have focused primarily on the fact that it applies only to wages and that the amount of the tax penalty is too inexact.

It cannot be presumed that the minimum necessary penalty to induce firms to avoid paying inflationary wage adjustments will be the tax penalty applied to any excessive payment. Either that penalty will be overly large or it will be imperfect in its antiinflation result. Probably the policy will lead to both situations as business prospects, the tightness of labor markets, and expectations about future inflation fluctuate.

Certainly the TIP policy would have a perverse effect from firm to firm. Firms with small tax burdens would find the incentive more annoying than harmful, and conversely. The suggestion that the TIP penalty should be made an excise tax rather than a corporate income tax would seem to be well taken. An excise tax would be uniform for all firms, could be adjusted with experience, and need not tie national corporate tax objectives to the subsidiary question of corporate wage policy.

Still, the problem of how to set the penalty level remains, particularly in those instances where the antiinflation goal is not achieved either because the tax penalty was inappropriately scaled or because corporate price behavior was out of tune with the wage policy induced. A partial answer might be for the federal government to guarantee that wage overpayments would not be subject to a tax penalty if announced inflation goals were unmet. But that announced policy would tie the government's hands on monetary and fiscal policy and still would not deal with the troublesome problem of excess profits and the resentment wage and salary workers would feel toward a program that controlled wages but not prices or profits. The matter is important because public support is necessary if wage-price controls are to be effective in their antiinflationary goal. The polls indicate that wage-price controls do not have strong public support. Therefore, in designing any controls program it is important to attempt to overcome this problem to whatever extent possible.

CONCLUSION

Wage-price controls, structured in traditional ways, can be effective and cost-effective, if applied in the proper macroeconomic setting. More than that, there have been and will be times when the only potentially effective antiinflation policies except wage-price controls already have been implemented. At that point the question is going to come: Is the fight worth the full measure of effort? If so, wage-price controls need to be considered.

Past control policies have had uneven success, often because too much has been asked of them. Controls have been expected to reduce inflation, but to do so in a macroeconomic environment of relaxed or relaxing monetary and fiscal policy. If controls are decided upon, and if the proper macro-environment for controls introduction is established, the control methods still should and could be improved upon. Abba Lerner, David Colander, Henry Wallich, Sidney Weintraub, Laurence Seidman, and others who have been working on control design deserve our wholehearted support. But the nonsequitur that wage-price controls represent an unwarranted interference in a world of perfect markets demeans the debate.

The current dilemma facing policymakers is illustrative of how and when wage-price controls might be used to help fight inflation. The Reagan administration has worked on supply-side issues, stimulating output incentives through tax policy changes and controlling government spending somewhat. The Federal Reserve has been holding fairly resolutely to its policy of monetary stringency. Saudi Arabia has done its bit by providing a pause in the trend of rising energy prices. Yet the public reaction on Wall Street and elsewhere is one of disbelief.

The public seems to feel that despite some reasonable progress so far, the Reagan-Volcker forces will fail later in their efforts to further reduce the budget, to get interest rates down, and so on. The possibility that the current antiinflation program could be successful is not given wide credence by the spending and investing public.

So the United States is confronted with the inverse of the paradox of thrift, which is the paradox of inflation-hedging. People fear inflation. This fear leads to a reluctance to loan at reasonable rates, advance buying, antique-collecting, hedonistic consumption, and so on. These actions conflict with productive economic activity and especially with capital formation. Ultimately they cause the inflation that is feared. The actions cause inflation by forcing the federal government into a position where continuation of a program of restrictive monetary and fiscal policy would be too damaging, both economically and politically. The expectation that antiinflation policy will fail promotes the failure.

It should be evident that in the context described low rates of productive capital formation stem from low savings rates and business pessimism. This is not fundamentally a tax problem and cannot be greatly helped by tax changes. It is an inflation-expectation problem. This is the phenomenon that wage-price controls might be used to help fight.

Florida State University

NOTES

1. Arthur M. Okun, "Efficient Disinflationary Policies," *American Economic Review* 68 (May 1968): 348–52.
2. I am indebted to Martin Bronfenbrenner, who was on General MacArthur's staff at the time, for this interesting sidelight.
3. Christopher Caton and Christopher Probyn, "The Inflationary Impact of the Productivity Slowdown," in Allen R. Sanderson, ed., *DRI Readings in Macroeconomics* (New York: McGraw-Hill, 1981).
4. The Emperor Diocletian introduced wage-price controls but did not restrict the process of monetary expansion taking place through debasement of the coinage. As a result, noncompliance quickly became quite general and he had to repeal the law, even though the penalty for violation of the wage-price edict was death. See, e.g., Naphtali Lewis and Meyer Reinhold, *Roman Civilization: Sourcebook II, The Empire* (New York: Harper & Row, 1966), pp. 458–60.
5. E.g., Otto Eckstein and James A. Girola, "Long-Term Properties of the Price-Wage Mechanism in the United States," *Review of Economics and Statistics* 60 (August 1978): 323–33; A. Bradley Askin and John Kraft, *Econometric Wage and Price Models* (Lexington, Mass.: Lexington Books, 1974); George L. Perry, *Unemployment, Money Wage Rates, and Inflation* (Cambridge, Mass.: MIT Press, 1966); Alan S. Blinder, *Economic Policy and the Great Stagflation* (New York: Academic Press, 1979); Christopher Probyn and Robin Siegel, "The New Inflation: Are Price Controls the Answer," in Sanderson, ed., *DRI Readings in Macroeconomics.*
6. Joel Popkin, "Incomes Policy," in Clarence C. Walton, ed., *Inflation and National Survival* (New York: Academy of Political Science, 1979).
7. Charles E. Rockwood, *National Incomes Policy for Inflation Control* (Gainesville, Fla.: University Presses of Florida, 1969); "The Economy at Mid-Year 1970," statement before the Joint Economic Committee, U.S. Congress, in

The 1970 Midyear Review of the State of the Economy, part 2, July 1970; "The Anti-Inflation Value of Direct Controls," in James H. Gapinski and Charles E. Rockwood, eds., *Essays in Post Keynesian Inflation* (Cambridge, Mass.: Ballinger Publishing Co., 1979).

8. Abba Lerner, "MAP: The Market Mechanism Cure for Stagflation," *Atlantic Economic Review* 7 (March 1979): 12–19; Abba Lerner and David Colander, "MAP, a Cure for Inflation," in David Colander, ed., *Solutions to Inflation* (New York: Harcourt Brace Jovanovich, 1979); Abba Lerner and David Colander, *MAP: A Market Anti-Inflation Plan* (New York: Harcourt Brace Jovanovich, 1980).

9. Henry Wallich and Sidney Weintraub, "A Tax-Based Incomes Policy," *Journal of Economic Issues* 5 (June 1971): 1–19; Sidney Weintraub, "Proposal for an Anti-Inflation Package," *Challenge* 21 (September/October 1978): 53–54.

11

Collective Bargaining <u>Is</u> Obsolete:

On Revising the Practice to Escape the Stagflation Madness

SIDNEY WEINTRAUB

Our stagflation mess of too much inflation and excessive unemployment is now a lusty fourteen-year-old. The contention here is that the Reagan budget slashes will do little to alter the madness and that we are condemned to the tragicomedy, with vast consequences for world well-being, unless our collective bargaining processes are revised. Unfettered bargaining, as conducted in the past, will maintain a predictable abject trauma to mark *a new economics of derision.*

Collective bargaining has an analogy in unions grabbing for a handful of money and drawing back a fistful of water. After completing publicized negotiations and winning a handsome pay settlement, unions are simply not able to shape the relevant variables that determine their relative earnings and the real buying power of their hard-won but illusory pay gains. The upshot is inflation. Thereafter, once the Federal Reserve superimposes its punitive actions on the economy, there follows the added misery of widespread unemployment. The concatenation of the twin evil soaks our economy in the bitter and vicious stagflation brew.

Criticism of collective bargaining, *as currently practiced,* should not be construed as an attack on unions: surely *both* unions and management engage in it! It would be farfetched to interpret the advocacy of a removal of an abscessed tooth or of a ruptured appendix as an assault on human life. Unions do many vital and good things; they are as entrenched in our democratic society as the right of association and free speech. They serve as a counterweight to an unbridled one-sided expression of business views. They serve all of us in their concern with health and safety at the work bench and in protecting labor's interests and airing grievances.

So it is possible to distinguish between unions and collective bargaining. It is the latter's aberrations that must be corrected if we are ever to lift ourselves out of the stagflation pit. A number of other bargaining modes can be installed to release us from the current morass.

The point compels reiteration, for it is too easy to misunderstand. Unions are one thing, and current collective bargaining practices are another. The two, too facilely identified as inseparable, can be segregated. They will have to be disentangled if ever we hope to restore a viable stagflation-free economy.

Generally, after being confronted by strikes, thoughtful bystanders, including strike victims, move to advocate resolution by fact-finding and arbitration. Too frequently the final settlement verdict splits the difference between competing claims. Historically, neither labor nor management has been willing to surrender its prerogatives to make strikes as dead as the dodo. Neither side is ever eager to place absolute trust in "judges" who, they suspect, may turn out to be for the other side.

Arbitration, nonetheless, shares the same faults as collective bargaining, for ultimately it is also *unable* to make the real thrust of its decision stick *because the key variables lie beyond its jurisdiction,* even when both labor and management abide the full spirit of the final judgment. Whether the decision is hailed as a victory for labor or a bloody nose meted out by management, the real settlement is invariably diluted by events that transpire beyond the bargaining table. There are chains of ramifications uncontrollable by either big labor or big management, despite their vocal contract bouts. Inevitably, after the settlement, some of the relative and real income gains slip away, as water from a clenched fist. Labor must always be at least partially stripped of its ostensible gains despite its elation over a "good" contract and no matter how amicable the negotiating climate. Management is bound to default partially on its participatory commitment despite its most honorable intent.

Several reasons for this partial collapse of bargaining prevent it from delivering what it promises by way of gains to labor. (1) As the wage changes percolate through the firms, industries, and the economy, labor's *relative* pay gains partake mainly of an illusion. The *relative* pay bonus invariably dissolves when it becomes shared almost universally. (2) As wages and prices spiral, the price excrescences fritter away some, most, or all of the hard-won real pay improvement: for its fighting pay gains labor moans over the ensuing price pains. (3) The progressive income tax nips away at the absolute pay hike as employees enter higher tax brackets. (4) As the Federal Reserve reacts and flails away at its money supply levers to curb inflation—with a conspicuous record of failure—the consequent unemployment dismembers labor's economic status.

It is this sequel which sustains the allegation that collective bargaining, as currently practiced, is obsolete. The economic facts of life render it an insidious institution that redounds to the detriment of labor and to a drag on the economy. The bargaining-table heroics perpetuate the *stagflation malaise,* and expose us to the *economics of derision.* Internationally, our dour outturn has supplanted the "British sickness" of jurisdictional strikes, tea breaks, and dwindling productivity as a subject of economic scorn.

Collective bargaining suffers from tunnel vision as a result of leadership concern solely with the terms of an agreement that will apply to the union membership covered in the bargaining sequence. Concretely, if the preoccupation of the United Automobile Workers (UAW) is with assembly-line auto workers, the agreement is intended to blanket just the people enrolled under the UAW banner. (Any other union can be substituted for the UAW in the illustration.)

Suppose the union bargains, and returns from the bargaining table elated at a big "victory," construed for illustrative purposes here as an annual pay gain of 10 percent over each of the next three years, amounting to a compound advance of about 33 percent. Once the terms are announced, with the revelry and jubilation pronounced, some of the gain is quickly discerned as illusory in both a real and a relative sense.

Assuming the original average pay of union employees to be $20,000 per year, the pay scale immediately swells to $22,000 as the annual pace. Nearly simultaneously, the pay of all other people within the firm or industry, such as nonunionized clerical help, is bound to ascend by about the same rate, for otherwise the gap would invite more unionism. Supervisory and middle-management people, perhaps after a bit of a lag, will be boosted by about the same percentage, maybe from an average of $30,000 to $33,000. Upper-management echelons follow suit with alacrity: the $100,000 and $500,000 executives, moaning about their "hardships" in making ends meet, will jump, say, to $110,000 and $550,000 respectively—or more. The union-sparked escalator will run irresistibly right up to the top level.

Obviously any *relative* income improvement is speedily eroded; production workers stay in about the same position in the pay pack as all other identifiable groups run at the faster tempo. In fact, on an *absolute* basis the pay discrepancies widen; in the illustration, the union pay gain is $2,000, and for the others it can be as much as $3,000, $10,000, or $50,000. Intrafirm and intraindustry *relative* income positions are rarely modified after the ripple effects of union bargaining bouts race the course.

This is only the beginning in the economic saga that spells out a story in real income frustration.

Manifestly, in the illustration, the firm's money wage costs climb by 10 percent. Product prices tend to rise immediately to reflect the new cost phenomena, for administrative pricing prevails almost universally in the market sectors exposed to big unions. "Administrative" pricing is the polite economic euphemism for monopoly and oligopoly positions.

Once the market price of products rises, some of the union pay gains are instantly diluted to the extent that workers are buyers of the firm's products. As matters stand, most of us normally spend only a tiny fraction of our income on the products we help produce; for example, as a university employee I spend nothing on the university's educational services beyond chipping in minor sums at the bookstore, cafeteria, or parking lot. For most workers the situation is practically the same, with minor differences in particulars. Still, there is *some* minor direct erosion of a pay gain.

A less subtle claimant on the pay hike is the tax collector. Normally there will be at least a proportionate bite out of the higher money income if employees stay in the same tax bracket. But pay gains over time are bound to push individuals up the progressive tax scale, which will tend to whittle the pre-tax boost. (The Reagan administration, especially Senator Robert Dole, Republican chairman of the Senate Finance Committee, plans to "index" tax rates so that these decline under inflation. At best, this would remove a lesser source of the money income gain illusion.)

Beyond the price move in the particular firm dispensing the pay gain, the big spin of the ineluctable wage-price spiral occurs at the next stage, in the roundabout indirect manifestations of the pay surge. It is on the roundabouts that the collective bargaining "gain" dissolves into smoke from an inflation fire and unemployment debacles.

Collective bargaining procedures take on their mirage features when parallel pay "victories" evolve in other industries. Given the pressures of envy released by one major settlement, analogous emulatory negotiations are set off in other sectors. At the finale, a more universal pay and price spiral marks the economic scene. The upshot: individuals in Industry A who buy the products of B, C, D, E, . . . find their buying power chewed up in the price outbreak, while employees of Industry B who are customers of A, C, D, E, . . . are aroused as their purchasing power is zapped. So it goes, across the full spectrum as the price binge follows the wage burst as night follows day. Some part of the break in the price dam occurs not so much because of cost pressures in industries of superior productivity performance but because of the greater nominal purchasing power of wage earners colliding head on with physical supplies in sectors such as farming, where prices are largely demand-oriented. Wages are, after all, not only the chief component of costs but also the mainstay of at least 85 percent of consumer demand.

As prices erupt along the line and in nearly all industries—in some sectors by more, and in other places by less—real wages are shaved. In the rolling process, prices seldom rise by as much as the ostensible pay boost, for under productivity growth real wages edge up.

The argument can be established more formally by invoking the Law of the Price Level. This is:[1]

Percentage Change in the Price Level *(P) equals*
Percentage Change in the Average Price Markup *(k) plus*
Percentage Change in the Average Money Wage *(w) minus*
Percentage Change in the Average Labor Productivity *(A)*

To illustrate with some sample numbers:

$$8\% \ P = 0\% \ k \text{ plus } 10\% \ w \text{ minus } 2\% \ A.$$

That is, if the average markup does not change—in fact, its change is generally so insignificant as to warrant our neglecting it—while the average wage mounts by 10 percent, and productivity advances by 2 percent, then the price-level hike will be 8 percent. Figures of this sort are especially pertinent for the last few years, during which productivity has frozen at about a nil or negative number, thereby accounting for price outcomes that have matched or surpassed the wage escalation. (*Real* wages will move directly with w/P, the money wage to price level ratio.)

The relation specified is a *general* law, and it applies to *all* goods viewed as an aggregate. Consumer prices comprise a large subset of the average of all prices. Some prices, such as those for new houses, cars, machinery, electronics, or energy, may be substantially *cost*-oriented and reflect pressures of unit labor costs (or OPEC oil rapacity) while

other items such as farm produce, old houses, or textiles may tend to
be more demand-oriented and poke up because of the higher purchasing power amassed by higher pay. But as an aggregate entity the general price level is a resultant of the elements specified in the formula.

It is a historical fact, amounting to *the most important empirical
law of economics,* that the *average* markup—not individual markups
in specified industries—tends to remain reasonably constant from year
to year. Over the long term, say of ten to twenty years or more, the
markup has tended to drift down modestly, in neither sharp nor steep
fashion.

Chart 1 (on semilogarithmic scale) depicts the course of the average
wage, average productivity, and the average markup over the period
since 1950. The slow markup *(k)* descent is apparent. Likewise, it is obvious that the average wage *(w)* has been outrunning the growth in
productivity *(A)*. If we tracked the course of the price level, it would
plot just under halfway between the *w* path and the *A* ascent, with
the discrepancy attributable to the downward price-level pressure im-
parted by the declining *k* markups. That money wages rise faster than
prices is of course a condition of improving real wages; over the long
pull this has happened.

The important conclusion is that if we are ever to realize a stable

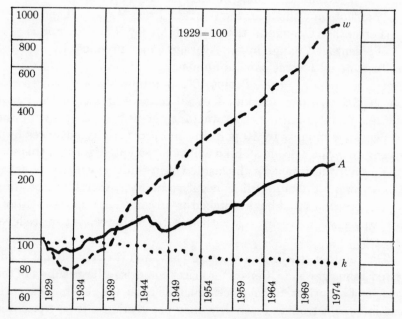

Chart 1.   Index numbers of *k, w, A,* 1929–75

price path, it will be necessary to align the average pay swoop with the average productivity gain. The average pay boost could be a trifle higher insofar as the k markup declined. But the main high-wire trick in price stability involves gearing w and A. Otherwise inflation *must* be our lot.

Money wages can thus leap ahead only in concert with productivity improvements if we are to escape the inflation madness. For those who have been making loud noises about "supply-side economics," the propaganda has put proper emphasis on productivity gains while scandalously disregarding the prerequisite of slowing down the pay escalator. In 1974, 1979, and probably in 1980, average labor productivity actually fell by 1 or 2 percent. Only a comparable *drop* in the average wage could have prevented the price orgy.

The caution is worth repeating: We are talking not of individual prices, nor of individual wages, but of all prices and the *average* of all wages. Individual prices might float around anywhere, either up or down. Some pay increases could be very large indeed. But on average they would have to conform to the average productivity movement to sustain a stable noninflation price outcome.

Unstated until now is the fact that the average markup is the reciprocal of the wage *share*. This means that if the markup is 2, so that prices go up by 2 cents when unit labor costs go up by 1 cent, the other way of looking at the sequence is to say that the wage share is one-half, or that out of every dollar of gross business product (GBP) labor gets 50 cents. This is close enough to the facts; about 53 cents of every GBP dollar typically goes to employees as wages or salaries.

The k markup, and hence the wage share, stays remarkably firm rather than fluctuating wildly, though we have noted some flex over time, tending to lower the markup or raise the wage share.

Profound implications adhere to this extraordinary fact. Despite the enormous transformation of our society since 1900, including the spectacular zoom in population from about 75 to 225 million, two world wars, the auto revolution from about nil to 125 million cars, air travel and virtual disappearance of the train and the ocean steamer, the ubiquity of television, radio, the telephone, the inroads of the computer on clerical help, the appearance of big labor, giant business, and the government economic Leviathan, labor's share of the national income has tended to stay remarkably close to where it was at the turn of the twentieth century. It would have been a prescient and unique soul who would have predicted this outturn if told, in 1900, of our pending technological, demographic, and institutional revolution.

We can be confident that a phenomenon which has survived the last eighty years of industrial, economic, political, and social development will persist into the foreseeable future. Labor's share of the GBP is unlikely to show much flex from its past trends.

It is thus a supreme delusion to think that collective bargaining for wage gains in excess of overall productivity improvements will somehow spell a rise in the wage share or spark an advance in real wages above the productivity norm. The pay "victory" will only spur inflation.

Each union, in focusing on its own collective bargaining negotiations, is engaged in a fight over its relative chunk of the economic pie that is destined for labor. If one union grabs a larger slice, other groups, by and large, will have to sacrifice, and be mulcted out of their usual share.

Thus, when the average wage jumps by 10 percent per year and productivity rises by 2 percent, so that prices mount by 8 percent, all labor groups with a pay boost of, say, 12 percent will eke out a 4 percent real advance. Everyone with a pay gain below 8 percent will feel an erosion of real income, absolutely *and* relatively. Those with a 6 percent pay hike will see their position undermined by 2 percent. The net result will be an important real-income shift among wage earners rather than from capital to labor en masse. Mostly it is just such an intrawage reshuffle that ensues from differential pay settlements in separate industries under decentralized and individualistic bargaining practices. The phenomenon thus too often involves an assault of *labor on labor* rather than a Marxian class combat of "labor against capitalists."

Fixed-income groups—and everyone is in a fixed-income class until his income receipts are corrected—lose out under any price lift. Those on welfare, unemployment pay, pensions, and social security, or under specific contract such as teachers, civil servants, and those who charge a customary fee, indeed a vast range of people, will watch their real income being nibbled away whenever prices outpace their own adaptations. Inflation thus strikes far, wide—and maybe deep.

Consider a fairer and saner alternative, of productivity growing by the same 2 percent and average pay up by 4 percent, with prices 2 percent higher. Groups getting 12 percent more now might win 6 percent, ending up with the same real gain of 4 percent. Those getting 4 percent will also be amassing real income. Laggards, however, would not be stripped nearly as hard because of inflation outrages. Losers in the inflation race would not be as prevalent; there would be less anguish for retired folks and smaller inroads on pension funds. The game would be fairer all around. Despite obvious winners and losers in the pay scramble, no group would be so decisively disenfranchised of their legitimate economic status.

Above all, moderating the pay madness would avert the unemployment drain which, in conjunction with inflation, menaces our economic system while wreaking havoc on so many lives.

The inflation and unemployment tangle constitutes our *stagflation malaise*. Unemployment emerges, and endures, by our resort to archaic and sadistic methods to fight inflation. The twin evil is essentially a product of the 1970s; the ominous threat of further disaster looms unless we alter our ways.

Inheriting doctrines inspired in a more agrarian age and under the thumb of a dogmatic sect of self-styled monetarists, the Federal Reserve System wields the money bludgeon to leash the money supply whenever prices gurgle or gush. The Federal Reserve lives by the classical creed that "inflation comes from too much money chasing too few goods," ignoring entirely the underlying mad money wage and productivity race. Its blinders prevent it from perceiving that once money incomes vault higher and higher, money *must* become more abundant to sustain the *same* volume of production and employment; if money supplies do not increase once money wages leap out of the starting blocks, we will have higher prices *and* unemployment. This is the essence of the stagflation fix that has become our lot.

Whenever the Federal Reserve thus enters the fray to assert its prowess—or lack of it—in inflation control, we experience skyward interest rates, driven to historic heights over the past decade. Production slows, especially in housing, autos, and big-ticket durable goods sales. Unemployment thickens, to the absolute levels of the late 1930s. Still, despite the flailing of the Federal Reserve, the price path wends its merry upward way, giving us, since 1968, our worst inflation binge in this century. Whereas we might have inflation without unemployment on a different set of policies, the Fed's huffing and puffing assures us of the worst of worlds, of stagflation or inflation plus unemployment. Rather than allowing the economy to suffer from only a kidney impairment (inflation), the Fed's flailing imparts a coronary arrest (unemployment) as it maneuvers to "protect" us from "disaster"—by *creating* it. Its benign intentions ensure malign results.

Of course, the Federal Reserve people regale us with the fable that they are merely "squeezing the inflation out of the system." Obviously its performance is execrable; the record reveals that we have the worst inflation in our modern history. The stagflation debacle comprises the worst of possible economic outcomes.

Collective bargaining, by provoking the Fed to its brutal ill-designed monetary maneuvers—which its self-serving public declarations proclaim as heroic and valorous—drops the other shoe by virtue of the self-inflicted unemployment wound. The toll of the jobless drives the jobless to the lowest rung on the economic ladder, with unions all the while clenching on tightly to the fistful of water.

This is the sordid impasse engendered by the exercise of unbridled individualistic collective bargaining. Because labor wants to "catch up" to *yesterday's* price increases—as labor's apologists call it—there is a demand for outsized pay increases today, to be implemented in the tomorrow. The result is a snowballing price upheaval, as in the last fourteen years, which is destined to spill over (on current policies) through the Reagan term unless there is a gigantic business collapse—an unedifying resolution indeed, for whenever we invoke monetary policy, we drive up interest rates, we deny funds to business for expansory operations, we dry up mortgage lending, and thus face the shock of unemployment. A double trouble is thereupon heaped on our price trauma by the benign preaching and calloused consequences of monetary policy.

Reason commends that we find a better method to cope with our pay excesses, and one which operates more directly rather than through the medium of the Federal Reserve which forces unemployment on so many innocent victims and solely for the ultimate purpose of curbing the extravagant pay creep brought on by the individualistic collective bargaining tactics. Although the Federal Reserve only perceives the price-pay relation dimly, it is pay subjugation that is the *only* channel through which its monetary mock heroics can subdue inflation: create enough unemployment by monetary denial so as to restrain the pay balloon. The whole operation is costly, indirect, imperfect, and irrational.

There must be a better and less debilitating way for labor to carve out its real-income gains, while assuring jobs for all, without sky rocketing prices and interest rates. The folly in the abortive Federal Reserve "fight" on inflation has already cost our nation over one and one-half trillion dollar production loss in the 1970s. This is the equivalent of over 20 million new housing units or about 10 years of our best housing efforts.

For all its emotional fighting talk, labor has conducted its collective bargaining practices as if everything in our economy occurs in a vacuum, and as if prices, other incomes, interest rates, and monetary policy will stay put after unions conclude their bargaining motions. Unfortunately, and to demolish this artificial premise, everything will be in flux, including prices, executive and nonunion income, foreign exchange rates, imports, and so on. In the mobile economic environment only the labor negotiations themselves partake of a static "victory" flush.

Anyone who retired in 1970 with a bank deposit of $100,000 has lost about $60,000 in purchasing power already, and the story is still not complete. Anyone who bought the "safest" investment of all, namely, government bonds, has now a market value of holdings of about $60,000. If they are sold, perhaps to settle an estate or to raise cash, they have a buying power closer to that of $30,000 in 1970. This is an index of the magnitude of our inflation tragedy to people of rather limited means. The plight includes labor's pensioners who imagined their retirement funds were viable for the misnamed "golden years."

Our awesome task is to eliminate the myopia and inherent contradictions of collective bargaining in a manner consistent with our market economy, and thereby to drop the mirage of one union shouting, "There's room for one more on the bus," and then watch millions of people clambering to get aboard. This is what happens under the existing uncoordinated collective bargaining; a union seeks only its own interest and in so doing provokes imitative behavior. It thus defeats its own purpose; its nimble scrambling can be effective income-wise only if other workers (or managerial people) are passive and inert.

On many occasions I have advocated TIP, a tax-based incomes policy devised by former Yale professor and now Federal Reserve governor Henry Wallich and myself. Briefly, this would target a corporate surtax on the largest 2,500 firms whenever they raised the *average*—not the individual—pay scale by more than 5 percent. The calculated average would include all employees, whether production-line, clerical, sales, supervisory, managerial, or executive. To ensure that the total corporate income-tax burden was not increased, the normal corporate income tax would be cut so that net corporate income would not be eroded.

The object of TIP is not tax revenue but a change in the tax base to mitigate inflationary conduct. The TIP tax could be likened to a fine on antisocial traffic violators. Inflation is certainly antisocial, victimizing innocent bystanders in extraordinary degree.

Without TIP or some analogue, the Federal Reserve will continue its wailing and flailing, mainly destablizing financial markets by decimating bond values and depressing the stock market, impeding capital financing and productivity improvement by business, and, saddest of all, augmenting the beleaguered army of unemployed.

Ironically, despite the Fed's bashing, until the deeper wounds of the 1982 recession the price escalation has not been arrested. Of course, by generating a catastrophic depression to rival the 1930s, the Fed might accomplish its flat-price trend mission. We do well to avert the havoc which is a "cure sure to kill"; recession and depression are a most circuitous and insidious route for stifling pay creeps in excess of productivity. Bankruptcies, job distress, and lost production are tantamount to burning the house to roast the pig.

The Reagan antigovernment legions still have a sublime faith in the efficacy of government expenditure cuts as an inflation antidote. Considering the arithmetic whereby an annual pay rise of 10 percent adds $180 billion per year to the wage bill and cumulates to about $800 billion in four years, the totals will abundantly *surpass* all federal government expenditures. The budgeteers are too prone to swat gnats while being trampled by elephants. Too, government expenditures are more the prisoner of market inflation rather than being the agent; every time prices go up, government must spend more to accomplish the same functions. At 1963 prices our near $800 billion budget would come to about $300 billion for precisely the same programs.

Sooner or later there will be widespread public, political, and economists' recognition of the money wage and productivity nexus as the inflation-maker. Thereafter we will have to devise a TIP plan, or something like it, to prevent chronic replays of our "stagflation malaise." Our country and the world cannot survive well under our unparalleled farce adding new chapters in the "economics of derision."

Joseph Heller, in his *Good as Gold,* satirized the double-speak that our political leaders purvey: "This Administration has decided to fight inflation by raising prices to lower demand to reduce prices to increase demand and bring back the inflationary prices we want to lower by reducing demand to increase demand and raise prices."[2] Heller might have gone further to lament how the Federal Reserve aims to *increase* employment by *decreasing* it, indulging us in a Humpty-Dumpty destroy-to-revive fantasy.

We are enmeshed in the economics of the absurd. Until we restrain money incomes from lunging ahead, while productivity inches ahead, we can count on a replay of the stagflation folly. Release will compel a revision of collective-bargaining practices.

University of Pennsylvania and University of the South

NOTES

1. Cf. my *Capitalism's Inflation and Unemployment Crisis* (Reading, Mass.: Addison-Wesley, 1978), Chapter 3.
2. Joseph Heller, *Good as Gold* (New York: Simon and Schuster, 1979), p. 203.

12

Lessons and Conjectures on OPEC

ROBERT E. KUENNE

Eight years have now passed since the effective activation of the pricing power of the Organization of Petroleum Exporting Countries (OPEC) in the international petroleum market. Fortunately, the initial sense of outrage, helpless frustration, and panic has subsided. Little is heard now of the wisdom of achieving energy independence. It has given way to sounder goals of conservation through market pricing, forcing those who benefit from oil to confront its market cost; of permitting those who seek to enhance domestic supply to reap typical market rewards; and of diversifying foreign sources.

Talk of an "oil crisis" is more restrained. These purported phenomena were never well defined, but they frequently implied imminent depletion of the planet's empowering resources, with bleakness beyond. One senses that such visions are being replaced by more gradualist expectations of rising energy prices into the future with attendant reductions in usage, substitution among types, and development of alternatives.

A calmer view of OPEC's strengths and weaknesses, and its capacity to afflict the economies of oil-consuming nations, is emerging. Fewer extreme views of the organization's potential stranglehold, on the one hand, or imminent dissolution, on the other hand, are being expressed. And recent research is revising downward the estimates of OPEC's part in stagflation in the short and medium run and emphasizing longer-term problems such as financing less-developed countries' oil-related balance-of-payments deficits, measurement of the social cost of oil imports, and the income distributional implications of alternative policies.

One may also be optimistic enough to believe—and admittedly with the aid of hope—that free market enthusiasts are learning the notion of "externality"; that environmentalists are approaching an appreciation of the meaning of "cost"; and that nuclear energy foes are grasping the concept of "alternative risk."

In short, the energy field today seems much quieter on a number of fronts. Indeed, as far as OPEC's future market power is concerned, we may have become too sanguine. The time seems ripe, therefore, to reassess OPEC's future implications for the international economy in the light of past impacts and its current nature. This is a formidable task, and I do not pretend to do the job definitively. Some ideas, however, seem to be central to understanding our present situation and medium-term petroleum prospects.

To what extent did OPEC's price-output strategies contribute to the stagflation of the 1970s? The answer is a difficult one for a variety of reasons. Inflation is a *process* which includes vitally within its dynamic induced money creation to support induced cost-push and price pressures, direct and indirect, initiated by external price increases. Its relation to real factors like growth is not as well understood as the Phillips curve once led us to believe. Hence, to be meaningful, our simple question becomes quite complex. What role did the nominal price increases of petroleum play in enhancing credit creation, inflationary expectations, income leakages, and responsive cost pressures during the decade? How did these induced price pressures, coupled with aggregate demand effects of international and national income redistribution, react upon jobs and output?

Answers become even more complicated when it is recalled that OPEC's disturbances were not inflicted upon an industrialized world at full employment with mild inflation and neutral monetary-fiscal policies. Industrialized nations were struggling to contain inflationary forces in 1972 and 1973; in general, fearing the inflationary tinder of the sharp petroleum price increases of 1973 more than the recessionary impacts of such increases, they actually tightened their monetary and fiscal stance in 1974. The doubling of oil prices in 1979 came in a world embattled against inflation. Therefore, the assessment of OPEC's stagflation impact in a world of neutral economic policy can only be made hypothetically.

Yet another problem in framing an answer is whether the OPEC impacts are to be measured only in the year or so that follow their introduction, or over their life cycle. A petroleum price rise transmits an immediate price shock upon refined petroleum products and spawns recessionary income leakages by shifting income to oil exporters and to domestic oil producers. However, over time, oil-producing nations will increase their imports from consuming nations, and domestic oil producers will step up investments in oil production. Over an even longer time frame, capital equipment will be altered to efficient configurations, reducing energy usage and making the national factor complex more efficient in goods production than it was in the immediate aftermath of the price shocks. Hence substantial "rebound" effects will offset immediate impact effects.

I do not think the definitive investigation of these complex questions has been published. Since 1977, however, my own suspicions have been that we have, in general, overestimated OPEC's stagflation effects and that we could focus more profitably on microeconomic aspects: conservation, supplies of energy goods, and international and national distribution effects. In a study for the Federal Energy Administration of the "optimal drawdown strategy" for the Strategic Petroleum Reserve in a period of oil embargo, we had used the INFORUM model of the U.S. economy to derive a gross national product (GNP) response function for oil deprivations.[1] As we simulated six-month supply interruptions to measure GNP impacts, we were surprised by the income rebound effects in the outyears, caused primarily by investment stimuli set in motion by the embargoes. Certain problems in detail with the answers led us to ignore the outyear impacts, but the strength of the rebound persuaded me that they were not negligible.

Early studies clearly foresaw the potentiality of rebound but could only speculate about its quantitative outlines.[2] However, some current studies are seeking to estimate the time patterns of a "permanent" adjustment to an OPEC price shock. John Tatom finds that a change in energy prices relative to the price of business output impacts the price level for four quarters, with a net effect of raising prices about 0.075 percent for each 1.0 percent rise in relative energy price.[3] His equation holds the supply of money and "high-employment" government expenditures constant and reveals a negative rebound effect in the third quarter after the price rise. Business output tends to decline about 0.09 percent for each percentage point rise in relative energy price. Hence, Tatom's equations show that a 10 percent rise in relative energy prices would raise the price level permanently by about 0.8 percent and contract business output by about 0.9 percent. The output reduction is the result of a direct productivity loss aggravated by an induced fall in the capital-labor ratio.[4]

Studies by the Organization for Economic Cooperation and Development (OECD) estimate that a 10 percent rise in oil prices decreases world industrial output about 0.3 percent and increases world inflation about 1 percent.[5]

The *Economist* Intelligence Unit, and the Wharton Econometric Forecasting Associates, forecast that if the nominal price of oil rises 20 percent in 1982, inflation in OECD nations would rise 1 percent, and GNP growth would fall 0.4 percentage points from their base case projections.[6] If we project a 10 percent inflation rate in these nations, the 20 percent hike in oil prices implies a real rise of about 10 percent.

Despite the variance of these estimates, they at least provide order-of-magnitude informed guesses as to direct and indirect impacts. From January 1974 through April 1979—a period of relative calm after the quadrupling of price in 1973 and before the doubling in 1979–80—the weighted price of OPEC oil in 1972 dollars rose from $9.59 a barrel to $14.40, or at an average annual rate of 7.9 percent. The OECD consumer price index (CPI) advanced at an annual rate of 9 percent. On the basis of the studies quoted, cumulatively, of the price index's rise by 57 percent over this period, only 3.5 to 4.5 of those percentage points were attributable to the rise in oil price. Even if the studies underestimate by a factor of 5, we are still able to account for only 18 to 23 of those 57 points of rise.

We have constructed an index of weighted industrial production for six OECD nations: the United States, Japan, West Germany, the United Kingdom, France, and Canada. It rose during this period at an annual rate of 3.5 percent. In the absence of the OPEC price rises at an average of 7.9 percent each year, the quoted studies imply that the industrial production of these nations would have run slightly higher, at about 3.7 to 4.2 percent.

These estimates are crude, and they apply to a period of modest OPEC price action. But they do serve to undermine the proposition that OPEC was a major factor in the past stagflation; by implication, they also challenge the notion that if OPEC's pricing power weakens in the 1980s, a major force will be in motion in overcoming the stagflation experience.

These conclusions do not dismiss OPEC as of negligible economic significance, even in terms of stagflation. An organization that can take advantage of supply reductions, and consuming nations' mistakes, to ratchet the price of oil up by 100 percent in a year can wreak short-run macroeconomic havoc. However, we may hope that 1979–80 has taught us that prices in the short run are driven by consumers' inventory policy and that the seeds of cooperation among consuming nations to avoid panic stockage, planted in the wake of that period of price runup, will take root. Quantum price leaps can then be avoided in the 1980s; price rises, if they occur, will be relatively smooth and restrained.

If so, then the worries about OPEC in the 1980s should focus upon: (1) its ability to tax world income for its own benefit, (2) the welfare loss inflicted upon consuming nations in adjusting to a price that is above marginal cost plus scarcity rent, and (3) the means of financing less developed countries' oil imports. Whether OPEC can survive does therefore matter. An answer requires an analysis of the anatomy and physiology of that organization.

OPEC is an elastic collusive oligopoly whose dominant policy is the setting of a price pattern for petroleum. It is important to stress that OPEC does not set "the" price of oil or a minimum price of oil. It concerns itself with the pattern of prices of a commodity that is differentiated in quality and location. It anchors this price pattern by setting the price of "marker" crude—Arabian Light 34° oil f.o.b. Ras Tanura—which in effect determines the price of the most common quality at a dominant location.

After this price has been negotiated, each nation adds a (positive or negative) quality premium reflecting the specific gravity, sulfur content, and nearness to markets of each type of crude that it sells. If the demand for its oil thereafter exceeds or falls short of a fuzzily determined market share acquiesced in by the organization, a country may add or subtract a market superpremium to bring its liftings close to its "just" share.

OPEC is a price-patterning oligopoly, not a cartel controlling members' outputs. It has never succeeded in obtaining agreement on prorationing, because to do so would demand an unacceptable sacrifice of freedom of action by member nations. To the extent stability of market shares has characterized OPEC's operations—at least until the Iranian revolution—it has been the result, I surmise, of such price patterning constrained by allowable sales restraints.[7] Saudi Arabia, in particular, would lose much of her power within the consortium if she accepted quantitative restrictions on her liftings.

Occasions have been rare, therefore, when member nations have announced autonomous restrictions on output unrelated to conservation or other rational usage restrictions. Rather, prices have been set and market demand satisfied at those prices, and when the amount lifted has encountered reduced demand in a soft market, real prices have been under great pressure to undergo reduction in order to protect pumping levels.

This point is demonstrated in Table 12.1, which lists the average daily liftings of eleven of the thirteen OPEC members for 1974 into the first five months of 1981.[8] From 1974 through 1979, OPEC output remained between 30 and 31 million barrels per day (mmb/d) with the exception of the deep recession year 1975. The slide in output that began in April 1980 and has accelerated since is wholly a result of reductions in amount demanded. The use of declines in real price per barrel to preserve the lifting level of about 30 mmb/d, and rises when demand strengthened, are also apparent in the data through 1979. The recent market disturbance is putting severe pressure on the super-premia whose expansion ran prices up in 1979–80.

Because OPEC sets price patterns, and because each member in it has a considerable amount of price flexibility, it has proved surprisingly durable. Two- and three-tiered pricing structures have emerged amid predictions that the organization would dissolve, yet it has been able to readjust patterns in the past with a good deal of flexibility. Thus I believe OPEC can survive severe price-pattern strains, because its fuzzy consensus on share entitlements gives it a blend of autonomy and cooperation that would be difficult to achieve among sovereign governments were it to seek rigid market prorationing.

My projection, therefore, is that OPEC can survive the prospective petroleum market conditions of the 1980s and exercise a substantial impact on price. By the same token, I doubt that the majority of mem-

TABLE 12.1: Average Daily Liftings of OPEC, Less Ecuador and Gabon, and Average Weighted OPEC Price, 1974–81 (in real terms)

	Average Daily Liftings (millions of barrels)	Average Price per Barrel, 1977 dollars
1974	30.084	$12.59
1975	26.603	12.37
1976	30.208	12.12
1977	31.018	12.36
1978	29.885	11.45
1979	30.442	13.89
1980	26.624	21.16*
1981 (Jan.–May)	24.133	n.a.

*For first half of the year only.
SOURCE: Outputs from *Petroleum Economist*, various issues. Price data are listed prices quoted in *Petroleum Economist*, various issues. Crude types are weighted by estimated proportion of each nation's output to obtain a notional price for each member; national prices are weighted by nations' liftings; and weighted average price is deflated by OECD CPI.

bers will sacrifice their ability to vary price and exploit short-run market conditions in favor of Saudi Arabia's proposed long-run pricing strategy which seeks quarterly price adjustments on the basis of OPEC's import prices, the foreign exchange value of the dollar, and the growth of industrialized nations' GNP. The Saudi proposal violates what I have interpreted as the functional essence of the organization; if Saudi Arabia should succeed in distress conditions in obtaining reluctant consent, I suspect the strategy will not long survive.

The General Economic Systems Project (GENESYS) Model of OPEC at Princeton University has constructed a microeconomic model that seeks insights into the structure and decision-making of the organization. It is *not* a forecasting model, but rather tries to project the price pattern that would emerge if each rival sought to maximize its own short-term profit plus the profits of its rivals discounted by factors that aim to catch each rival's potential to affect its own profits. In short, the model attempts to build in the oligopoly power structure as well as the maximum and minimum bounds on output, nation by nation.

Based on my belief that very strong forces exist in OPEC to exploit the short run, our base case seeks to measure whether, in fact, it has done so to its full capability or whether longer-term noneconomic factors have tempered its myopic urges. I envision a short-run normal in which world industrialized activity returns to a prosperous level, inventories are drawn down to normal, and Iran and Iraq resume most of their lifting capacity. Under such conditions, what would the pattern of prices and output be?

The model projects that the average OPEC price would rise to about $69 in current dollars, or roughly *twice* the going price, and that production would fall to 22.520 mmb/d. Saudi Arabian marker crude's price would rise to about $67, but her production would continue at its maximum sustainable level.

Several caveats are in order in interpreting the model. Demand functions for member nations' sales were fitted to only seventy-eight monthly observations available at the time. Those data do not reflect recent conservation moves by industrialized nations, which we consider later. The power structure was included by methods as objective as we could devise, but the process was inescapably judgmental.[9] And the lower bounds on sales were taken to be, rather arbitrarily, at one-half sustainable capacity.

Recognizing the shortcomings, I shall limit myself to qualitative conjectures that arise from large quantitative differences in the model's solution.

First, there is a great deal of short-term profit pressure in normal periods to raise prices substantially higher than the present figures—high enough for most producers to reduce sales to their lower bounds. The magnitudes of these lower bounds therefore become important to consuming nations. Programs that commit OPEC nations to large-scale development are to be welcomed.

Second, although Saudi Arabia's short-term interest is to keep the price low enough to set sales at her capacity output, the country has a collusive profit incentive to roughly double price.

Third, the differentials between the prices of Gulf crudes on the one hand, and African, Venezuelan, and Indonesian crudes on the other, can be substantially higher than they are at present. Hence the pressures that revealed themselves in 1979 and 1980 to widen the quality premia margins, and as market superpremia seem to be endemic in the price structure, the forces that make multitiered price problems probable should persist. New refineries, and the retrofitting of old refineries that are more tolerant of sour crudes, may weaken these forces, but they should persist through the 1980s.

Longer-term tempering of OPEC's pricing power has occurred, largely under the aegis of Saudi Arabia, at some cost in short-run profits. If most OPEC members are driven to the extent I believe by the short-run, and if world demand for OPEC oil approaches the 30 mmb/d at current prices that it experienced in most of 1974–79, we may anticipate a continuation or intensification of upward price pressures and price-pattern conflicts in OPEC's operation. But by the nature of its structure, OPEC should hold together as an entity, especially because Saudi Arabia's own short-run gains in compromising tend to allay somewhat what she perceives as her longer-term losses as prices rise.

Will world demand for petroleum in the 1980s afford OPEC the same opportunity for price hikes that it had in the 1970s? The question springs from an optimism concerning a demand reduction for energy in general in the industrialized nations, substitution toward natural gas and coal specifically, and increased supply from non-OPEC sources.

Table 12.2 lists some relevant data for 1979 and 1980 on petroleum product usage. It is worth noting that the reduction in total petroleum consumption in 1980 below 1979 was about 2.76 mmb/d and that the industrialized world's 3 mmb/d reduction was offset by an increase in that of the industrializing nations. From Table 12.1, OPEC's liftings fell by 3.18 mmb/d over this time period, which would imply that the drawdown of world stocks, the increase in non-OPEC, non-Communist

TABLE 12.2:   Consumption of Petroleum Products, 1979 and 1980, with Percentage Changes

	All Petroleum Products (mmb/d*)		
	1979	1980	Percentage Change
Industrialized nations			
U.S.	17.130	15.580	−9.0
Canada	1.730	1.680	−2.9
W. Europe	13.930	12.950	−7.0
Australasia	.730	.710	−2.7
Japan	5.130	4.650	−9.4
Subtotal	38.650	35.570	−8.0
Industrializing nations			
Latin America	4.080	4.150	+1.7
Africa and Mideast	2.670	2.870	+7.5
Indian subcontinent	.790	.810	+2.5
Other Asia	1.920	2.010	+4.7
Subtotal	9.460	9.840	+4.0
Total inland consumption	48.110	45.410	−5.6
Total bunker oil usage	2.190	2.130	−2.7
World total	50.300	47.540	−5.5

*Million barrels per day.
SOURCE: *Petroleum Economist*, August 1981, pp. 329–30.

world production, and a cutback in Communist-world consumption accounted for a net decrease of about 0.42 mmb/d in this period.

Non-OPEC, non-Communist world output rose by 1.02 mmb/d during this period. If we assume the Communist world's production and consumption were in balance, this would indicate a buildup of world stocks of about 0.6 mmb/d, or about 219.0 mmb over the year. Although accurate data on total world oil stocks are not available, 5.0 to 5.5 billion barrels is a useful order-of-magnitude estimate, indicating about a 105-day supply. Hence, on balance over the year, world oil stocks were enhanced by about a 5-day supply. Because this magnitude is negligible, we shall ignore it.

Therefore about one-third of OPEC's output reduction in calendar 1980 resulted from an oil substitution and two-thirds reflected recession and price- and other-induced conservation. Fully 56 percent of the total consumption cutback occurred in the United States; however, much of this must be viewed as a once-for-all reaction to an average price for crude that rose under decontrol from $19.87 to $32.69 per barrel during the year.

A weighted industrial production index for six major OECD nations, used earlier in this essay, reveals that an output slump began in April 1980, continuing to the present. For 1980 as a whole, the index slumped 0.9 percent, but for the second half of the year the index was down 3.5 percent from the second half of 1979. Recession must be responsible for a sizeable amount of the decline in consumption.

In the first five months of 1981 the drop in OPEC liftings continued. Output averaged 24.13 mmb/d, down 4.47 mmb/d from the same period in 1980. The industrial production index was off 2.8 percent for the same intervals, while non-OPEC, non-Communist world output *expanded* by 0.22 mmb/d. The greater severity of the current experience seems, in good part, the result of inventory decumulation because of very large holding costs brought on by record interest rates, and the widespread fear of falling oil prices. An estimate by the Petroleum Institute Research Foundation is that worldwide inventories (October 1981) are being depleted at rates as high as 1.25 mmb/d when they normally climb by 2.00 mmb/d, for a 3.25 mmb/d net reduction in demand for current output.[10]

To summarize, short-run factors—once-for-all price pass-throughs in the United States, the rise in the exchange value of the dollar, recession in industrialized nations, and cost-induced inventory depletion—seemed to dominate the petroleum market in late 1981. With their passage it is quite possible to envisage an OPEC sales rebound in 1982, or 1983, to 26 or 27 mmb/d with steady growth to 30 mmb/d (or more) in the remainder of the decade. That seems to be a level at which substantial OPEC pricing power will exist, within which non-OPEC, non-Communist world production will be content to shelter as it rises.

OPEC in the 1970s has functioned as a price pattern-setter in the world petroleum market, with a longer-run cautionary Saudi Arabian policy constraining the short-run motivation of most other members. The inevitable frictions between these goals have created considerable divisiveness in the organization's operation, but it seems well designed to tolerate these strains.

OPEC should therefore function into the 1980s as an effective pricing power, with the overly sanguine hopes for its demise being born of the shorter-run demand slump. Nonetheless, OPEC's impact on world inflation and recession has been exaggerated in the past. Even if it pursues a steady target real price increase of 4 or 5 percent per year, the macroeconomic impact on the world economy will be tolerable in most economies. Microeconomic impacts, however, may well call for greater international coordination.

Princeton University

NOTES

1. Robert E. Kuenne, Jerry Blankenship, and Paul F. McCoy, "Optimal Drawdown Strategy for Strategic Petroleum Reserves," *Energy Economics* 1 (1979): 3–13.
2. See, e.g., Edward R. Fried and Charles L. Schultze, eds., *Higher Oil Prices and the World Economy* (Washington, D.C.: Brookings Institution, 1975).
3. John A. Tatom, "Energy Prices and Short-Run Economic Performance," *Federal Reserve Bank of St. Louis Review,* January 1981, pp. 3–17.
4. John A. Tatom, "Energy Prices and Capital Formation: 1972–1977," *Federal Reserve Bank of St. Louis Review,* May 1979, pp. 2–9.
5. Cited in Ferdinand E. Banks, *The Political Economy of Oil* (Lexington, Mass.: D. C. Heath, 1980), p. 19.
6. *London Economist,* September 26, 1981, p. 76.
7. This stability of market shares has been made the basis of a Markov process approach to the explanation of OPEC behavior by Richard F. Kosobud and Houston H. Stokes. See, e.g., "Short-Run OPEC Market Share Behavior and Its Implications," *Energy Economics* 2 (1980): 66–80.
8. Data limitations in earlier periods forced me to exclude the outputs of Ecuador and Gabon. Their combined lifting is only about 1.5 percent of the OPEC total.
9. For the derivation of the power structure, see Robert E. Kuenne, "Rivalrous Consonance and the Power Structure of OPEC," *Kyklos* 32 (1979): 695–717.
10. *New York Times,* September 15, 1981.

PART FIVE

INTERNATIONAL DIMENSIONS

INTRODUCTION

SIDNEY WEINTRAUB[1]

Francis Seton, Senior Fellow at Nuffield College, Oxford University, traces the stagflation ordeal in the United Kingdom in recent years, after providing a good background briefing on past economic growth in the initial industrial wave. Recent history under both Tory and Labour governments has been an uninterrupted series of "stop-go" antics on jobs and production, and "go fast and faster" on inflation in periodic episodes that top the abysmal stagflation league in the decade just closed. Seton, too, sees "the faint outlines of a remedy" in Tax Incentive Plan (TIP) policies, which he sees as capable of being supplemented by more direct types of sanctions on employees and their sponsoring unions. While Seton has English practices mostly in mind, the concepts—with due modifications for institutional disparities—are transferable to the United States and other large industrial nations.

Jan Kregel, now of Groningen University, Netherlands, but equally at home in the United States, Belgium, England, and Italy, offers a keen focus on the interdependence of Western economies through trade, interest rate, and foreign exchange interactions. In trade the United States, for potentially better and too frequently worse, retains its motivating power as the "economic locomotive" capable of pulling up European jobs and production or jolting our interlocked economies by sudden low gear or recessionary reverses. He is particularly skeptical of what he detects to be a too frequent U.S. attitude of "benign neglect," whereby the foreign shocks of our revised economic policies are assigned low priority by American policymakers, to the chagrin of our allies appraising our mutual global fortunes. Kregel's welcome contribution should also sensitize readers to European dismay over our almost unbridled reliance on monetary policy; he offers his own brief advocacy of incomes policy, or social contract guidelines for wage behavior and for use in public expenditure contexts. His own discernment is fortified by some poignant quo-tations from the recent *Annual Report of the Bank for International Settlements.*

Arthur Donner, whose most recent experience consists of background advisory studies for briefing high-level Canadian policymakers, reported on the desultory stagflation aberrations of our friends and neighbors to the north. For those unaware of the facts it will come as a surprise to learn that the record in Canada is even more distressing than the sorry misadventures in the United States, on both the job front and the inflation front. Donner is especially effective in illuminating the interactions between our money markets and interest rates which often aggravate the Canadian foreign balance position and touch off exchange rate disorders or underwrite Canadian dollar volatility. Rising U.S. interest rates draw funds from Canada, press down on the Canadian currency, and thereby menace import prices and the Canadian home price level.

The Canadian experiment in energy independence, even to the extent of urging and acting for greater energy nationalization of drilling firms, is bound to have direct and numerous subtle ramifications on our own energy position. One of the more pessimistic surmises is that the nationalistic rash will operate toward perpetuating double-digit Canadian inflation in the years ahead, while the escalating interest rate binge poses a formidable obstacle to sustained growth. While Donner has been an eminent proponent of a TIP-type incomes policy for Canada, he is not sanguine that Canadian policymakers have the stamina at this time to devise and implement a feasible program.

Readers of these three essays must come away with a deeper awareness of the global nature of the stagflation trauma and the attendant widespread misery already endured, with more in prospect by the U.S. failure to provide imaginative leadership to abate the madness. Our political leaders are the modern Candides, complacent with obsolete practices and a wish for a historical miracle through inadvertence. They fret only too seldom over the lingering economic debilitation that may mean 25 million unemployed in Western economies.

The international essays deserve a wide readership, for they alert us to the price that the world economy pays for our addiction to the "economics of derision" under the new Reagan cast assembled for a rerun of our stagflation fiasco.

University of Pennsylvania and University of the South

NOTE

1. Professor Werner Hochwald served as chairman of this session. Difficulty in reaching him in Germany, where he is undertaking some official and personal research, prevented his contributing his assessments in this introduction.

13

Thatcherism in Britain

FRANCIS SETON

Thanks to her head start in industrialization, bringing Britain to the threshold of economic "maturity" as early as 1837[1] (fully two decades before France and half a century before Germany), the country enjoyed a per capita income some 50 percent greater than its industrial rivals in the last quarter of the 1800s. While overtaken by the United States by World War I, Britain remained ahead of Western Europe by 10 to 15 percent throughout the first half of the 1900s. With population barely doubling between 1850 and 1950 (while that of the United States more than quintupled), Britain defied Verdoorn's Law by achieving an average growth-rate of 1.15 percent per year, less than three-fourths of one percentage point below that of the United States. It emerged from World War II only some 30 percent below contemporary American levels per capita. It was not until the early 1960s that Britain began to be overtaken by the average country of the European Community. Since then, the relative decline has seemed irreversible; by the 1970s the country was 20 to 30 percent behind France and Germany, barely ahead of such traditionally disadvantaged runners as Finland, Italy, and Ireland.

Yet Britain remains one of the best countries of the world to live in. The scope for individual freedom and idiosyncrasy is generous, the rule of law universal—the bureaucracy incorruptible and, by and large, humane.[2] Even in the 1970s British consumption standards were nearly two-thirds those of the United States, her saving and investment ratios about the same, and the export growth noticeably faster. How is it, then, that the current recession has hit Britain more severely than the rest of the world? What accounts for the prevalent impression of sclerosis, morbidity, and Balkanization that is damaging the country's self-image?

Tables 13.1 and 13.2 show Britain's performance lag more pro-

TABLE 13.1: The Current Scene—Average Annual Rates of Growth (%)

	Gross Domestic Product[a]				Industrial Production[a]			Hourly Earnings (Mfg)[b]		Unit Lab. Costs[c]		Consumer Prices[e]		
	1	2	3	4	5	6	7	8	9	10	11	12	13	14
	1970–73	1974–79	1980	1981[d]	1970–73	1974–79	1980	1969–79	1980	1981[d]	1978–80	1961–70	1971–77	1978–80
U.K.	3.7	1.3	−1.4	−2.0	2.7	0.7	−7.0	14.9	17.8	10.0	15.5	4.1	13.9	13.2
G.F.R.	4.4	2.1	1.8	−0.5	4.7	1.1	0.5	8.7	6.2	6.0	8.9	2.7	5.6	4.1
France	5.6	2.8	2.2	1.6	6.0	1.6	—	13.7	15.1	15.0	10.5	4.0	9.0	11.2
Netherlands	5.0	2.5	1.0	—	6.7	1.8	—	10.6	4.6	4.0	5.2	4.0	8.3	4.9
Italy	4.2	2.2	3.5	—	5.1	2.1	5.5	20.2	22.5	21.0	17.6	3.9	13.1	16.0
U.S.	3.5	2.6	−0.3	1.7	4.1	2.6	−3.5	7.7	8.7	10.0	9.0	2.8	6.6	10.8
Canada	5.8	3.3	−1.0	1.0	6.1	1.9	−2.0	10.3	10.1	11.0	8.3	2.7	7.5	9.4
Australia	3.5[g]		2.1[g]	5.8[g]				12.4	10.9		2.4[f]	2.5	11.0	9.1
Japan	5.4[g]		3.5[g]	3.4[g]				14.1	8.1		3.3[g]	5.8	10.7	5.1

[a] U.N., E.C.E. *Economic Survey of Europe in 1980* (New York, 1981), p. 7.
[b] Manufacturing only. *OECD Economic Outlook* 29 (July 1981): 43.
[c] U.N., *Economic Survey of Europe in 1980*, p. 23.
[d] Forecast.
[e] *OECD Economic Outlook* 29 (July 1981): 46.
[f] "Real Labour Costs" projected for 1980–82, ibid., p. 39.
[g] Ibid., pp. 16, 17.

TABLE 13.2: Symptoms and Thermometer Readings

| | Change in Consumer Prices (%)[a] | | | Components of Price Change 1980[b] | | | | | Rate of Unemployment[g] (%) | | | | |
| | | | | Total | Of Which | | | | | | | | |
	1978	1979	1980	Total[c]	Wages etc.[d]	Gross Profit[e]	Net Tax[f]	Import Prices	1969–73	1973–78	1979[h]	1980[h]	1981[i]
U.K.	8.3	13.4	18.0	17.4	9.7	2.1	2.9	2.7	2.9	4.3	5.4	8.8	10.2
G.F.R.	2.7	4.1	5.5	6.0	2.1	0.9	0.3	2.7	0.8	3.2	3.1	4.0	3.7
France	9.1	10.8	13.5	12.7	6.1	−3.1		3.5	1.5	3.7	6.4	6.8	7.0
Netherlands	4.1	4.2	6.5	9.6	1.6	1.2	0.7	6.1	1.6	3.6	4.1	5.9	6.4
Italy	12.1	14.8	21.2	9.6	1.6	1.2	0.7	6.1	4.8	5.7	7.7	8.1	7.6
U.S.	7.7	11.3	13.6	9.6	1.6	1.2	0.7	6.1	5.0	6.6	5.9	1.4	7.2
Canada	8.9	9.2	10.1	9.6	1.6	1.2	0.7	6.1	5.6	6.8	7.1.	7.4	7.2
Australia[k]	7.9	9.1	10.2	9.6	1.6	1.2	0.7	6.1	2.0	6.2[j]	6.3[i]	6.1[i]	5.5
Japan[k]	3.8	3.6	8.0	9.6	1.6	1.2	0.7	6.1	1.2	2.2[j]	2.1[i]	2.2[i]	2.1

a U.N., E.C.E., *Economic Survey of Europe in 1980* (New York, 1981), p. 24.
b Ibid., p. 23.
c Implicit price deflation of total final expenditure.
d Compensation of employees.
e Gross operating surplus.
f Indirect taxes less subsidies.
g Ibid., pp. 16, 17. Unemployment as percent of total civilian labor force.
h December figures.
i Standardized rates. The 1981 figures refer to the first quarter of the year. *OECD Economic Outlook* 29 (July 1981):ibid.
j Standardized rates for 1978; ibid.
k Ibid., pp. 140, 142.

nounced as we move from physical indicators to the "value parameters" of the market, or the components of the incentive structure and signalling system—from the anatomy to the "physiology" of the system. They reveal some symptoms of a more deep-seated malady in social relations and responses which makes us vulnerable to shocks and to spreading infections.

It is no wonder therefore that most diagnoses of Britain's ills have fastened on social relations rather than on production-related capacities of a physical or mental kind.[3] It has been argued, for instance, that our traditions of tolerance and consensus politics have produced excessive respect for vested interests, a disinclination to control historically overdue accessions of power, with too little regard for checks and balances. In the pursuit of freedom our intolerance of authority, whether that of government or the market, has grown to the point where we are bound to lose out in efficiency compared to countries who are prepared to follow decisive leads and enforce discipline. Immunities almost absentmindedly conferred on trade unions are only one example of this tendency; the vested interests of business and monopoly, whether private or state-run, have received similar kid-gloved treatment. When consensus is threatened, we take refuge in appeals to "voluntary restraint," the "common sense of the majority," or the "fairmindedness and sense of responsibility of the free individual," rather than "impose solutions from on high." This very vocabulary, which has gained common currency, is symptomatic of a state of mind. No doubt it has stood us in good stead through long periods of history; it may do so again in the future; it does not serve us well at present.

Policymakers must have something more concrete to bite on, some tangible and well-defined disorder amenable to treatment on the spot; economist-diagnosticians have responded to this need with almost unseemly enthusiasm. In doing so they have created tricky dilemmas and the state of chronic "dither" which has characterized British economic policy for the last three decades. It is possible to cure obesity by physical exercise, but only if you do not also suffer from heart disease. It may be possible to combat lethargy with extra doses of blood sugar, but only if you are not also diabetic. A state of general sickness tends to become chronic when diseases occur in mutually reinforcing pairs, where the only known cure for one is bound to aggravate the other. A skilled physician may be able to contain the situation by ministering to the more threatening disease, until his ministrations have brought the other to such a pitch that all resources must be thrown over to the second front, thus forcing him to shuttle from one breach to the other without ever winning the battle, let alone the war. This will eventually demoralize him and undermine the patient's confidence, making the diseases even less amenable to cure.

It may not be too fanciful to describe the British economy of the last three decades in these terms. There were abrupt changes of tack, U-turns, and sheer vacillation in at least three aspects of economic strategy and performance:

1. The "stop-go cycle" with the longest history is a form of Keynesian peristaltics whereby a varying mix of monetary and fiscal policies is invoked to blow hot and cold in succession, reacting to a poor growth performance by pumping demand into the economy, thereby opening up a dangerous foreign trade deficit, and then going violently into reverse to "get out of the red." Thus between the mid-1960s and 1974, domestic spending was jacked up from £123 to nearly £160 billion (in real terms), causing the current foreign balance to plummet from +£3 to −£6 billion in a matter of thirty months. This was followed by a three-year squeeze that brought domestic spending down to £144 billion by mid-1975, lifting the current account out of the red by the third quarter of 1977. By that time, however, a new expansionary phase had already been under way for fifteen months or so, and while domestic spending topped the previous record in early 1979, the current account once more plunged into the red.

Advocates of this type of "fine-tuning" argued endlessly about the relative merits of fiscal and monetary measures within the policy mix, the left wing generally favoring the first and the Conservatives pinning their hopes on the second. But both evaded the basic incompatibility between internal and external balance.

2. A second series of hiccups stemmed from recurrent attempts to tackle inflationary pressure directly through various forms of incomes policy in a social environment highly suspicious of erosions of traditional "differentials" between various types of labor. If wage restraint could be imposed for limited periods—and who could hope for more?—its beneficent effects were quickly undone in the subsequent scramble to regain lost positions in the pecking order. A single centralized trade union organization acting for half the workforce, and used to settlements spread throughout the year, constantly spurred by the threat of imminent government intervention, offered a certain recipe for this type of pernicious periodicity.

The 1960s rang up the curtain on the famous "pay pause," followed by a "guiding light" from the National Incomes Commission. This was followed by the guidelines of 3 to 3.5 percent in 1965–66 under the

Prices and Incomes Board (PIB). The next two years saw the uncompromising "squeeze," followed by "severe restraint" during which the PIB was put on a statutory basis. Thereafter the annual rise in money wage settlements took off to 15 to 16 percent in 1970 and 1971, only to be nipped to single figures by the six-month freeze of "Stage 1" in 1972–73 and the complicated statutory provisions of "Stage 2" (maximum increase of £1 + 4 percent with a total limit of £250 per year).

"Stage 3," with its statutory limits of £2.25 per week or 7 percent (whichever was the greater) and £350 per year, with "threshold payments" linked to price increases, was broken by the miners' strike in early 1974 which forced a change in government as voters recoiled from the miseries of Edward Heath's three-day week.

In the resulting scramble, wage settlements soared above 30 percent, and the Labour government felt compelled to resort to incomes policy in 1975, this time under the voluntary discipline of trade union guidelines endorsed in a government white paper. The workforce then accepted a £5 limit on wage increases, with a zero limit for those earning over £8,500 per year, thus exerting a savage squeeze on time-honored differentials.

This commendable restraint brought settlements down to single figures again by 1977. The subsequent Callaghan norm of 5 percent (limited to a range of £2.5 to £4.0 per week) caught the workforce already straining at the leash and invited settlements up toward the 20 percent mark in 1978 and early 1979 to forestall the guillotine. After a "winter of discontent" led by a recalcitrant wing of the trade union movement, James Callaghan's government was sent into the wilderness to muse on the wisdom of 5 percent versus 10 percent. Margaret Thatcher's administration was voted in, to try with the whips and scorpions of monetarism and expenditure cuts what the velvet glove of persuasion had failed to achieve.

3. A third type of seesaw was built into the exchange rate. Governments getting cold feet about exports, profits, and private investment seemed irresistibly attracted to a dose of depreciation before the resulting rise in import prices, with another bout of inflation, would send them scuttling back to the opposite policy. Thus, if the value of sterling, adjusted for domestic exporters' costs, is set at 100 at its pre–North Sea oil peak in 1972, we observe at least one peak of 96.7 in 1966 and no less than three well-defined troughs considerably below 90 (1968, 1974, and 1976) before the barometer starts its relentless upward surge in 1977–80.

In the face of these distressing symptoms of schizophrenia, the public was ready to take refuge in unicausal explanations of the nation's ills. One of the more influential was Professor (now Lord) Nicholas Kaldor's famous inaugural lecture of 1966. He laid chief blame on the secular drift away from manufacturing to the less "productive" and innovative service industries. This produced a spate of "antiservice" measures, such as selective employment taxes and premia (SET, SEP) and discretionary cash grants for investment favoring manufacturing, export industries, and manufacturing equipment.

The other diagnosis that caught the public imagination was the famous Robert Bacon and Walter Eltis tract of 1976, whose message is proclaimed in the title "Britain's Economic Problem: Too Few Producers." They argued, plausibly, that our miseries are due to the inexorable shift in the distribution of the gross domestic product (GDP) from company profits to the provision of unmarketed public services, a view which Mrs. Thatcher already pronounced in 1975: "The private sector creates both the goods and services we need to export to pay for our imports and the revenue to finance public services. So one must not overload it. Every man switched away from industry and into government will reduce the productive sector and increase the burden on it at the same time."

Such diagnoses have at least the virtue of concentrating the mind. But on what? "De-industrialization" and "de-marketization" may be mythical dragons, and if they are not, do we really possess the resourcefulness or courage of St. George? The SET and discretionary investment grants signally failed to fulfill their promise, and no one knows a way to roll back the tide against company profits without courting political disaster.

And so we seemed condemned to shuttle backward and forward, not between one extreme policy and another, but between dither and overkill. It is no wonder that the private sector, constantly harassed by government and the unions, lost its bearings and much of its morale, causing the perennial sluggishness in investment which imperils the country's industrial future and never fails to be denounced by the left as a "capitalists' strike."

The Conservative government burst upon this desolate scene with a refurbished ideology and a great new resolve: The mixed economy had swung too far toward collectivism, both in production (nationalization) and in consumption (welfare provisions). This tide had to be rolled back to restore incentives to individual and entrepreneurial effort and to generate private funds for productive, economically motivated investment. Only this could revive growth, solvency, and employment in an increasingly competitive world. But nothing, absolutely nothing, could result in sustainable change until the evil of inflation had been banished.

The battle against inflation, therefore, was given priority over all other objectives—over full employment, growth, forward-looking interest- and exchange-rate policies, and even the maintenance of living standards already achieved. *The prime weapon was to be the monetarist prescription*—to throttle the annual increase in the money supply, thus forcing employers to resist wage demands on pain of plant closures and bankruptcy, coupled with the necessary concomitants of high interest rates and axe cuts in the government deficit, now identified with greater accounting precision as the Public Sector Borrowing Requirement (PSBR). The policy is embodied in the Medium-Term Financial Strategy (MTFS) announced by the government as a unique and unprecedented forward commitment for four years to reduce inflation to 4 to 6 percent per year and jack up the real GDP growth to 2 to 4 percent per year.[4] Essentially, it entails slowing the growth of the money stock ("sterling M3") to 4 to 8 percent per year and cutting the PSBR to just over 3 percent of GDP at market prices.[5]

It is difficult to decide at this stage whether the policy is clearly unsuccessful or merely irrelevant. To some extent it merely carried forward the 7 to 11 percent target range for sterling M3 set by the new Conservative government for 1980 by mechanically reducing the previous (Labour) government's target of 8 to 12 percent set for the year ending April 1979—a target which was actually met. But sterling M3 was a most misleading figure at the time, for British banks were then operating under a system of monetary control known as the "corset," which penalized them on a steeply rising scale for exceeding preset limits on the growth of their interest-bearing deposits, thus driving them to substitute nondeposit-creating transactions for normal deposit creation (e.g., expanding bills in preference to overdrafts) and distorting the M3 reading in the process. When the "corset" was eventually abolished in June 1980, the effects of removing this window dressing (which had been seriously underestimated in the previous year's target-setting) swamped the effects of genuine monetary restraint and discredited sterling M3 as a suitable policy target. The Bank of England, which in its dislike of the MTFS appears to have connived at this result, thus helped spread the impression that the policy would founder on the government's inability to control the money supply as such—a most damaging impression, given the fact that its success so largely depended on the hoped-for mitigation of inflationary *expectations* for which credibility was an absolute precondition. Several of the government's critics who advocated a shift from sterling M3 to "money GDP" as a more appropriate target seem to miss the point, since money GDP is no more amenable to government manipulation than any of the monetary stock aggregates that may be selected as the control proxy, with the additional shortcoming that its variations are compounded of a notoriously unpredictable mix of price and quantity effects.

Nor has the problem of reducing the PSBR proved any more tractable. From a level of 5.8 percent of GDP in 1978, it actually increased to 7.6 percent in the first year of the new government and shows every sign of remaining stuck in that region. The largest component, the Central Government Borrowing Requirement, was boosted to an estimated £9.4 billion by the civil servants' dispute in the first eight months of the financial year 1981–82. Apart from public sector disruption, the PSBR is subject to an upward "dole pull," which boosts transfers through increased needs for unemployment and other welfare benefits, and an "inflation push," which increases local authorities' need for central government grants in the face of their inability to meet rising costs by local tax increases. It is proving difficult to foist government-dictated economies on local councils elected on different platforms with a political composition which often differs markedly from that of the central government.[6]

The much-heralded deceleration of inflation came later than expected, preceded by an actual acceleration in the first two years of Margaret Thatcher's government largely from renewed pressure for wage-increases which the MTFS was unable to mitigate. During early 1981, however, there was some fall in the level of wage settlements, and by June the underlying increase in average earnings had been reduced to about 11 percent, barely one percentage point above the average of other countries. Since then, however, there has been no further deceleration, largely due to the long-delayed fall in the exchange rate (by 12 to 13 percent) from the unnatural heights of 1980, except for the most recent fall to 9.4 percent in April 1982.

The outstanding fact that seems to emerge from this experience is that the modality through which monetarist manipulations bring about variations in wage settlement is the thoroughly undesirable one of trouncing output and employment rather than moderating expectations and improving the climate of bargaining over wage rates. To the extent that monetarism succeeds—and this is problematic in the best of times—it does so through its nefarious effects on economic activity and welfare and not through any theoretician's magic exerted through shifts in portfolio composition, the relative attractiveness of assets, or money burning greater or smaller holes in people's pockets. In the perception of many, monetarism has by now become merely the official instrument to chastise labor by unemployment, reductions in benefits, and cuts in social services (mostly hitting those who had no part in strike threats or excessive wage demands); it offers us a series of savage and largely irreversible bloodlettings which could equally well be enforced by a variety of nonmonetary means. At the same time the only obvious advantage of monetarism, which is its relative political anonymity, is scuttled by the rigid truculence of its chief advocates, who have by now become its prisoners.

Not the least of the blandishments of monetarism in Britain has been the fostering of the illusion that incomes policy can be dispensed with totally and forever and that the good fight must be fought against the inflation enemy with one weapon only. This has enabled its advocates to present themselves in the borrowed plumage of defenders of free collective bargaining, and their opponents in the odious light of officious meddlers harboring sinister designs on the birthright of the British working class. It has, moreover, deflected attention from the painful nettle which will in the end have to be grasped, namely, the need for legislative reform in the field of industrial relations. Without this the divorce between power and responsibility, which enhanced union power and militancy have brought about, will continue to wreak its havoc unchecked in the context of a welfare state. It should be recognized that the sacred cow of free collective bargaining in Britain has yielded nothing but poisoned milk in the last decade; legal privileges and immunities granted to organized labor by successive governments have, in logic and in practice, ceased to be compatible with a system that seeks to combine social justice with political freedom. They have created a situation in which powerful sectional interests have exacted concessions that the economy cannot deliver, hiving off the responsibility for the resulting slump on government and the general taxpayer and shifting the real costs of the breakdown on to the shoulders of the unemployable young, the superannuated old, and the more exposed ethnic minorities.

The faint outlines of a remedy may be discernible in a combination of legislative reforms bearing on union obligations to their members with the fruitful proposals for novel forms of economic leverage variously known as inflation taxes or tax-based incomes policy (TIP).[7]

There may be something to be said, however, for shifting the point of impact of this taxation from the employers of labor, as usually pro-

posed, to the initiators of wage increases, on the grounds that employers already have an incentive to resist excessive wage demands to protect their cost structure, while unionized labor has none. Moreover, the
dispensation might be devised in a way to appeal to the solidaristic ide-
ologies of the trades union movement by legislating for more, rather
than less, integrated responsibility of unions for their members. It
could, for instance, be made mandatory to include in every membership
contract a guaranteed monthly payment from union funds during the
member's first year of unemployment, geared to the member's current
wage, including the latest wage increase from which he would have
benefited in employment, his length of membership, age, and so on. The
unions would thereby be on notice that high wage demands could hit
them financially both through the larger numbers of newly unemployed and the increased benefits becoming payable from union funds.
Job losses induced by factors other than negotiated wage increases or
work concessions would of course need to remain the responsibility of
general government.[8]

Notwithstanding the difficulties of interpretation, legal wrangles,
and so on, likely to emerge, only an arrangement of this sort could
enjoin the renewed and much-needed sense of responsibility on both
parties to the wage bargain which could convert it from the annual
exercise in competitive bluffing, ransom-demanding, and political ex-
tortion—which it now threatens to become—into a rational updating
of contracts serving the long-term interests of labor, employers, and
consuming public alike. Within such a framework the unions could
return with full vigor to their legitimate function of promoting the
concerns of their members as workers and employees without preju-
dicing their interests as citizens and consumers.

Nuffield College, Oxford

NOTES

1. The date is the notional one when the U.N.-defined level of $200 of per capita
   GDP would have been reached. It was obtained by projecting observed
   growth rates backward in time from 1952–54. See Simon Kuznetz, *Six Lec-
   tures on Economic Growth* (Glencoe, Ill.: Free Press, 1955), p. 27.
2. Exceptions have occurred, particularly in the field of immigration and na-
   tionality, and have been duly publicized.
3. The excursion into amateur sociology or politics which follows may be disre-
   garded by positivists without doing violence to the rest of the essay.

4. Her Majesty's Stationery Office, London, March 10, 1981.
5. Economists and politicians have wavered between M1 (notes, coins, and current bank deposits), sterling M2 (M1 *plus* deposit accounts), and M3 (sterling M2 *plus* foreign currency accounts), and various other aggregates (including building-society deposits and various forms of short-term paper). All these can show divergent movements.
6. It took the highest courts in the land to discipline the Labour-controlled London authority into desisting from the government-proscribed course of cheapening urban transport at the expense of local rate-payers.
7. Thanks to the original Wallich-Weintraub proposals, first unveiled in the *Lloyds Bank Review* (January 1971), pp. 1-12 and in the *New York Times* (November 1971) and subsequently expanded and given theoretical underpinnings in Sidney Weintraub, *Capitalism's Inflation and Unemployment Crisis* (Reading, Mass.: Addison-Wesley, 1978), such ideas are now more familiar in the United States than elsewhere, even though they were first consistently and successfully implemented in a European country. For descriptions see, e.g., Jan Adam, "The System of Wage Regulation in Hungary," *Canadian Journal of Economics* 7 (November 1974): 578-93, and I. Friss, ed., *Reform of the Economic Mechanism in Hungary* (Budapest: Akadémiai Kiadó, 1969), esp. chaps. by B. Csikós-Nagy, I. Konya, and I. Friss.
8. This proposal, under the somewhat fanciful name "DIP" (dole-based incomes policy), is spelled out in greater detail in the author's article in the *Journal of Economic Affairs* 2, no. 3 (April 1982): 171–76.

14

The Interaction
of United States
and European Policies

J. A. KREGEL

For the European Economic Community (EEC) as a whole, nearly 9 million people (over 8 percent of the active population of the member countries) were registered as unemployed in July 1981. In Italy, the Netherlands, France, and Belgium nearly half those unemployed were under twenty-five years of age. At the same time, the EEC average rate of inflation (as measured by gross national product deflators) is about 10 percent. Clearly the "depression" element is gaining dominance over the "inflation" element of European "stagflation." Yet few European countries—with the obvious exception of France after the election of President François Mitterand—are acting decisively to expand output and employment. There are internal reasons, but more important is past and present U.S. economic policy. The aim of the following discussion is to identify the U.S. contribution to European stagflation conditions.

Europeans have been widely critical of the so-called policy of "benign neglect" of the U.S. external payments and exchange rate position practiced in the 1960s and early 1970s. This policy was linked to a belief that the weak U.S. trade performance was primarily due to an overvalued dollar. The "refusal" of the Europeans to allow a full-scale readjustment via appreciation of their own currencies drove them to buy, and hold in their official reserves, increasing quantities of dollars.[1]

This situation created a conflict in these countries between control over exchange rates and control over growth of internal liquidity. Germany, in particular, was forced frequently to choose between appreciation and the uncontrolled expansion of liquidity that accompanies the defense of exchange rates against speculation before the final unilateral declaration of independence on August 15, 1971 by Richard Nixon. The concomitant actions of the rundown in Vietnam, Kissinger's new foreign policy of regional dominance, the unforeseen Middle East October War, and the OPEC (Organization of Petroleum Exporting Countries) price revolution meant that the monetary disagreements between Europe and the United States, papered over in the Smithsonian Agreements, were never fully discussed, nor were alternative policies proposed—except for periodic escapes and squirming through floating exchange rates. But this was less a studied remedy, despite the academic discussions of the 1950s, than the prudent response of central banks finding their reserves inadequate to the new international monetary conditions.

The ill-fated Smithsonian Agreements were quickly replaced by local European arrangements, first in the "Snake" and most recently in the European Monetary System (EMS). In this regard, one of the implicit goals and logical outcomes of the success of the European integration process which was initiated with the Treaty of Rome was the stabilization of community exchange rates, the coordination of national monetary policies, and ultimately the creation of a common currency area. At the same time, as member countries agreed not to use exchange rates to influence their competitive position, they also committed themselves to the coordination of monetary policy via exchange rate stabilization.

The major European complaint against U.S. monetary policy was (and still is) that it caused disturbances in intra-EEC exchange rates that were independent of either trade or capital flows within the community. It thus contradicted the goals of the EEC. Since speculative pressure against the dollar was expressed primarily through the markets for gold, Swiss francs, and Deutsche marks, Germany, the strongest member of the EEC, was faced with a Hobson's choice of revaluing, not only against the dollar, but in varying degree against all the EEC currencies, usually to Germany's competitive disadvantage. To attempt to preserve existing EEC exchange rates would make German monetary policy move out of step with the rest of the community; higher rates of relative money growth would promote expansion, and a trade deficit that had nothing to do with relative competitive conditions within the EEC but with the position of the DM in international speculation induced by the weak U.S. external position.

The EMS might thus best be interpreted as a method of redistributing this burden throughout the EEC by provoking other member central banks to respond in tandem with the Bundesbank when speculative pressure causes \$/DM rate adjustments which produce divergence from ruling intra-EEC rates. For the Benelux countries, because of their close trading and manufacturing links with Germany, such cooperation had always existed by necessity. It was far less true for the "Latin" members. Since joining the EEC, the United Kingdom has resisted any such monetary cooperation.

Of course, the Europeans also brought pressure to bear on the United States to recognize the importance of its role as the producer of the Nth currency in a dollar-based exchange system. The usual response of the United States was simply that the issue concerned the equitable sharing of the adjustment burden for the U.S. deficit. Germany was accused of exhibiting traditional surplus-country behavior of trying to force the entire burden of adjustment onto the deficit country. The U.S. policy of benign neglect thereby forced Germany to bear a fair share of the burden via exchange appreciation and/or increased monetary expansion.

The Europeans constantly argued instead that the United States had abused its position as the issuer of the Nth currency in the system, effectively usurping the monetary sovereignty of the other participants. (DeGaulle had preferred a return to gold under which, he thought, the franc would become an equal partner.)

After the 1973 oil crisis the European position also focused on the dual nature of the adjustment problem—one side concerned the U.S. deficit, the other the OPEC deficit. While the former might be aided by parity adjustment, the second could not, (a) since the OPEC countries had nearly nonexistent capacities to spend (this proved to be wrong) and (b) since OPEC exports were denominated in dollars rather than in their own currencies the traditional adjustment mechanisms of appreciation of the surplus countries' currencies leading to higher imports was impossible, as was the reduction of exports which in the short term were technologically fixed. Indeed, depreciation of the dollar *reduced,* rather than increased, the price of their exports to the rest of the world and left them unchanged in the United States.

The European case against exchange adjustment also concerned the supply effects of a declining dollar, which meant a lower real price for oil in terms of international purchasing power, leading either to increases in U.S. dollar prices or ultimately to decisions to limit production (a reaction that Paul Davidson saw with exceptional prescience in 1965).[2] The Europeans thus accused the United States of using ex-change-rate policy to avoid internal adjustment to the OPEC surplus and to endanger future oil supplies to the benefit of U.S. energy re-serves.

The combined pressure of OPEC's threat to use a basket of curren-cies to set prices and control supply, as well as the more positive U.S. policy of adjustment during the Carter administration (along with the appointment of a "banker" as chairman of the Board of Governors of the Federal Reserve System who was more open to the arguments of European central bankers), led to the "October Revolutions" of 1978 and 1979 and some recognition of the relation between domestic mone-tary policy and exchange rates.

The feelings of European central bankers toward U.S. policy is most visibly represented by Federal Reserve Chairman Volcker's pre-mature departure from the 1979 International Monetary Fund meet-ings in Belgrade. The Europeans did not, however, limit themselves to visible attempts at jawboning. They were also actively at work to change the terms of the Hobson's choice they faced. As they were in-creasingly forced to accept exchange appreciation, the detrimental ef-fects of this action on internal costs and their international competitive position became acute in the export sectors of these economies. At the same time, appreciation brought the benefit of dampening (or in Ger-many's case eliminating) the impact of the rise in petroleum prices. This led to more conscious policies to control nonenergy input costs, especially wages, and to increase access by manufacturing industry to finance.

Given strict liquidity controls, this agenda meant increased atten-tion to government deficits. The attitude produced the much envied "virtuous circle" syndrome: Rates of inflation in Germany, Benelux, and Switzerland were lower after 1976 than they had been *before* the 1973 petroleum crisis. At the same time, the growth and unemploy-ment rates were not adversely affected (see Tables 14.1, 14.2, and 14.3).

The United States' benign neglect, which effectively forced EEC central banks from their policy target of exchange stabilization through coordination of monetary policy, thus initiated a greater reli-ance on implicit or explicit wage or incomes policies and government spending controls to control export costs and money markets. Table 14.4 shows the marked reduction in nominal wage rates and, given sta-ble or rising productivity, the translation into sharply reduced unit labor costs for European producers. The United States' attempt to de-value its way to a surplus in competition with the Europeans clearly

TABLE 14.1:   Annual Percentage Changes in Gross Domestic Product
Deflators

	1973	1974	1975	1978	1979	1980
Germany	7.8	7.7	4.7	3.3	5.3	5.9
Belgium	6.2	13.6	13.3	4.3	3.9	6.5
Netherlands	8.7	11.9	11.0	4.8	5.4	7.1
Switzerland	8.8	8.9	4.5	0.9	3.7	4.2
Italy	16.1	26.1	11.6	13.8	18.2	23.8
France	8.0	15.4	9.0	8.3	9.9	12.4
U.K.	11.9	22.3	22.9	9.5	16.7	15.5
U.S.	7.6	12.0	7.0	7.9	8.5	9.6

Terms of Trade Component

	1973	1974	1975	1978	1979	1980
Germany	1.1	−0.9	0.9	−0.5	1.3	0.5
Belgium	−0.7	1.4	0.7	0.1	−0.3	1.5
Netherlands	0.3	2.6	−0.2	−0.3	1.5	1.2
Switzerland	0.7	2.0	−2.6	−2.7	1.7	2.2
Italy	3.0	2.3	−1.4	−0.3	1.9	3.5
France	0.0	3.2	−1.3	−1.5	0.1	1.7
U.K.	3.8	2.7	−1.9	−1.0	−1.5	1.3
U.S.	0.1	1.0	−0.5	−0.3	1.6	−0.2

SOURCE: Bank for International Settlements, *Annual Report 1980*, June 1981, p. 15.

TABLE 14.2:   Annual Percentage Changes in Consumer Prices

Changes over 12 Months Ending:

	12/73	12/74	12/75	12/76	12/77	12/78	12/79	6/80	12/80	81
Germany	7.8	5.8	5.4	3.7	3.5	2.5	5.4	6.0	5.5	5.6[b]
Belgium	7.3	15.7	11.0	7.6	6.3	3.9	5.1	6.2	7.5	7.4[b]
Netherlands	8.2	10.9	9.1	8.5	5.2	3.9	4.8	6.6	6.7	6.2[b]
Switzerland	11.9	7.6	3.4	1.3	1.1	0.7	5.1	3.3	4.4	5.6[b]
Italy	12.3	25.3	11.1	21.8	14.9	11.9	19.8	20.7	21.1	19.9[b]
France	8.5	15.2	9.6	9.9	9.0	9.7	11.8	13.5	13.6	12.5[a]
U.K.	10.6	19.2	24.9	15.1	12.1	8.4	17.2	21.0	15.1	12.0[b]
U.S.	8.8	12.2	7.0	4.8	6.8	9.0	13.3	14.3	12.4	10.0[b]
Japan	10.0	22.0	7.7	10.4	4.8	3.5	5.8	8.4	7.1	6.2[a]

[a]March.
[b]April.
SOURCE: Bank for International Settlements, *Annual Report 1980*, June 1981, p. 9.

TABLE 14.3: Annual Percentage Changes in Real Gross National Product and Unemployment

	Changes in Real GNP 1977–80					Changes in Unemployment 1970–1980		
	1977	1978	1979	1980	1980 IV	1970–75	1975–80	1970–80
Germany	2.8	3.6	4.5	1.8	−0.5	4.0	−0.9	3.1
Belgium	0.7	3.0	2.1	1.7	—	2.4	4.2	6.6
Netherlands	2.4	2.5	2.2	−0.3	—	4.1	0.6	4.7
Switzerland	2.8	0.3	2.5	2.8	—	0.3	−0.1	0.2
Italy	1.9	2.7	4.9	4.0	0.5	0.5	1.7	2.2
France	3.0	3.7	3.5	1.2	−0.4	1.5	2.6	4.1
U.K.	1.0	3.6	1.1	−1.4	−2.9	1.3	2.9	4.2
U.S.	5.5	4.8	3.2	−0.2	−0.3	3.6	−1.4	2.2
Japan	5.3	5.1	5.6	4.2	3.5	0.7	0.1	0.8
Austria	4.4	1.0	5.1	3.6	—	—	—	—

SOURCE: Bank for International Settlements, *Annual Report 1980,* June 1981, pp. 28, 30, 33.

was more beneficial to Europe than to the United States. One of the basic reasons was that the existing wage policies allowed the OPEC transfer burden to be met out of real wages, and terms of trade improvements, rather than from profits and investment.

A sharp division developed in concert within the EEC between those countries most able to compensate for the upward pressure on their exchange rates by reducing domestic costs (Germany and Benelux) and least able (France, United Kingdom, Italy). Inflation in the former was confined to the 5 to 7 percent range, while in the latter it averaged 10 to 20 percent.

A crucial point was reached at the Bonn summit of 1978, when Germany (and Japan) agreed to a "convoy" approach by joining the "stronger" international economies in expansionary policy. The full force of this decision can be seen in the tables on the following pages.

As a result, the 1979 petroleum price rises met German domestic conditions of internally generated expansion. The "second" oil crisis has been characterized by a concentration of current account deficits in the "low inflation" European countries, making the recycling of the surplus much easier. This created a paradoxical situation in which surpluses are located in high-inflation countries that clearly were not willing to risk further expansionary adjustment policies; simultaneously, relative differences in inflation rates did not suggest that currency ap-

TABLE 14.4:   Annual Percentage Changes in Hourly Earnings and
Productivity

Hourly Earnings

	Nominal				Real			
	1973	1974–75	1978	1979–80	1973	1974–75	1978	1979–80
Germany	11.1	10.2	5.7	6.1	3.2	3.6	3.1	1.0
Belgium	16.1	20.8	6.6	8.0	9.6	7.5	2.3	3.4
Netherlands	13.6	15.1	5.0	4.2	3.9	4.3	0.7	−1.4
Switzerland	9.2	9.7	3.7	4.5	0.2	1.3	3.1	0.2
Italy	25.4	22.2	16.1	22.1	10.5	5.6	3.2	2.5
France	15.9	17.6	12.6	14.6	7.6	4.9	2.7	3.6
U.K.	13.0	24.4	13.4	19.5	3.0	2.3	4.7	4.0
U.S.	6.6	7.4	9.2	8.4	−0.8	−1.5	1.5	−1.2

Productivity

	1973	1974–75	1978	1979–80
Germany	3.6	3.5	3.8	0.2
Belgium	9.7	7.8	13.2	3.0
Netherlands	4.9	4.6	11.7	−0.3
Switzerland	5.4	4.4	3.7	1.2
Italy	11.1	1.5	12.2	5.7
France	0.3	3.7	10.3	4.4
U.K.	2.6	0.7	1.3	0.3
U.S.	−1.6	2.9	0.8	0.8

SOURCE: Bank for International Settlements, *Annual Report 1980,* June 1981, p. 18.

preciation would be in order. Deficit countries sensibly claimed that
contraction of their economies would be undesirable and depreciation
ineffective. When the new Reagan administration declared an antiinflationary policy based on monetary-control procedures, with its impact
on interest rates and exchange rates viewed as unimportant, it was natural for the Europeans to sense that the Bonn agreements had been
betrayed. Indeed, the policy of *conscious* neglect was no different in its
effect than the previous policy of benign neglect, except for the theoretical justification of the independence of national monetary policies in
a world of floating rates. Again, the United States had failed to recognize that such an assumption contradicted the very foundations of a
united Europe.

The results of U.S. policy were, however, just what the Germans had recommended in 1976–77 when they called for a sharp reduction in the rate of expansion of U.S. liquidity. Continued European criticism obviously reflects the different context in which monetary policy is viewed.

Tinbergen's *Theory of Economic Policy* suggests the necessity of matching policy instruments to targets; it is normally applied to a single economy. If this proposition is considered on an international level then the divergent views on the role of monetary policy in the United States and the EEC have produced an "assignment contradiction." The United States is using money policy to control prices through its impact on internal demand, while the EEC countries have reserved monetary policy for stabilizing exchange rates. The former leaves interest rates and exchange rates free to fluctuate, while the latter seeks their strict control. The two policies cannot succeed simultaneously. Given the position of the U.S. economy and the dollar in world capital markets, EMS countries have had to operate monetary policy so that their interest rates matched or exceeded U.S. levels, if sharp depreciation of their currencies was to be avoided. This has meant increases in terms-of-trade inflation due to the depreciation on the one hand and, given their initially lower than average rates of inflation, real rates of interest so high as to discourage internal growth, and adjustment and increases in government deficits due to sharply increased interest payments on government debt, higher social security due to rising unemployment, and costly government

TABLE 14.5:   General Government Net Borrowing

Annual Average as Percent of Gross National Product (Minus = Deficit)

	1970–73	1974–76	1977	1978	1979	1980
Germany	0.2	−3.6	−2.4	−2.7	−2.9	−3.5
Belgium	−2.2	−4.2	−5.7	−6.2	−6.7	−8.8
Netherlands	−0.1	−1.7	−1.5	−2.1	−3.0	−3.3
Italy	−7.4	−9.6	−7.9	−9.7	−9.4	−7.9
France	0.8	−0.7	−0.8	−1.8	−0.6	0.3
U.K.	−0.3	−4.6	−3.4	−4.3	−3.3	−3.7
U.S.	0.2	−1.5	−1.0	0.0	0.5	−1.2
Japan	1.0	−2.0	−3.8	−5.5	−4.7	−4.0

SOURCE: Bank for International Settlements, *Annual Report 1980*, June 1981, p. 36.

support programs for bankrupt "strategic" industries. The paradox of exchange-rate adjustment departing from inflation-rate differentials, and purchasing-power parity in the face of the assignment contradiction, has led to a deflation-dominated European version of stagflation.

For the Europeans, the problem is no longer directly one of inflation but one of attempting to reduce the real rates of interest associated with realistic U.S./EEC exchange rates. One avenue is the rapid elimination of payments deficits through increased international competitiveness—a solution which has reinforced dependence on wage settlements. In 1981, nominal hourly earnings in the Netherlands and Germany were up 4 percent and 5 percent respectively, producing real reductions of −1.75 and −0.75 percent in earnings.[3] Table 14.6 gives forecasts of the results of such action on export performance.

As the depressive effects of such policies tend to increase government transfer expenditures and decrease national income growth, the share of the deficit to national income rises. This also implies that the proportion of government claims to private claims on the private capital markets rises. Thus the choice between appreciation and liquidity control is replaced by a choice between further depreciation and liquidity control to stabilizing the deficit as a proportion of GNP.[4] Since depreciation has a similar impact on inflation to loss of control over liquidity, the preferred choice has been to restrict liquidity. This,

TABLE 14.6:   Relative Export Performance* (Percent Change from Previous Year)

	1979	1980	Forecast 1981	Forecast 1982
France	1.6	−3.1	0.25	0.00
Germany	−2.3	−1.2	3.50	8.50
Italy	−1.4	−10.1	−3.50	0.50
U.K.	−7.9	−4.2	−10.25	−2.00
Belgium	−7.6	−3.0	−2.00	−0.50
Holland	−1.7	−4.1	−0.75	0.25
Denmark	−0.5	3.3	2.50	1.50
U.S.	0.4	5.7	−6.75	−15.50

*Defined as difference between growth in export markets and growth in export volumes, e.g., German exports in volume terms are forecast to grow 8.50 percent more rapidly than the markets in which it sells exports.
SOURCE: *OECD Economic Outlook*, Dec. 1981, p. 18.

coupled with real wage reductions and reduced government stimulus, has had sharply depressive effects on employment levels. The rates of increase in unemployment for July as reported by the EEC Commission (average *rate* of unemployment in excess of 8 percent) were:

Belgium	14.5%	England	6.4%
Luxembourg	12.2%	France	3.4%
Germany	10.7%	Denmark	0.7%
Holland	10.1%		

Thus, the only alternatives to adjusting to the U.S. inflation rate and abandoning the principles of the EEC in the face of the impact of U.S. monetary policy on interest and exchange rates are sharply deflationary policies.

From its effects on unemployment, budget deficits, and private investment, the Europeans argue that U.S. policy is inappropriate in an international context because it will lead to a continued decrease in world activity, on the one hand, and a rise in average inflation, on the other—manifestly, stagflation on a world level.

At the same time, U.S. policy is considered inappropriate on the domestic level. Again following Tinbergen, U.S. policy implies the use of a single instrument for all economic objectives, or the belief that stopping inflation will lead the way to economic recovery. The Europeans have always been perplexed by the Reagan mix of severe credit restraint and fiscal stimulus resulting from the tax cuts and defense appropriations. There is a strong belief in the interest-rate impact of a rising deficit on a falling availability of private savings which accompanies falling real GNP—or more simply a *rejection* of the supply-side aspects of the program. The current *Annual Report of the Bank for International Settlements* puts it this way: "Countering inflation may indeed be primarily the responsibility of monetary policy, and the improvement of control procedures is important. But equally at issue are the risks which may be associated with an inappropriate policy mix. Interest rate levels may be higher than necessary if monetary restraint is not supported by appropriate fiscal policies and where possible, also by incomes policies."[5] Further,

> The monetary policies applied in recent years have been designed largely to counter inflation. But as usual they had substantial repercussions on output. The impact of monetary policy on interest-sensitive components of aggregate expenditure could be seen last year in some countries in the behavior of stocks and house-building. Fixed

investment generally proved fairly resilient, perhaps because of long-term inflationary expectations but also because of the shift to energy-saving outlays.[6]

Particular criticism is leveled at the use of fixed monetary norms:

> Where published monetary targets are viewed as a cornerstone of strategies for controlling inflation, there is a risk that failure to ad-here closely to them may weaken the credibility of the authorities' resolve. Yet money-demand relationships and the exchange of mar-kets are often unstable, and in many countries norms have been fixed on the basis of fairly simple considerations which may prove to be in-appropriate.[7]

In support of this, the Report also notes, "It is not easy to establish close *ex post* statistical relationships between government borrowing requirements and rates of monetary expansion or interest rates." Thus although "it may not be unreasonable to associate the current high le-vels of real interest rates in many countries . . . with the fact that gov-ernments' financing requirements are already large and are likely to rise further,"[8] it would be inappropriate to link nominal interest rates to high inflation rates.

Noting that much of the U.S. failure to control money aggregates is put down to institutional changes, the Report states:

> however, large quarter-to-quarter fluctuations in rates of monetary expansion were also experienced, under different systems of mone-tary control, in countries where there were no major institutional changes. . . . Even with improved procedures it may in practice be im-possible for the central bank to smooth out short-run fluctuations in rates of monetary expansion. To attempt to do so may place unneces-sary pressure on interest rates and exchange rates.[9]

The European monetarist position is then summed up as follows:

> Severe monetary restraint, if not supported by appropriate policies in other areas, may actually tend to impair an economy's supply po-tential. It may, for instance, encourage capital inflows, currency ap-preciation and a weakening of the current account. High interest rates and weak overall demand continuing for a protracted period may result in a serious loss of productive investment. . . . However, in the real world the costs of relying on monetary restraint alone and the hazards involved can run high. These costs may be justifi-able, even unavoidable, if supporting measures to combat inflation have for various reasons to be ruled out. Nonetheless, they can often

be reduced significantly by recourse to a more eclectic policy approach.[10]

A policy of constantly pressing down aggregate demand in response to these repeated price and cost shocks poses many risks—political, social and economic. In economic terms, the greatest risks are of creating high levels of unemployment and low rates of industrial utilization which reduce current levels of activity and ultimately undermine profitability and the incentive to invest. . . . Some more direct form of anti-inflation policy—be it known as concerted action, social compact or incomes policy—can contribute to the maintenance of real income growth.[11]

Certainly, it cannot be denied that, for both larger and smaller countries, responsibility, most especially for preventing and combating inflation, begins at home. However, when the world economy is already burdened with payments imbalances as acute as those it faces in the wake of the second oil shock, it is all the more necessary that in whatever is done on a national level sufficient thought should be given to the effects on the rest of the world—and this in no way applies solely to the United States. The connection of these imbalances and the simultaneous rolling back of inflation call for a high degree of international cooperation.

   Indeed, such cooperation may be considered as the most effective bulwark against a repetition of the kind of events witnessed in the 1930's, which ultimately resulted in a disintegration of the world economy.[12]

Thus, from the European point of view, U.S. policy is not only misconceived, failing the internal and international "assignment" test, but it also produces the risk of preventing European adjustment and thus provoking a world crisis. Varieties of "monetarist" policies have been practiced in Germany and the Benelux countries throughout the 1970s. It is perhaps relevant to the current U.S. experiment to recognize that such policies, in the view of their European practitioners, can succeed only if supported by some form of incomes policy or social contract which also sets guidelines for the growth of wages and government expenditure.

Unfortunately, it may be Europe and the world economy which must pay the cost of U.S. policymakers learning that such policies are necessary.

University of Groningen

NOTES

1. The U.S. position was also explained by some economists in terms of foreigners' demands for dollars to be held as international reserves "causing" the U.S. deficit. If this had ever been the case, most Europeans would claim that such "demands" had ceased by the late 1950s and were virtually nonexistent by the time full convertibility was reestablished in Europe and the Treaty of Rome ratified.
2. Cf. Sidney Weintraub, *A Keynesian Theory of Employment and Income Distribution* (Radnor, Pa.: Chilton, 1966), p. 110n.
3. OECD *Economic Outlook,* Dec. 1981, pp. 43–44.
4. This was the original Reagan objective in 1981. The portending 1982 growth in the deficit is creating pressures on the administration (early 1982) to reverse its tax-cutting tactics in favor of the euphemistic "revenue enhancement" tax increases of a regressive variety.
5. Bank for International Settlements, *Annual Report 1980* (Basle, June 1981), p. 51.
6. Ibid., p. 61.
7. Ibid.
8. Ibid., pp. 68–69.
9. Ibid., p. 71.
10. Ibid., p. 75.
11. Ibid., pp. 22–23.
12. Ibid., p. 168.

15

Perspective on Canada's Stagflation Economy

ARTHUR DONNER

The origin of Canada's stagflation is similar to the affliction of other industrial nations. Many difficulties can be traced back to the fourfold increase in world petroleum prices. The dramatic Organization of Petroleum Exporting Countries (OPEC) price shocks affected the Canadian economy directly and indirectly. Stagflation swept in both because the oil hikes induced slower growth and higher inflation in the U.S. economy and because the direct effects of the associated relative price changes in Canada spurred price increases and a slower growth in domestic demand.

Even though the federal government devised an elaborate low-price energy scheme to insulate the economy from the full brunt of these external shocks, at present Canada faces sharply higher escalations in its domestic energy costs. The Canadian government response to the stagflation dilemma has been nationally characteristic in the sense that there was an attempt to cushion the impacts and to impose a gradual adjustment to world levels. And while Canada officially adopted monetarist central banking practices, and began monitoring government spending back in 1975, it also imposed full formal wage and price controls between late 1975 and early 1979. The total mix of these policies can be regarded as restrictive.

The gross national product (GNP) tended to grow at about a 5 percent annual rate during the twenty years preceding 1975. Similarly, output per worker tended to increase at a 2 percent per year average rate, while a 5 percent unemployment rate was regarded as high in Canada prior to 1975. Since 1974 the real GNP growth rate in Canada ranged from zero growth in 1980 to a 5.5 percent high in 1976, with the average rate at 2.8 percent per year. Including estimates for 1981, real GNP per worker posted no gains at all since 1974, and the unemployment rate rose to an average of 7.6 percent between 1975 and 1981; the peak rate of 8.6 percent was centered in mid-1978.

Thus far in 1981, the consumer price index has been advancing at about a 12.4 percent annual rate, averaging an increase of 9.6 percent since 1974. The Canadian inflation rate is presently 3 to 4 percentage points higher than in the United States. The Economic Council of Canada expects double-digit inflation to continue over the whole of this decade. Real wages have tended to decline for the past three years in Canada.

Canada's policy response to stagflation, and even its version of monetarism, is different from the U.S. policy response partly because of the vulnerability of the Canadian currency on international markets. The federal government and the Bank of Canada have been operating under a severe balance-of-payments constraint—in particular, the concern that a weaker Canadian dollar would set off higher domestic inflation. The balance-of-payments constraint has meant that Canada has not only required high interest rates to reduce its money-supply growth rates, but on many occasions higher than warranted interest rates were required to protect the external value of the Canadian dollar because of high and volatile U.S. interest rates. Moreover, Canada recently introduced policies to encourage a major internal restructuring of its energy industries toward a greater degree of domestic ownership and control (the Canadianization policies). Since 1975, the Canadian authorities have been ambiguously committed to monetarism in terms of its domestic money-supply implications.

Canada's economy is far more foreign-trade oriented than the U.S. economy; trade, for Canada, represents about 25 percent of GNP as compared to less than 10 percent of GNP in the United States. As well, Canada's current account component within the balance of payments is much affected by Canada's net international debtor status; in contrast, the United States is a net creditor.

Canada's debtor status in some respects resembles a capital-short developing country rather than that of a mature industrial economy. Federal governments in Canada have always been sensitive to changing the structure of the trade accounts, favoring the industrial trade potential at the expense of resource development.

The structural reality of Canada's balance of payments is that Canada usually earns a large surplus in its merchandise trade, with huge surpluses in resources and large deficits in manufactured goods. Offsetting the goods surpluses are the extensive deficits in the service side of Canada's current account statement. Indeed, the service account deficits have increased rapidly because of net interest payment outflows which have swelled under the pressure of record-high interest rates in 1980 and 1981.

Despite a surplus in its direct energy trade when one includes electricity, natural gas, and petroleum products in these calculations, Canada is presently a deficit country in its direct oil trade, though its petroleum self-sufficiency far exceeds that of the United States. The service account deficit in the balance of payments reflects Canada's debtor status, with interest outflows in excess of dividend outflows.

Lately the Canadian government has taken a more nationalistic position with respect to foreign ownership. Two policy initiatives were introduced in this field—the FIRA (Foreign Investment Review Act) back in 1975 and the NEP (National Energy Policy) in 1980. Contrasting policy objectives have always tugged at government policymakers; from the Canadian perspective there is always a continentalist position favoring free trade with the United States, including unimpeded capital knit between the two countries. In contrast, there is a loosely known group of nationalists which favors buy-back schemes from foreign ownership in Canada. It was the nationalist tilt which spurred the FIRA and the NEP.

Since the mid-1970s, the federal government has practiced an ambivalent intervention with respect to the U.S. exchange rate. Substantial net inflows of foreign capital—primarily from the United States—have usually been encouraged; recent nationalist policies have worked the other way. The shift of the federal government toward the nationalist left is an overt attempt to change the foreign ownership composition of the petroleum industries, and on several occasions in 1981 these initiatives led to sharp outflows of capital and a series of mild exchange crises. For example, the depreciation with respect to the U.S. dollar in 1981 at no time exceeded 5 percent; in contrast, the European Economic Community (EEC) currencies devalued about 25 to 30 percent during the first half of 1981.

Some time after the second OPEC price shock deflated the world economies, the federal government introduced its National Energy Policy (the NEP) in October 1980. This provided extensive tax incentives to Canadian companies to take over nonresident equity positions in Canada; extensive disincentives were placed on nonresident-controlled petroleum companies covering exploration and development in Canada. In 1980, about 60 percent of petroleum assets in Canada were under control of nonresident corporations and individuals. The policy also in- cluded a continuation of Canada's gradualistic energy price hike strategy. The NEP impact was strongly resisted by both domestic and foreign companies, and the Province of Alberta. Critics saw this program as a grand money-grab by the Federal government from the petroleum industry, a sector which usually fell under provincial jurisdiction. Some argue that the expansion of the government-owned "Petro-Canada" was in fact "socialism." Opposition to NEP continues, though a Canadianization of this sector is generally popular.

An agreement negotiated in September 1981 between the Alberta government and the Federal government resolved their impasse over pricing and revenue distribution but left industry dissatisfied. The result was a schedule for domestically blended oil prices to move rapidly toward world prices by 1986. The underlying assumption is that world oil prices will average about a 13 percent annual increase until 1986. The two governments each claimed a larger share of the expanded petroleum revenues—about $14 billion for the federal government, $10 billion for Alberta, and $8 billion for industry. It is widely expected that the agreement will improve the federal revenue flows considerably, permitting a reduction in the federal deficit, but that in the process it will deepen the stagflation problem in Canada and provoke higher inflation as well.

The macroeconomic fallout from the steep increases in oil prices are well understood—indeed, Canadians have already gained considerable experience in adjusting to these effects. A hike in oil prices increases the cost of living in Canada and simultaneously reduces national productivity and production below levels that would otherwise have been attained. At the same time, the additional oil revenues will go some way toward reducing the national deficit. However, the revenue gains are modest during the first two years of the agreement, and Ottawa's fiscal problems will not ease that dramatically in 1982. The additional $8 billion flowing to the Alberta government, and the $10 billion to the oil and gas producers over the next five years, will stimulate both national savings and investment. But real consumption spending will be retarded as domestic prices move up to world levels. The identifiable losers from this agreement are the Canadian consumer and Canadian industry to the extent it loses its low-cost energy supplies. The agreement's impact on inflationary expectations must be regarded as negative, especially when contrasted with the U.S. deregulation experience.

To sum up, the typical investor and wage earner in Canada will expect at least double-digit inflation in the years ahead because of the extra inflationary effect of the Alberta-Ottawa agreement.

While many of the economic problems engulfing the Canadian economy in the 1970s and in the 1980s are not necessarily of the making of the Canadian policymakers, the Canadian government and the Bank of Canada did embark in a monetarist policy direction back in late 1975 which has had its own distinctive flavor.[1] Canada adopted monetary growth targets in 1975, and at the same time the central bank stated that it would no longer be as expressly concerned with interest-rate determination; in fact, since 1978 its attention to interest rates has remained particularly keen due to its use of interest rates for supporting the external value of the Canadian dollar. Despite the fairly clear monetarist tone at the Bank of Canada, Governor Gerald K. Bouey protests the monetarist label.

> There does seem to be an impression around that a few years ago some of us in the Bank of Canada were struck down on the road to inflation by a blinding light—the word "blinding" is sometimes emphasized—and experienced a sudden conversion to a new far-out religion called monetarism. I have to confess that I was there at the time and that nothing quite so dramatic happened.[2]

Bouey has also pointed to the exchange-rate management role as a practical example of Canada's independent monetary policy. But Ottawa's exchange-rate fixation has spurred accusations that the Bank of Canada is simply operating as the thirteenth Federal Reserve District of the U.S. monetary system. This charge has some credibility, for the Bank has aimed at shoring up a weakening Canadian dollar in this era of high world inflation and high U.S. interest rates. Considering the extraordinary erratic interest rates in the United States since 1978, the Canadian economy never seemed far away from a foreign-exchange crisis.

The irony in this statement is that in 1975 a monetarist supporter of the Bank called it the most monetarist central bank in the Western world. He has since recanted these views. While the Bank's stress on interest rates for foreign-exchange rate purposes represents a mild departure from pure monetarism, nevertheless interest-rate intervention appears always poised to tighten, seldom to ease.

Monetarism encompasses more than the simple proportionate relationship between money-supply growth and inflation. There are, at least, three other facets to monetarist theory: (1) the natural rate of unemployment hypothesis, and the view that any deviation from the natural rate will only be temporary; (2) the view that fiscal policy has no impact on macroeconomic performance other than through induced shifts in money-supply growth; and (3) the thinking that the "natural rate of unemployment" can be improved only by supply-side policies. There seems to be no easy way to assess the acceptance of these remaining propositions by the central bank and the government; their public releases are vague. Certainly there is a willingness to tolerate higher unemployment than in the past.

Since the Bank of Canada adopted its money-supply targeting rules, the federal fiscal authorities also chose to tighten the budgetary position, but here matters are complicated. In Canada there has been a large imbalance between the budgetary positions of the central government and some of the western provinces, particularly Alberta. On balance, Canadian monetary policy has been restrictive over the post-1975 period, particularly when measured in terms of real money-supply growth or in terms of real interest rates. Fiscal policy at the national level has not been all that restrictive. The impact of the total government sector was therefore restrained after 1979.[3]

The sum total of the Canadian policy responses, and the deteriorating international environment since 1974, has meant real economic growth considerably lower than at any time since the 1950s. The national unemployment rate has been surprisingly low in view of the sluggish growth pattern, though clearly there is much disguised unemployment because of the extraordinary poor national productivity performance. The national unemployment figure fell to 7.0 percent in August 1981, whereas several years ago it was as high as 8.5 percent.

Between 1976 and 1979 there was the predictable drop-off in housing activity, consumer spending, and business investment. Indeed, tight monetary policies (and high interest rates) significantly curbed nonenergy investment between 1976 and 1978, so that when economic growth resumed in 1979, the economy encountered industrial bottlenecks despite high unemployment.

Since 1979, energy and nonenergy investment boomed.[4] High real and nominal interest rates in 1980 contributed to a recession, but investment held strong in 1980 and 1981. Energy flows have created additional inflation problems as labor and capital have been pouring into the thinly populated economy of western Canada. The strength of this westward shift has provided the illusion that investment in Canada defies high interest rates.

But tight monetary policies and unusually high interest rates have sown the seeds for further inflation and unemployment by destroying the incentive to invest in the nonenergy sectors of eastern Canada. A case can be made that given the unemployment and excess capacity Canada would have been better off with an easier monetary policy and a tighter fiscal policy since the mid-1970s. But one is hard-pressed to argue that there has been an insufficient shift in aggregate demand toward investment, the supply-side view on how to contain inflation.

Still, Canada's brand of monetarism is mild compared to its more extreme cousins in Britain and the United States. Ironically the greatest monetarist threat to Canadian economic prospects stems from U.S. monetarism and its impact on Canada's economy via the export of high U.S. interest rates, rather than from Canada's imitation of U.S. economic policies. Because of tradition and possibly necessity, Canada has tied its monetary policy to that of the United States, and the U.S. Federal Reserve has been imposing high and erratic interest rates that are damaging economic growth and unsettling the foreign exchange markets.

It would probably be more advantageous to the Canadian economy if the central bank allowed the Canadian currency to fluctuate more freely (or on occasion to devalue further), rather than accepting the intolerably high interest rates from the United States. The Bank of Canada seems to be attempting to stabilize the Canadian dollar somewhere above 83 cents U.S.; its recent low point of 80 cents U.S. made the Bank uneasy and drove interest rates at the Canadian Chartered banks to as high as 22.75 percent. These interest rates were much higher than was warranted in terms of achieving domestic monetary growth targets and were certainly high in real terms.

In a Reagan-like posture the Canadian government also set in motion policies to shrink the public sector. In 1975 the federal government committed itself to restrain its expenditures to below the growth rate of Canada's GNP. That commitment has been continuously reconfirmed, and it has also been effectively enforced at the provincial and municipal levels through revenue-sharing arrangements. The spending limitations were introduced because critics have denounced the federal bureaucracy as being too large and inefficient and charged that the government was playing too large a role in society. But this rigid acceptance of the federal spending guideline has placed government spending in the perverse position of always reinforcing cyclical downturns in the economy.

Like most industrial countries, Canada has suffered from unpredictably high and volatile interest rates stemming from the monetarist policies of the Federal Reserve. These high U.S. interest rates have passed into Canada virtually unchecked because the Canadian central bank approves of these high levels or is unwilling to offset them by allowing the Canadian exchange rate to decline. In fact, it did permit a mild decline in 1981 and tried to support the Canadian dollar through currency intervention. But its foreign currency holdings are too thin to carry out much of a defense through this route. The official policy has therefore been to encourage Canadian interest rates to fluctuate more or less in line with U.S. interest rates. A decline in the Canadian dollar is directly inflationary, for it results in higher import costs.

In summary, Canada's economy has been badly hurt by erratic, high, and unstable interest rates since 1979. The sharp month-to-month changes in interest rates are costly and damaging and defensible, at best, by exchange-rate considerations. Inflationary pressures intensified in Canada in 1981, yet real economic growth has occurred despite the high real interest rates. But the current wave of inflation in Canada is alarming since it occurs in the midst of an international recession and a background of highly restrictive monetary and potentially more restrictive fiscal measures. The new oil agreement adds fuel to the ongoing inflation. Canada's inflation has worsened in absolute terms and relative to the United States since the 1979 slowdown began. Since demand-pull causation makes little sense in explaining the inflation in Canada, analysis points clearly to money wage acceleration and a surge in unit labor costs even as the economy was confronted by higher food and energy prices.

Money wages in the present inflationary setting in Canada are a very sensitive issue. Real wages in Canada have been contracting now for several years, and they are presently in some type of a catch-up phase. Indeed, one often hears Canadian politicians arguing the justice of the catch-up effort, but no matter how justified this development may appear, wage acceleration generates another spin of the price-wage-price spiral.

Food and energy prices are on inflationary roller coasters of their own. While food prices are typically more cyclical than other prices in Canada, food prices between 1950 and 1973 nevertheless did not accent the general inflation. But this longer-term stable relationship seems to have changed with the heavy energy component in food production.

Under the present mix of policies, Canada risks higher inflation in the future. One should not understate the importance of Canada's new energy pricing policy. The "cold turkey" policy in the United States of moving quickly to higher energy prices encouraged various sectors to quickly substitute lower price alternatives for higher priced fuels. The Canadian energy pricing strategy had not provided that imperative, and this has been more inflationary. This calls into question the gradualist energy price rises implicit in Canada's program, and the wisdom of four to five more years of chasing world energy prices.

John Cornwall has argued that economists require separate theories of inflation and unemployment and that the Canadian economy seems always poised for more inflation when provided with any type of economic stimulus, whether from exports, domestic investment, or expansionary fiscal or monetary measures.[5] The asymmetry in the Cornwall thesis is that weakening aggregate demand translates primarily into output and employment losses and has *little or no* impact on inflation.

Perhaps such market asymmetries have always been there. The Weintraub thesis that wage inflation is largely exogenous seems to fit Canada far better than the United States.[6]

Unfortunately it takes a supreme effort to be optimistic for Canada's inflation. The missing policy variable at this time is a wage policy—but the Canadian government seems unwilling to accept the political risk necessary to go that route. Perhaps Reaganomics may save Canada from its inflation future. As it stands, most economic observers project a stagflation scenario. Indeed, the Economic Council of Canada has forecast that on current policies double-digit inflation is possible throughout the 1980s.

Arthur Donner Consultants, Canada

NOTES

1. Arthur W. Donner and Douglas D. Peters, *The Monetarist Counter-Revolution: A Critique of Canadian Monetary Policy 1975–1979*, Canadian Institute for Economic Policy (Toronto: James Lorimer, 1979).
2. Gerald K. Bouey, Remarks to the Empire Club of Canada, Toronto, November 13, 1980, *Bank of Canada Review*, November 1980, p. 8.
3. In absolute terms, total government deficits in Canada ranged from $3.2 billion to $7.1 billion between 1975 and 1980. As a percentage of GNP, the variation was between a low point of 1.7 percent in 1976 to a high point of 3.1 percent. However, estimates of the cyclically adjusted position of all governments show a balance in 1980.
4. The national unemployment rate rose to 8.2 percent in September 1981.
5. John Cornwall, "Do We Need Separate Theories of Inflation and Unemployment?" *Canadian Public Policy*, April 1981, pp. 165–78.
6. Sidney Weintraub, "The Missing Theory of Money Wages," *Journal of Post Keynesian Economics* 1 (Winter 1978–79): 59–78.

POST KEYNESIAN ECONOMICS

Sidney Weintraub and Marvin Goodstein, eds., *Reaganomics in the Stagflation Economy*

CWI

DATE DUE

OCT 1 9 1983	MAY 1 2 1999
NOV 1 6 1983	NOV 1 1 2004
DEC 1 4 1983	
MAR 2 8 1984	JAN 1 9 2004
	NOV 0 9 2009
NOV 2 1 1984	
DEC 1 2 1984	
APR 1 7 1985	
APR 2 4 1985	
AUG 2 8 1985	
DEC 0 3 1986	
12/16/87	
FEB 2 4 1988	
MAR 2 8 1988	
APR 2 0 1988	
MAY 1 0 1 1994	
MAY 1 0 1 1996	